GLORY FOR ME

GLORY FOR ME

MacKinlay Kantor

SPEAKING VOLUMES, LLC
NAPLES, FLORIDA
2017

Glory for Me

ISBN 978-1-62815-607-2

TO
GEORGE I. HARKAVEY

> *"When all my labors and trials are o'er*
> *And I am safe on that beautiful shore . . .*
> *O that will be*
> *Glory for me!"*

CHARLES H. GABRIEL

GLORY FOR ME

i

FRED DERRY, twenty-one, and killer of a hundred men,
Walked on the width of Welburn Field. The cargo ship
Had set him down in noontime haze of early spring.
He smelled the onion farms:
He heard the trucks in Highway 52,
He saw the signboards, and the ugliness
That was a beauty he had dreamed.

Fred Derry, green of eye, with lids pale-washed in pink
(The way the eyes of bombardiers and gunners grow)—
Fred Derry, middling slim and round of shoulder,
But alert . . . possessed by jaunty weariness
That could be taut when life demanded it—
He stopped beneath a 26's wing,
Took off his coveralls, and with a handkerchief
He wiped the one small smear of grease
That marred the bottom of his pinks.
He brushed himself; fastened a pocket flap,
Saw that his wings and ribbons looked all right.
And he was toughly proud of all that color on his chest:
The D.F.C., its oak-leaf cluster . . . other bronze
On other ribbons.
                    Purple Heart.
He shrugged. It was an easy Purple Heart—
A blighty Purple Heart, the Raf would call it.
A 20-millimeter shell had stove the nose,
And pulverized some chunks of Plexiglas
And put a piece of copper in Fred's arm.
Strong arm. . . . They sewed it up again.
He wore a crimson bathrobe only sixteen days,
For he was young and hard and mean
And glad to wear the Purple Heart,
And holy glad that he was lucky when he got it.

His fingers drew his cap bill down—
The sloppy Air Force cap with grommet taken out

3

And crow rubbed to a yellow polish.
Then, with his zipper bag in hand
And coveralls across his arm,
And chute and harness in the other hand,
He went to Operations.

The counter where the crews dispatched
Was crowded front and back.
The people waiting for a hitch stood silent,
As if hoping in their silence to attract benevolence
From bustling stay-at-homes who held
The power of their transportation—
Who brought the waffles closer by three days,
And you in bed with Evelyn on Tuesday night
Instead of three nights later.
They waited, and the sergeant's voice went up:
"Who hasn't got his name down? . . . read the list again."
He read the eastbound list . . . the people going south,
And names were added.
West . . . he read the names:
One spoke for Tulsa, three for Albu-q,
And more for the Pacific Coast.

Fred Derry took his turn, he gave his name,
Wrote: "Derry, 1st Lieutenant F."
He put his bomb group down, the 3-0-5th,
And said that Mitchel Field was home.
He lied. The sergeant knew he lied,
And almost everyone was lying. . . .
Civilians, now; they hadn't any home
In Army, Navy or Marines.
They hadn't any place in life this moment,
And they knew it well.

The sergeant's voice was grim again
Above the twitter and the talk,
The chatter of the telephones
And instruments connecting with the planes aloft,
The mumble that two Wacs were making
As they talked about their dates on Saturday.
The sergeant spoke: "Now, listen here.
I haven't asked to see your passes,
Haven't asked for AGO cards—
I ain't no MP,
I'm not a provost. But remember this:

You want your rides, you take your turn.
I'll call the names just once
When space is ready, and you got to be here!
I just ask, please: stay away from this here counter.
We got a lounge next door; there's lots of room outside;
We'll call you on the amplifier.
Please don't gang up inside the door!"

Fred Derry hadn't specified.
He just said West;
And West might mean a lot of things.
K.C. was good; St. Louis was a little better;
He could get a bus;
He might make home before the morning if he got a bus.
He went outside and smoked a cigarette.
He looked back in, and he was hungry.
"Where's the PX?" he asked of other men.
They told him where to find it,
But he didn't like to go:
He might miss out. He waited.
Once he had hitch-hiked up from Drew—oh, long before.
He wished that this were Drew;
Down on the line, they had free coffee,
And some orange juice, and stuff like that.

He went inside and hung around the door of Weather,
Pretending he was looking for a guy he knew.
The sergeant saw him sharply,
But then looked away . . . for new men came
To hope, to want their rapid ride
(The chocolate cake, the beer at Billy's Bar,
And sex with Emily, and kisses from some babies
They had never seen.
They wanted Home, as quick as they could get there).

. . . Sergeant's voice again:
"No chute? I'm sorry: we can't help you here.
We can't give chutes. Right up there it says so:
That directive:
'No more chutes to be signed out at Welburn Field.'
You better try to get aboard a train;
The main gate has a bus in twenty minutes. . . .
Sorry, sir. You got to have a chute."

An hour passed for Derry; then he thought,
"The hell with it."

One Lib went out for Dallas,
And that was too far south.
A cargo ship was headed east;
Those two ships took a lot of guys away....
Crowd was much thinner now, and hungrier.
Fred went to the PX. A couple other fellows went along—
One was from Mediums, the other in the Navy.
They ordered malted milks and sandwiches.
The sandwiches were pretty good, especially the pork.
Fred Derry bought another: pork on white bread.
It was swell.
He went around the counter,
And he took the ketchup that he saw,
And spread his sandwich red and thick.
He walked back to the Line alone,
The other guys gone on before.

He saw a dandelion, butter-bright,
One tiny piece of sun
Upon this thin wet grass no other sun could find.
He thought of dandelion greens.
(His grandma sent him with a silver knife
Across the neighbors' lawns ten years before....
They had to be the smallest and the earliest:
The fragile, baby dragon-tails.)
He thought of greens, fresh-cooked, the kitchen steaming,
And once again he smelled the steak.
They had it only Saturdays because the price was high ...
And grandma dead—how long before?—
When he was flying PT 6's,
Weeks before he washed out as a pilot.
Oh, long ... how long? His grandma dead—
How long? ...
The plaintive mass and little funeral flowers....
How long since? The house was changed....
And how long since he met Marie?

He went forever, and he left
The flower metal-yellow on the grass.

ii

BACK UP to Operations. He walked faster;
There were some words upon the amplifier.
They were calling names.
                    Bryan. Smoak.
The sergeant broke his word and called the name again.
He called it twice . . . again. But never answer.
Ostwick. Hall. And then he called Fred's. *Derry.*
Fred went inside, and breathed hard in excitement.
The scornful envy of the sergeant swept him,
Saw all his ribbons, and regretted all the things
The sergeant had not seen and done,
And hated Fred for seeing them and doing them instead.

"Where you for?"
                    "Well, West. . . ."
"Boone City do you any good?"
Fred swallowed. No, it wasn't true!
His voice was shrill as he replied,
"Wizard! I'm for Boone."
"Look, sir. You be sure, or you'll be sorry—
It's hard to get away from there—
Not much stuff going out."
"By God," said Derry. "That's the place I live!
I'm in like Flynn!"
"O.K.," the sergeant said, "sign here.
You ask the pilot when he's going out."

His motion marked a red-head boy
Who stood in coveralls, down at the other end.
Fred Derry signed, and hurried to the pilot's side.
"Boone City?"
"Yeh," the pilot said. "You got a chute?
Swell, Lieutenant. We'll be leaving—twenty minutes—
If that gas is in. You haven't got a pal along, or some-
        thing?
I could take a couple more.
It's 23," the pilot said.
"That F, down at the end behind those Mitchells.
You can wait for us and ride down in a jeep,
Or you can walk. There's plenty time."
"Roger," said Fred. "I'll walk."

As he went toward the door
He heard the sergeant speak again
Upon the amplifier:
"Room for two," the hollow tone was saying,
Deep and scratchy and impressive,
The squawk-box voice you heard through several years of
    war,
The voice without a soul or conscience—
It rose to break your dreams and make your task,
And order every second that you lived.
"There's room for two," the squawk-voice said.
"Boone City. Room for two. . . ."

A man came in the door, and walking fast:
A big guy . . . infantry . . . a sergeant.
And his pants were four shades lighter than his blouse,
And he was almost out of uniform
The moment that he put them on.
A big guy—tough and smart—and he was old.
The dust of hard male years
Was on the hair that showed beneath his cap.
Buck sergeant: silver rifle and a wreath
And double deck of ribbons.
Derry looked. He saw the ETO.
This joker walked to war in Germany
While Derry flew.

"Boone City, Sergeant? Did you say Boone City?"
The big man's voice was low
And smooth and wholly courteous
But hard as concrete underneath.

"That's what I said—about a dozen times!
You want to go? You got a chute?"
The dark-faced sergeant nodded
And he held it up:
A heavy back-pack of the kind they always sign
To transients somewhere along the line.
He held it unfamiliarly;
He had not held so many chutes before.
"O.K.," the little guy with stripes was saying,
In his scorn and hatred
Of the men who'd done what he had longed to do.
"O.K. Sign here."

Fred Derry waited in the sun which shafted out
To gild the luckiness that now possessed him.
The sergeant came, and—
                    "Hey," said Fred.
The sergeant threw him a salute. Fred threw it back.
"Forget the rank," he said. "You just signed on for
    Boone?
That's where I live."

The big brown face made up a smile.
The black and silver mustache, thinly cut,
Twisted above the lip and went aloft;
The eyes were glinting,
But the eyes were hard and dark.
"Yes," said the voice, grown rugged from the war,
But with its undertone of courtesy,
Its native culture that a dozen wars could not destroy.
"I live there too."
And Derry nodded.
                    "Whereabouts?"
"I haven't seen it, sir. It's on Grand Avenue.
My wife moved there the year I left.
We had a house. But you know—with the war and all—"
"I live on Brighton," Derry told him.
"Brighton Drive."
                    "Where's that?"
"Just south of Wildwood Park."

He didn't tell him Brighton Drive was only one block
    long,
And ended in a clay ravine.
The little house, the scabby house,
Like those that grow behind the subdivisions
Where the well-to-do are housed....
The pavement ends, the road has noble name;
It's lined with sumach suddenly
Instead of curbs and velvet grass;
The road grows rough and full of clay—
The little houses come from hiding,
And the boys who live in them
Go up to cut the velvet grass
On richer lawns.

That's where Fred lived.

"Of course," the sergeant told him,
"I know Wildwood Park.
Say, what we riding in? A 17?"
Fred told him Yes. An F.
"Well, I don't care," the sergeant said,
"Just so we get there.
Are you married?"
"Yes. Are you?"
The sergeant nodded.
"I have a girl and boy," he said.
"The girl is twenty."
"Jesus Christ," Fred Derry said.
"You don't look old—
Say, are you Out?"
The sergeant touched the pocket on his breast,
And whispered, "Papers. . . . I got scared
They wouldn't let me ride."
"Balls!" said Fred Derry.
"Half the guys that hitch the rides these days are Out.
I guess that Operations knows it well enough.
What difference
If we get a ride and get Home sooner?"
"Yes," said the sergeant,
And then he spoke those very words again:
"We'll get Home sooner."
They held a pleasure and a menace all in one:
The whisper of a wedding night,
The doom of taxes and the dentist's chair.

What waited them they did not know,
But they could guess.
Their guesses would be wrong.
They knew it well,
And so did many million other men.
They were afraid. They were resentful,
But they wanted Home.
They didn't trust the people they had left;
They'd have to learn to trust them.
They'd have to learn the U.S.A.
Like any immigrant who tries to speak
His bits of history aloud before a flag.

They walked across the apron.
There were many types of aircraft—
All the hit-or-miss assemblage

Of a flight line on an ordinary field.
The stubby fighters waiting dumb—
P-47's, with their noses large and blunt—
That 40 from some air-field, straying far,
Its nose around the wind-screw painted red
To mark the squadron letter or the number;
And no chance now to ever see the German war,
And small chance now to ever burn aloft,
Or sink its redness in a land where men had hated it.

The 24, the 25, the 26,
The cargo ship with rows of seats depressed,
The fuselages twin, and all the Piper Cubs,
With folks in coveralls that walked among them,
And one lone screw that turned.

The men who wanted Home walked on.

"My name is Stephenson."
"Mine's Derry. Where you been—in Germany?"
"Yes. Gone three years, almost."
"You must have seen a lot."
"I see you got hit—"
"You sure bought the ribbon counter:
Silver Star, Bronze Star—"
"And all the GI crap," said Stephenson.
"You got a few yourself."
"Well, coming home—" said Derry.
The sergeant looked at him and grinned,
A sage old grin:
A grin that knew that Sergeant Stephenson
Was old enough to be his father.
"Do you mean," he asked, "you didn't wear them over
    there?"
And Derry said, not caring,
"Hell, yes, sure I wore them;
We all did.
Those babes in London—"

"Those babes everywhere," said Sergeant Stephenson.
They laughed.

And then, a Wac.
She wore her coveralls,
She walked with purpose, and the pride
Of little woman doing little job.

But still the coveralls could not conceal
The charm and molding of her flesh.
Fred Derry looked, but Stephenson
Was staring straight ahead
As if he saw a metal pillbox, and his love beyond....
As if he had to walk through every sort of oily death,
With every sort of flame to scorch him,
And every sort of metal heretofore devised
To open holes within him.
But they didn't. Here he was on Welburn Field.
He had a ride.... Some other guys would never ride.
So many other guys would neither move
Nor roll from out their solitude again.

...
iii

AL STEPHENSON asked where Fred worked before the
        war.
        "In Bullard's."
Bullard's was the biggest drugstore,
And the best, in all the downtown of Boone City.
Fred was there from seven in the morning until school;
From five p.m. to ten, three nights a week,
From seven to eleven other nights.
He was a sandwich man, a soda-fountain helper:
He got four bits an hour.
He was looking for a better job....
And then—on Sunday afternoon
When he had slept all through the frightened news,
He woke and heard the radio. His father wasn't home.
His father's second wife was playing bridge.
No one was home. He went downstairs.

(It's hard to think that you are young when you are
        seventeen.
It's hard to think that you could ever be just seventeen,
When you look back from twenty-one,
And know that you have killed a hundred men or more.)

He went downstairs. The radio talked on:
It spoke of Hickham Field as he stood in the door.
Pearl Harbor Sunday....

Thursday he was In.

These things he did not tell the older man
Who walked beside him now.
He only said he worked at Bullard's.
"Where did you—?" he asked.
The sergeant said, "The Cornbelt Bank."
The 1st lieutenant studied him.
"Were you a janitor or something?"
He spoke with brusqueness and such crudity
Because he was not old in ways of people civilized,
But only old in ways of people wise in war.

Then they both saw, before the sergeant could reply,
Another figure.
This was never Wac in coveralls:
This was a death—one piece of death,
Alive on its right side, and dying, jerking on its left.
It walked with pain and twisted muscles.
It was so young . . . it had a face without a beard.

Its name was Wermels, Homer,
Seaman Second-Class,
But working as a gunner's mate the night torpedoes
    struck.
He went In as a child, as many went.
He came Out as a monster.
In his brain a little telephone was doing things
And all so wrong, so very wrong indeed.
A little telephone said to his arms,
"You do not have to swing the way that arms should
    sway."
A little telephone spoke to his leg
And told it foolish things to do.
Spasticity, they diagnosed a dozen times,
But Homer's head was jerking none the less.
He held it on one side, and when he spoke,
He used a method of the men who tell the jokes—
The harelip tales, the jests that people speak
With lips held tight against their teeth.
So that was how he talked,
And that was how he'd talk till he was right again,
If ever he was right.

Nineteen years old, but twenty soon:
His yellow hair was tufted at his ears.

He had a sweep of whitish fuzz around his chin,
And bright blue eyes that looked with love on life,
Because he'd never thought to taste it more.
He dragged his foot; his shoe was built so thick
He'd drag it twenty days before the sole wore down.

The men could not believe.... "He walks abroad,"
Each muttered in his mind.
"This shouldn't be. What goes on here?
Who is this, wearing cloth
Worn only by the strongest and the best,
The straightest and the ruggedest,
The fine?"

They saw his ribbons. Purple Heart ... the ATO.
The yellow bar of South Pacific duty,
And green and brown and white—
The blotches of the ETO
With one big star upon it.

"... Right off Oran," he told them later.
"We should have flushed our tanks at Liverpool.
The old man said, 'By God, we'll miss the convoy if we
    do.'
And everybody said, 'Let's go!' and everybody went."

They caught the convoy,
And they traveled down outside Oran.
They hove to, miles outside. A blinker brought them in;
And one by one they turned and made for shore,
Each in its turn, with guarding planes above.
It grew dark. Still the blinker talked.
The skipper said, "That's us."
And words and numbers went from bridge to engineer
And back again. They swung to starboard;
All their tanks were thick with fumes.
(They would have missed the convoy,
If they'd flushed those tanks at Liverpool.)
And then it hit. The first one aft,
The second dead ahead, and missing them,
And Homer said he got an order,
And he started down a ladder,
Feeling rungs.
            The rungs dissolved beneath his hands.
And he was spastic
When they woke him up in nine more days.

All this he told them later in the 17.
He chattered like a monkey, with his lip drawn tight.
He couldn't know the life ahead
Because he had so little life behind.

Just now he came out plaintively,
Walking with half a run,
His black shoe dragging on the ground;
His thick shoe made a worser squeak
When once he walked the concrete.
"Say," he said. (That wasn't how he said it.
No more S. But that was what he tried to say.)
"Where do I go to try to get a ride?"
They looked at him hardboiled,
And knowing he was part of death, but only part;
And each declared within himself
He'd rather die than be like that.

"Where to?"
              "Boone City, sir,"
And he kept grinning up at them.
They both looked out across the field,
And each was glad he didn't have to drag himself around,
And each was glad that he was there,
And going to Boone City.

"Got a chute?"
              "No."
In that harelip whine,
But smiling still . . . his eyes so bright . . .
Like marbles he had played with, years before,
Like bits of broken teacup, or a twist
Of ribbon on a girlie's lingerie:
Pale blue, and rather soft and feminine and kind.
"Oh, no, I haven't. But they'll let me ride
Because I'm wounded, don't you think?
Say, don't I get priority or something?"

"Are you Out?" asked Stephenson, so old and grim,
So mighty, so alive and lean.

The sailor tapped his chest, and grinned.
"Oh, sure, I'm Out," he said.
"I'm sick of hospitals.
I'm getting better, too.
But, gee, it's kind of slow."

"Boone City," said Fred Derry. "Three of us. . . .
By God, I bet there's room.
Look, Sergeant, gimme!"
He picked up the chute, and Stephenson gave back a
    challenge.
"I'll leave mine," said Derry. "You wait here."
He left them there, and hurried up the Line
And found the Fort marked 23—
One GI lying on his back, asleep beneath the wing;
A greasy sergeant walked atop the other wing;
He stood and stared, and Derry waved.
He climbed aboard, back in the waist.
He dropped the chute of Stephenson
Beyond the tail-wheel housing.
There were some other chutes, some coveralls,
The clothes of officers they'd hung up forward;
All the good silver walls; the windows and the guns
    taped up;
The smell of 17, B-17,
And somehow different from the smell of any other
    plane,
Or so he thought with pride, as airmen do.

Fred hurried back;
He found the two. The sergeant still said nothing,
But the sailor talked. Fred wished he'd quit.
"Look here," he said. "They'll have to put you on the
    list.
Come on along, and keep your mouth shut.
When they ask about your chute,
Just let me do the talking."
The sailor said, "Gee, thanks," and scuffled on behind,
And Derry went ahead,
And Stephenson just grinned, and understood,
And smoked another cigarette, and strolled.

They met the pilot coming out,
And he put Homer Wermels on the list.
"You got a chute?" the pilot asked of Homer.
"Here," said Derry, and he held his own,
The peanut pack, the little olive chute he'd had before.
The pilot said with doubt, "Look here, where's yours?
We haven't got an extra chute aboard, and—"
"Christ!" Derry said.
"We left our parachutes aboard your Fort already.

Where the hell you been?
The sergeant and I want to get to Boone!"
The pilot grinned. "Eager? Let's go."
They followed on; and Homer followed last of all,
And thought about the food he'd get this very night;
He'd thought of veal loaf many, many months . . .
And brown potatoes . . . cabbage slaw. . . .
He shuffled quick behind;
His heart was full of tunes.
He thought he'd talk, but no one listened.
He made his sounds alone, and no one listened,
But his eyes were bright.

There was one moment, after they had climbed aboard:
Derry talked fast. The Crew Chief was perplexed.
"Counted just three back here," he said,
"Where's yours?"
                    "Right over there."
                                        "Where's yours?"
"Somewhere aboard," said Stephenson, with ease.
"I guess I put it up ahead
In radio," Fred Derry said
Above the warming of five thousand horses.
"It's up ahead. It's there."
The Crew Chief went to see,
And there were other chutes.
He got balled up. This was too much for him.
He found himself a harness, then a chute square-packed;
He held it up and read the number.
"This one's yours?"
                    "Sure. Sure," said Derry.
So the Crew Chief went away,
Perhaps believing, and perhaps he didn't care at all.
So many guys to climb aboard the 17's, these days,
Or anything with wings, these days.
It wasn't like a while ago. . . .
The world which war had built was breaking up.

The Crew Chief yearned for Bridgeport in Connecticut.
Another month and maybe he'd—

So they took off: three points, tail down.
And Homer Wermels drooled and dripped. . . .
One thing about spasticity: you always seem to drool.

He laughed and wiped his chin, and said that he was
    glad.
"And, anyway," he said, "the last time that I rode a plane
They signed me out a chute.
I had to sign it back....
But I'm so kind of little, and so light,
They said they'd have to shoot the chute,
And fill it full of holes,
Before my weight would bring it down!"
He laughed and mumbled in the room
Where they sat on the floor through take-off.

They were borne by air.

Fred saw his watch: two-twenty-three.
He stood up, and he put his face against the Plexiglas;
The field went low behind—
The runways patterned there,
The clover leaves cut flat at intersections,
And distant towns, all smoky and serene behind.

"How long?" the sergeant shouted up at him,
And Derry guessed three hours.
Nearly right ... but longer
If a headwind held them back.
The 17 was climbing.

iv

Later, much later, Derry went, crowding the cat-walk,
    Crowding where bombs had been,
    Wearing his coveralls again to save his uniform.
He crawled across the round flat plate, top-turret bottom,
Where once a gunner peppered death.
"It's sure beat up," he told the pilot,
Leaning there above his chair.
"Got combat time?"
"Oh, sure," the pilot hollered at his ear.
"She had a lot of time down in the South Pacific.
What was yours? What theater?"
Fred cried, "The 8th Air Force, in Britain."
"Oh," said the pilot.

Derry went under—crept in the nose,
Wormed past the Crew Chief, sound asleep
And passive with his chute beneath his head.
You couldn't hear him snore. The engines bustled on.
Derry went forward in the nose, till all the world
Was Plexiglas around him. . . .
No automatic flight control,
And that was rugged on the pilot, Derry thought.

There were the guns, with cumbrous tape around them,
And the guts were gone.
He drew the charging lever on the cheek gun at the right:
It came back lifeless, lazy, with no spring to check.
Fred clicked the top and there was nothingness:
An empty metal shell, where death had lived.
Unhooking cord, he brought the gun around;
It pulled against the balance and the spring.
He flicked the little catch from left to right,
Put it on "Fire," and held his eye behind the ring-sight
But the forward sight was gone.
He swung the gun again and snapped it up.
It swayed there empty, fit for nothing now. . . .
He thought it like a bombardier,
And like himself. He'd learned so many things:
The toggle knobs, the business of the double grip,
The rate and drift, the hairlines into place,
And all the many things you'd do
When you were working Norden bombsights. . . .
Eleven thousand dollars worth of well-tooled steel
And glass and jewelry.

What could you do against this patterned world beneath?
What could you do that men might pay you well?
That men might cheer your name in inky print,
And hang applause upon your chest—
An oak-leaf cluster for each several missions?
What might you do in life that needed not
The plunging weight of all the destiny you held?
Six thousand pounds of destiny,
So well encased, kicked loose from cocking shackles.
To plummet down on Lille and Kiel
And Bremen and the rest.

So many he had killed, when smoke went high;
So many walls and girders puffed away.

He'd taken railroad trains with his small finger,
And poked them into nothingness and dust.
So many times the mask across his face,
The heavy hose, the red ball bobbing high—
The white lips of the blinker closing, opening—
So many times the kiss of cold about his ears—
The fear that went to bed and stayed with you,
And never left your side when you were clothed
In leather and electric heat and wool of lambs.

"I was a bombardier," he told himself,
A whisper that the engines shouted back.
"I was a bombardier and did my job.
Now I am alive and Clark is not,
Neither is Stein, nor March, nor Callahan,
Neither is Olsen.... Bailey's dead, and Payne.
Gadorsky's dead, and Holloway is down.
I am up here, and going on to Boone,
And going Home to what?"

The engines mourned.

Dwelling in space where once the bombsight lay,
He held his nose above the Plexiglas,
And watched the wads of villages and farms
And larger towns.
He saw a highway, and the folks
Who rode in painful crawling cars:
He saw them all.
He wondered fleetingly about the rest:
The men he'd never known—
The ones who came anonymous from colored dots
    beneath,
From mother's house, Aunt Mollie's place,
From Home....
A million homes he'd pass above, this day.
He wondered fitfully about the rest,
And what would wait ahead of them when they were
    Home.
But only for an instant:
He was generous by nature, and in thought sometimes,
But he was young. He loved himself.
He was the best. He was Fred Derry.
All of Fred Derry's life was bound in Fred,
Now that the Bomb Group ceased to live for him,

Now that the 3-0-5th was but a name:
Something to be embraced when you were older,
Fit for reunions when your waist was fat,
And gray was in your hair.
Good for the past, good for the future,
But worth nothing now.

He slept.
          The props turned on,
The inboard engines groaned,
The outboard engines, nearer wings at either side,
Turned on as dull and rugged as before.
He slept.
          He had a little dream—
Something about the British people whom he knew:
The girl called Beatrix—
And she was Lady Tillman.
That was real.
He'd never thought
That titled people lived, outside of books,
But he had made merry with a Lady.
Not so bad....
A Flight Lieutenant relative:
That's how it came about: a Raf.
Fred Derry knew him. They had worked together.
"And when you're up in London," said the Raf,
"Why don't you give my Sis a buzz?"
And so he did.
He'd danced with Lady Tillman;
They went out, hunted their cab with flashing pocket-
     torch,
Had biscuits and another drink at home, up in her flat
Near Grosvenor ... and all the rest.
A thing like that Fred Derry'd done—
The sandwich boy from Bullard's. Soda jerk!
Two-hundred-eighteen pounds within his clothes,
Pounds sterling: multiply by four, and you have dollars.
That was a time he'd won;
Sometimes he'd lost.
The crap games roared, on nights before an op;
Sometimes he had a lot of dough, a lot of pounds,
And sometimes nothing.

He dreamed a little ... broken dreams:
His nights with Lady Tillman.

Mixed round with riding on a crowded railroad train,
And eating carrots.
Something about some bolts that lay
Lost in the grass by a dispersal point. . . .
The fragment dreams that never meant a thing;
Better than nightmares, though.
He had those too.
Sometimes he saw the fighters coming in,
Sometimes he froze to death,
Sometimes he fell,
Sometimes he fell and fell and fell and fell.

v

"F ORTY-FIVE minutes more," the pilot said.
"We've got a twelve-mile tailwind now—
That's Illinois—
Forty-five minutes more: we'll let you down at Boone!"
Al Stephenson slid back into the waist,
And talked with Homer Wermels, waking up.
"I've got to go," said Homer. "Where's the head?"
There wasn't one. They asked the Crew Chief, and he told
About the cup and tube, and where they were.
Al helped the best he could; the door swung back;
The wind came through the cracks of bomb-doors;
Homer pitched and tottered on his perch;
He couldn't manage tube and ropes together.
"Hell," said Stephenson,
"Just you forget that tube. . . ."
The boy looked Thanks,
And leaked against the bomb-bay door.

Derry came to them in the waist . . . he yelled
The time: just half an hour. They were clustered
At the right waist-port; the gun was there,
And Homer hung against it, crying joy.
They saw a river; they all knew it. All had fished
That gleaming brown, had walked those woods. . . .
The spring trees with their savage name,
The legend . . . buried bones of Pottawatomies. . . .

The red of farm barns, and the white of homes,
The windmills stippled up from black. . . .
And white the ribbons of the concrete laced,
And small the cars disported there,
And green the winter wheat shone in its squares.
Beneath were robins and the dots of cows,
Beneath were clustered roofs that made a town.
"That's Sperryville." "No, Midland Falls!"
"That must be Willow Fork," cried Homer, twisting up
    his mouth.
They let him call it Willow Fork. It didn't matter much.

So many other towns where men came Home,
So many men who didn't come to other towns—
To any towns. (So many shell-bursts in a Norman field,
So many tom-guns on the Dutch frontier,
So many subs, so many Messerschmitts.)
Goodbye to Ed, and Charlie too;
Make a memorial in the month of May.

But these were back and breathing, and each saw a room
And someone sitting there.

The Crew Chief called out from the door, and beckoned
    them.
"Going to let down," he said. "You'll have to sit."
They traveled forward, and they hunched, awaiting
    shock.
Their ears hurt. Derry blew his out,
And showed the others how.
Their ears got thick again; the Fort banked slow;
It traveled in, it rubbed against quick surfaces,
"Another buck for Goodyear," Derry said.
The Crew Chief scowled; he'd heard that crack
A hundred times before. The tail went down;
The 17 had slewed around. A yellow jeep came out to
    lead—
Its *Follow Me* so pert and sparrow-like.
The big Fort followed
To the Line.

(Did Caesar see the smoke of Rome
With staring eye, and think
That only half of him was there?)

vi

I<small>T WAS</small> all new. This Base was built
While they were far beyond the seas.
They didn't know the bleak green shacks,
The tower or the hangar roof.... The highway:
Number 2—it went to Sperryville. "The old golf course,"
Said Stephenson. "They used to call it Bonnie Dell."
"Yeh, this is it," said Derry.
"And all those farms beyond," said Al.
They walked with chutes, while Homer dragged along.
Above, beyond, in thinning brown,
The dust of sunset fired hot.
They saw Boone City's smudge, five miles across the
. fields,
They smelled a packing plant, and spring within its
stain.

The dome of their state capitol: gold leaf, it was a gem
Within the muddled soot. They saw the signs
For selling Camels, cokes and Essolube....
Boone City: population, 1940 census, just about
One hundred eighty thousand souls,
Including Milly, Peg and Rob for Stephenson;
Including Fred's Marie and all her selfishness,
Including Patrick Derry and the liquor that he drank.
Including Homer's Ma, and cabbage slaw,
And Wilma Jacobson next door,
And Epworth League, where he and Wilma used to go.

They left the 17
(Farewell, big metal friend,
Farewell to rudder, flap and fuse;
God keep your turbos strong
Until you need them not again).
The red-head pilot came behind,
And three men thanked him for their ride.
He saw two chutes.... "Where's yours, again?"
He asked of Fred.
"I lost it in the ETO," said Fred.
"Forget it, chum. We're here!"
The pilot made a face. "You're Out,"

He said with grim conviction.
"Well, I wish I was!
Duration plus six months." He made another face,
And thought of Oregon.
                    The little farm
Was lean and poor, but noble as he dreamed.

Homer was hoping for a bus.
How often did they run? He asked MP's;
They couldn't understand a word he said;
One stood embarrassed, pitying,
While Homer asked for muss or uss
Or something strange.
Al Stephenson signed back his chute;
He came to find the sailor jigging down the steps
So nervous, sensing Home,
That he could scarcely speak at all.
"Forget the bus," said Al. "We'll take a cab.
Where's the lieutenant?" Derry came
From buying cigarettes. They went to the main gate.
Al carried Homer's bag; he had none of his own.
He'd shipped his stuff Express from the east coast.
He had a razor in his pocket, one small comb,
A toothbrush and some photographs.
He had them in his pockets. That was all.
Perhaps a bag would hold him back. . . .
He wasn't used to bags, but used to packs,
Accustomed to the GI dirt and battle dress—
Even so far away from war, he felt bereft
Without a pack and carbine,
And a helmet on his head.

They found their cab. "Eight bucks," the driver said.
"Jesus," said Fred, "we're Home, and how!"
"Listen, my friend," the driver told him,
"If you don't like it you can—"
Al was inside and sitting down.
"Shut your big face," he said, "and drive."
The driver shut his big face, and drove.

vii

THIS wasn't war. It never happened here.
The maple buds were never snipped away:
Boone City never had a battle
Since painted Sioux had ridden by with arrows.
The Belt Line cars still jangled out to 33rd
Without a Mark IV tank to match their ugliness.
Never a dead child lying in the road,
Never a cat with furry paunch distended,
Never a shell to spoil the Fifth Street Bridge
Or spray the Sinclair station into pieces.
Bazookas never puffed across the roofs
Of Bide-a-Nite Motel or Butch's Place. . . .
And people said the war was getting rough
When ration boards refused to give you B's;
You saved your A-gas and you took your Chevrolet
On weekends to Rock Springs and greyhound races.

Never a war. It couldn't happen here.
There wasn't anything to scare your fancy.
You gave a pint of blood, and got a button;
They had the war-bond posters in the locker room;
A lithographed, drowned seaman long accused you
Of telling secrets you had never known, to tell.
Home Front . . . The Man Behind the Man Behind the
    Gun.
Welders Are Wanted . . . Back the Attack. Please Do.
Give bundles to the French if they are Free;
Give bundles to the British and the Poles;
Withholding income tax, and paper salvage,
And flat tin cans, and help the USO. . . .
And telegrams that came sometimes
(O wicked little windows, stamped with stars).

Boone City never had a war: the town was whole.
The malted milks still whirled at Bullard's store;
And Oppenheimer-Stern announced their sale
Of new spring rayons just as sheer as nylons.
And telegrams were made of worded tape:
"Deepest regret" and "Service of his country."
A woman out on Elm Street closed the door,

And held the yellow telegram, and spread it flat,
And read it once again, and saw the hall go spinning,
And called out, "Eunice..." in a tiny voice;
But still Boone City never had a war.
And other telegrams, from 1941
Clear up till now, clear up till '45—
To Woodlawn, Stanley Drive and East 19th
To make the stars turn gold.
                              The older folks
Often wore black. The younger seldom wore it.
Boone City never had a war—
Because the Christian Science church
Was quite intact; and so was Temple Sholom;
So were St. Thomas's... and Butch's Place.

O long, O long the midnight sky
Unwashed by searchlight fan and tracer stream!
United Airlines sent their Flight 16
Above the roofs, and no one ever ducked.
The sirens shrilled in February, '42;
A few times more: just once in '43....
The air-raid wardens studied long directions;
They took First Aid at Wilson Junior High;
Some of them got their helmets. Some
Had only arm-bands for their pride.
And sand-pails stood in upstairs hallways
Of the Hotel Daniel Boone....
O long, O long forever—night unscorched
By Heinkel, Dornier, Junkers and the rest!
The air-raid wardens took their arm-bands off—
Ready to die if need be. (They would have died
As bold as London ARP's)
They didn't have to die.
Their little boys played War with wardens' helmets;
And Red Cross pamphlets stood forgot
In upstairs bookshelves next to *Freckles, Tish,*
And *Stoddard's Lectures.*
                              Never war in Boone.

Thus D-Day came, and people drank,
And some were praying.... *Yanks Advance in Normandy.*
The queer French names again. The Legionnaires,
The stay-at-homes today, they talked of Toul and Brest,
And tried to think of things forgot; and envied youth....
So what did *vin blanc* taste like, anyhow?

Thus Paris fell, and radios were full
Of drama, caution, brag and platitudes.
The pictures spread in *Life* and *Look* and *Click,*
The newsreels at the Alamo and Orpheum,
The commentators busy always on the air—
(Brim-full and spilling over, radios)
And BBC re-broadcast to the States
A tale of robot bombs. Boone City heard the bombs.
Re-broadcast bombs are not so frightening to hear.
The Siegfried Line was breached, the Rhine was crossed,
And robots ceased to buzz. There came a day . . .

In German street there was a burned-out tank.
"Look out," said Al.
"O.K.," said Pascowitz. "I'm looking out."
They passed the tank.
Two soldiers came behind them slow.
"Look out. That window over there." Al looked.
The mine went off.
There wasn't anything to do
For Pascowitz.
Al couldn't figure what it was
He wiped from off his helmet rim—
It was so round and wet and firm.
A piece of bone?
He nearly slept, that night,
And then he bounded up,
Disturbing Smith and Beecher.
Half awake, he knew:
Yes, Pascowitz, the all-State end—
The glamour boy, the jitter-bug,
The master of a hundred dames.
("Only God," the boys would say,
"And Pascowitz
Can make a tree.")
And now Al knew. Yes, yes—oh, yes—
The pink and dangled little thing
With veins and stuff attached:
A testicle.

So Homer shook and quavered on his bed,
And Fred went back on Bomber Operations,
And Al sneaked on through Germany.
There'd come a day . . . with flags displayed at Home,
And whistles blown for long, for long

Atop the Midland Tin & Type,
Atop the oat mills, and the Ford assembly plant,
But still it never was a war in Boone.
It hadn't happened there. No mortar fire
At the Western Ball Park nor on Cherry Street.
No girl of ten or twelve, to slip up dirty-faced
And say, "Hello.
You got a cigarette?
You give me cigarette—
I play so nice with you."
No war in clover, none in corn,
Nor in the cottonwoods along the streams.
The sun went down in pretty haze of spring
As when the Pottawatomies were there.

viii

HOMER was first. He lived on 17th.
    The taxi turned from Black Hawk Boulevard
    And passed the school where Homer used to go.
The street was lilac in its lengthened ease—
Some maple trees, some elms, a vacant lot,
And houses set above their sloping lawns. . . .
And boys rode bicycles in circles
With auto traffic thin.
An old man walked; he turned to talk
With someone sitting on a porch.
It was the sober, verdant kind of street
Where God is middle-class (the devil keeps a maid)—
One house is rich, but none is poor,
And cupolas adorn the elder roofs,
And stained glass lights the narrow hall,
And four-o'-clocks are bright in summer yards;
And there's a card-tray on a table top
Containing pins, one stamp, a Yale lock key
And rarely anybody's card.
The hitching-post still waits by Mrs. Engle's curb:
An iron darkey holding bridle-ring
(The carriage never comes. It has not come since 1912.)

So Homer Wermel's taxi scraped and stopped.
Al got out first; Fred held the little canvas bag.

Al checked the number: 1525—
That was the way he'd understood it,
And told it to the driver.
"This the place?"—
And Homer beamed and drooled.
He squeaked; he nearly fell, a-getting out,
But Derry caught his arm.
                              "Say—
How much did he say?
This taxi—" Homer tried to claw
His money out.
"Aw, Christ," said Fred.
"Come on, Mac. Let's go."

They started up the concrete steps.
A woman came and trembled on the porch—
The door left open—inside sounded running feet
And screams. *He's here! That's him!*
Oh, Dad—it's Homer—
Homer's mother could not move
Her feet;
She stood and looked.
A girl came out: Luella, just thirteen,
She skipped and cried—
Then came the father, and Aunt Sade—
An audience of horror on the porch.

They hadn't known his arm would flap like that.
They hadn't known he'd throw his leg around—
The letters he had sent to them were sane
And written with his good right hand.
No one had thought his face would pull and squeeze
Until the baby mouth was tightened out of shape—
No one had known he'd flop and dance
So gaily as he walked.

A little dog that lived two doors away:
A wire-hair. Its name was Jinx.
It came to run and sally,
Bark and challenge, growl and shake its head;
This was a clown, a thing to worry,
To make advances at, to whirl away,
To dive again and try to bite—
A relic of the Homer that it knew,
Somewhat forgotten, partly loved,

And partly like a game to play—
A garbage-man to check, a tramp to jeer,
An enemy uncouth, a crazy thing.
Arr-warr-warr-warr. The dog came back
So many times, no matter how
They called its name. *Here, Jinx! Here, Jinx!*
Luella wailed as she was pleading with the dog.
Derry kicked out. The villain snarled and dodged.
Nice Jinx! Oh, go away—
Luella came to Homer first. She cried his name.
She bellowed into tears.

The Jacobsons heard noises in the yard
And Wilma Jacobson, next door, came out to see....
He'd taken her to Epworth League,
One high school dance, to movies seven times;
And she had Homer's picture on her dresser,
And called him hers. Her sailor. He was hers
To gush about, to cry about, to love,
To spat with in the letters that she wrote,
To build imagined marriages....
And they were not engaged:
They were too young,
They didn't know a thing.
She was His Girl, and wore a Navy pin
On her school sweater.

So she came out upon the porch
And witnessed Homer, coming Home.

There was a silence, after tears—
Beginning of the longer silence that would come.
Derry and Al took mumbled thanks, and fled
Back to the taxi....
Didn't speak.
They smoked.
The taxi went
To 17th and Cottage Grove.
"Go over west," said Al,
"And back on 20th.
That goes clear through to Grand."
"No, 21st," the driver said,
Humble and somehow scared,
And never knowing why.
"I'll drop you first," said Al to Fred.

"I go out west to 34th."
"Roger," said Fred.
They didn't talk again;
But Homer stayed before their eyes a while.

ix

... The dusk was darker. Derry saw
A house above the turn in Wildwood Park.
He used to think it like a castle:
All brick and pointed gables: manor house.
No castle now, nor manor house,
But just a place in Wildwood Park
Where lived the local agent for the Phoenix Mutual.

He saw it with a sour eye.
Something was wrong. This wasn't as
He'd thought to come. Something was cockeyed—
Snafu and fouled and mixed around—
When houses shrank and trees grew small,
And cities lost their spice and strength
(The hotel here was once a dream
Of luxury too rich to be attained
By common men ... he'd seen it now—
This hour: sixteen stories high,
Its dismal red electric sign—a wretched thing.
How sweet the age of Claridge's!
How fair the Mayfair and Savoy
In any rationing, in any fall of bombs)!
And all the people docile here in Boone—
Oh, thin-lived folks who didn't know a thing
About the wizardry of life and death—
Life was their bridge club and their profit on the books;
Death was a siege of gallstones
At the age of sixty-two.

The taxi swam the curving avenues....
"Hold it," said Fred. The driver stopped.
"This it?" asked Al.
　　　　　　　　　　"Just down the road."
Fred pointed to a winding sluice,

And said some more—about its being difficult
To turn around down there.
                              Now he was out;
He had his harness and his chute,
His zipper bag.
                 Al watched him.
Each was afraid, somehow, to leave the other.
Like children, infant playmates, side by side,
Exiled in kindergarten at the age of five—
They huddled close in spirit, and they stared,
And found a comfort in their fear together.

"What will you do with that chute, now?
Keep it forever for a souvenir?"

"No, it's signed out—a guy named Weeks.
He's still at Mitchel. It goes back Express."

"Well, good luck, sir," said Al.
The *sir* came out before he thought.
He saw those bars. The *sir* came out. . . .
"Hey. Wait—I'll get this cab—"

"I've got a lot of nice *per diem*
Burning up my pants," said Fred.
He gave the driver Ten. The man dug down
For change. "O.K., O.K.," said Fred
With irritation in his voice,
And went away amid the dusk
And didn't wait for change.

He heard the tires humming far,
The switch of gears.
                      He walked along;
His feet slapped on the sloping road;
The pavement ceased; Fred walked the ruts
Half-dried from early springtime rain.
New curbs-and-gutters ran beside him,
White in the gloom. Some day they'd pave that street.
He saw a window yellow-lit—
Macgregors' house, it used to be;
Maybe some other people lived there now.
He noted water running through
A hillside drain: hollow it went
Into a culvert. Lights of the town
Spotted the other hill beyond.

A freight train filled the east with sound,
And cars honked fitfully.

O God, O somber God in sunset dust—
Now I come Home,
But I am nothing like
The green and hopeful thing that went away.

x

Hıs father had a little face,
Small for his height.... Rough eyebrows,
Raw mustache, and hair that seldom felt a comb.
His voice was nasal, kindly ... he apologized
Each breath he drew.
                "By golly, Fred, I'm sorry
That you never wired us. We would of had
A decent dinner. We ain't got so much tonight.
Mother was kind of tired; we just thought
We'd open up a can of salmon—
Stuff like that. I sure am sorry
You didn't let us know—"
                His father
Had a black crust on his hands—
The crust that printers get, and press-men.
He was a press-man—Union—Local Number 2.

His father wiped his eyes a little
When Fred came ... let his hands shake....
They shook more than they used to shake.
His hair was paler. Gin was a fog
Around him. His long underwear
Made rims of sodden gray around each wrist.
Pat Derry—forty-nine,
But looking sixty-odd.

The woman who ground open cans
At the big opener upon the wall—
A widow, Mrs. Newburger by name,
Before she married Patrick Derry
When Fred was aged sixteen.

Her neck was red; the straying hairs
Stood out in fuzz. She could have bathed
A bit more frequently. She had no humor
But she laughed a lot. She played bridge
Twice a week, and went to Bingo parties
Other afternoons.
"Gee, you sure are the nuts!"
She shrilled in antique slang.
"Look at his medals, Pop—those ribbon things!
Freddy, you look so grown-up
That Mother hardly knew you."

"Forget that Mother stuff," said Fred.
He didn't mean to hurt her,
But cared not if he did.
"My mother died when I was twelve.
Your name's Hortense. I'll call you that."

First she looked frightened, then annoyed.
"You used to call me Mom before you went. . . . "
"The hell I did," said Fred.
"That Mother stuff was yours.
You're still Hortense to me."
Her little nitwit brain decided
This was funny, and she squealed with laughter.

Derry walked back into the living room.
His father twisted knobs upon the radio:
The stations made their fragment sounds.
"Listen," he told his Dad,
"Give me the gen about Marie again."

"The what?"
                "Sorry. Tell me again
About Marie, and tell it slow."

"Well, just like I said, she didn't like it here.
We didn't get along so good and—
Her and me—we got along,
But she was kind of cross with Mother.
You know how women are. They used to fuss
And bicker all the time. Then—well—Marie—
She got a job: cashier down at the Alamo.
You know—the ticket office?"
He made a plaintive question with his voice.

"That's what she used to do:
Sell tickets in a movie
When we first met, at camp," said Fred.

"Yes. Well, she got so sort of uppity.
She had a lot of money—
Guess you sent her some— And buying clothes, and all.
Well, she and Mother had a row,
And yelled, and everything.
Marie, she just lit out. She moved.
Packed up her things one night and went."

Hortense had lingered near the door
To hear the tale. She heard it.
There was more she could have told,
But Fred's rebuke still hurt her ears;
She was perplexed, and hurried back
To put the salmon on a plate.

"Well, Fred, she isn't at the Alamo—
Not selling tickets any more.
She's got a night club job—"

"Where?"
        "I don't know
Which one it is. We got a lot of bars
And places opened up since you been gone.
All these defense folks, they sure spent the dough;
But now I guess a lot of them
Won't have so much to spend—"

"Well, where's she live?"

"At Pine and 23rd.
Tnat building on the corner.
Kitchenettes. . . ."

"Yes," said Fred Derry
"It was built before the war:
The Lorelei." There was so much
He might have asked—so much
He might have said.

He'd known Marie for seven days
Before they married. They had spent

Twelve nights together; only twelve.
After the twelfth night he was gone away.
She wrote him she was pregnant,
And he had her move
Up to Boone City with his folks.
She wrote again. A false alarm, she said....
But she kept living there.
Four times she'd cabled, telling him
She needed money. Each time he sent
The money that she asked:
Eight hundred sixty bucks in all,
Besides the regular amount each month.

The boys he flew with knew her face;
He had her picture on the wall
With Lana Turner, Hildegarde, Priscilla Lane,
And nameless girls with satin skin
And slinky gowns from out *Esquire.*
The boys declared Marie to be the best;
They whistled wolf-notes at her gleaming hair
And black chiffon—
Woo-woo, they yelped.
They called her *Derry's Diamond-studded Tail.*

"Hey, listen—that's my wife—"

"Yeh?" said Gadorsky.
"How's about her number, when I finish up
And go back to the States? I'll call her, Derry.
How's about the telephone? *Woo-woo!*"

Gadorsky finished over Vegesack.
It was his twenty-second op.
They burned up all the way,
And Derry watched them burn.
In times like that
You thought the oxygen was out.
You couldn't breathe.... *Woo-woo.*

xi

THIS night he lingered not for long.
The canned salmon, the canned beans—
The stuff he'd seldom had abroad—
The common food of lower-class that seemed
So horrid when you had it every day,
But such a prize in Britain. . . .
Patrick Derry asked
His thousand questions. Quite intelligent they were.
He was a man who thought a lot
About a world that baffled him,
And found retreat from all perplexity
In gin.
      Fred got away
As soon as he was able;
Went to the bathroom, shaved,
Rubbed up his shoes.
"Well, Fred," his father said,
"I guess you're off—"
Derry said, "Yes, I'm off."

"Be home tonight? I guess the bed's made up
In your old room—"
"I don't know," the boy replied
With honesty. "Expect me
When you see me. I'm sure much obliged
For that swell supper."
      "Gee!" cried Hortense.
"That wasn't much. Tomorrow night
I'll get some hamburg—fix it up
With onions, just the way you like!"
"Thanks a lot, Hortense." He made a smile;
He looked at her and saw a sweetness
In her empty, sagging face
That he had never seen before.

Both sweet,
He told himself . . . the futile, nameless people
Of a hundred lands. They meant to do
The best they could. They were enslaved;
They fought the wars, they conquered,

They were led, and ordered on
To fresh enslavement. They had boasted
In this country every chance;
And still they never had a chance
Because they were themselves.
                              God pity them,
His spirit wept.
                    His mouth made jokes.
"Be seeing you in church,"
Hortense was calling as he closed the door.

God pity them and bless them all.
God pity them . . . the short, the tall. . . .

He walked the road. He saw Marie
Before him in illusion . . . he had dreamed of her
In black chiffon. . . . By God, forget
This Jesus stuff. What business have I got
Condemning folks or blessing them?
I'm twenty-one. She is my wife, by God.
Eight hundred sixty bucks. . . . a night club?
Lorelei? . . . . I'll sleep with her tonight,
Or I'm no credit to the 3-o-5th.
I've got to take up slack,
And do some double sack-time for some other guys
Who'll never do their own.
                          Marie!
He heard his voice
Go gasping in remembrance, as he lay with her.

He walked the road
In chilly darkness. Over Vegesack
He saw Gadorsky's Fort go down.

xii

WHEN YOU come out of War to quiet streets
You lug your War along with you.
You walk a snail-path. On your back you carry
it—
A scaly load that makes your shoulders raw;
And not a hand can ever lift the shell
That cuts your hide. You only wear it off yourself—
Look up one day, and vaguely see it gone.

You do not see yourself in malformation.
The men and girls who have no shells
Of War upon their backs— You count them well de-
formed.
You recognize the other snails by eyes or ribbons;
You speak your perfect language to their ears,
And they to yours. You look with solemn eye
On those without a shell. You do not scorn,
You do not hate, you do not love them for it.
You only say, "They have no shell."

With other snails you crawl the quiet street
And wonder why you're there,
And think of folks who aren't.
You polish up your shell for pride
Until you tire of it.
And one day it is gone if you are wise.

xiii

THE TAXI stopped the third and final time,
And Al got out. The driver said, "Good night."
"Good night," said Alton Marrow Stephenson the
3rd,
Harvard the class of '24, great-grandson of a man
Who met John Tyler face to face,
Who knew Van Buren very well.

"Good night," said College, Bank and Country Club,
Said elder Baptist faith and Sound Investment
And late Republican and Isolationist.

They called it Casa Blanca. Neon dripped
Sedately round the vestibule.
The light came down
From seven stories of Venetian blinds
And light-anointed windows.
There were two junipers beside the steps
And cars two-deep along the half-moon of the drive.
The doorman wore a phony uniform
Like comic-opera Latin general.
Al didn't like the place. This wasn't Home.
He thought of Home—three miles beyond
The end of Grand, in brushy hills, and rented to
A fellow from the East who came out there
To manage war production
For the Midland Tin & Type.

This wasn't Home,
But it held Milly and the kids.
He walked inside. The doorman called
A sharp command—polite, perhaps,
But full of small authority.
Another man in uniform
Came out to block Al's way.
"Who is it that you wish to see?"
Al turned; he halted there; he spoke the name
Of Stephenson.
                "That's 7-A. The penthouse.
Is Mrs. Stephenson expecting you?"
"Oh, more or less," he said, and started on.
They called again—a sharper tone;
They ordered him to wait.
"Listen," he said, and speaking slow,
"I'm Sergeant Stephenson, her husband.
Don't you touch that telephone.
You want to spoil it all?"
                He laughed.

They didn't laugh. They looked at him
In servile snobbishness and doubt.
"You're Mr. Stephenson?"
                "Sergeant," he said.

And suddenly he hated every inch
Of carpet and terazzo stairs—
He hated every fake and fraud
In pictures, lamps and Spanish furniture.
He hated oaken chest and useless leather seat,
And all who managed such a cheap attempt
At made-to-order elegance.

"Just a buck sergeant. What did you
Expect? Lieutenant-colonel?"

The elevator man had ducked his head;
He tried to make a joke. He said
Something about his boy in the Pacific.
Al didn't listen. Floors went by. . . .
He saw the painted numerals
On grimly-antiqued doors.
Now he was here. The panel slid.
"First on the right, sir. Glad you're back!"
Descending now . . . hydraulic depths.
Al felt a shame; he didn't turn around
Or say a word.
He pressed the bell beside the door.

Long, long he waited, hearing clean
Electric summons in the little rooms beyond.
He waited seconds studied into years
As he went through the puzzle of his past:
The hasty draft in '42. In 1942
The nation fumbled in a dismal doubt;
Selective Service boards were all confused,
And in Boone City they called pampered men like Al—
The well-dressed golfers who had desks in banks
And Scotch in lockers at the Black Hawk Club. . . .
So smugly tailored in their small-town way
They'd be a joke as soldiers!
                              Stephenson
Was forty—married—with two children.
He tried for OCS and had no luck;
But when they started jerking men past thirty-eight,
He found himself in Africa, a Pfc,
And proud as hell the day he got another stripe.

Eternity . . . he waited: fifteen seconds, surely.
He saw a boy who longed to run away

To swat the Kaiser in another war.
He heard his father's careful voice:
                                          "I know
The way you feel. I wouldn't mind, myself.
Your mother's heart is pretty bad ... that lesion ...
Doctor Smalley said she mightn't last till spring.
It's up to you. But stay in high school if you can."
He stayed. His mother lived until July.

Now boyhood opened up a door to him.
Al heard the heavy feet approach
And wondered with a sudden jealousy
What man was there.
                        Rob turned
The iron knob ... stood five-feet-eight
And growing taller. Hair like Al's own,
In burnished black; the Adam's apple, too;
The little freckles got from Milly.
He was fourteen. His eyes blazed wild
As when his father saw him last.
(The baby face extended on the neck
And torso of a coltish man)—
Rob let his jaw go down; he sucked in breath
For one hyena howl of glee.

Al had a hand across Rob's mouth.
He squeezed and hugged him
As they struggled there. *Keep still, keep still,*
Don't let your mother hear.
"All right," the changing voice
Assented with a strangled squeak,
But still the boy was hugging him.

"Where's Mom?"
                        Rob motioned to the living room.
"Where's Peggy?"
                        "In the kitchen, fixing toast—"
They heard her voice. She had a little radio
Out there; she sang duet with Lena Horne.

Milly called out against the songs;
Her paper rustled. "Rob,
Was that a Special—
Or a telegram?—"
                        The paper made a noise

Again. The Capehart played Sibelius
Which did not chord with Lena Horne.
Al reached the door. Rob pushed him back,
And saw the coast was clear,
And drew him on again.
                              Five times
He'd called, Long Distance, since he landed
In the States. They were expecting him;
They didn't know the day or hour.
                              This was it.

The mortars missed him close in Rhineland rain.
The bullets missed him other times;
The shells and booby-traps and mines
Had finished Pascowitz and Sloane
And Maxon, Hancock, Rosenberg,
And twenty-seven more from his platoon.
But this was it.
                    Al looked at Milly:
She was in a chair. She had her glasses on;
She read the *Tribune* . . . couldn't see her face,
But still her hair was curly, live and fair.
She wore the skirt of her blue suit,
A blouse he'd never seen before,
And little shoulder straps all pink and slick
Beneath the tender cloth.
He saw her legs: the lovely knees,
The ankles just a bit too full
But meaning much to him. (He'd thought of them
In worship and in fury. Thirty months of thought
And long denial, nor caressing them.)
He saw her feet and knew their size:
Four-and-a-half, or Five, and B.
(The slippers he had bought so ardently,
Silly with silk and fur—the golden mules)
He saw the slim and stilted heels
Fashioned of patent black, made by a man,
Made by machine, but seeming part of Milly
When she wore them. . . .
And his slow passion was the maddest miracle—
Like thunder, wind and hard bright star—
As honest as the dirt, and clean as ice—
The happy lust good men can feel
When they love loins and morning voice
And secret rapture shared a thousand times;

And, in a bargain, have created flesh
Of the same woman.
                    Milly turned,
She saw him standing there; she didn't say a word.
Her face began to work. The tears broke loose—
He came to her—she came to him—
Belatedly she squawked his name again, again
Amid her sobs.
                  Their daughter hustled,
Slipping and banging, from the kitchen;
Knocked off a platter from a shelf.
It didn't break. The Scotty came behind—
He'd begged his head off in the kitchen—
Now he barked it on again.
                            He danced
And stepped across the rug, a crazy wad
Of noisy fur and dripping tongue
And tartan collar. Peggy tried
To climb Al's back, the way she used to do
When she was six.
                  Sibelius droned
In morbid passages. The toast burned black.
Down yonder in the kitchen, Lena Horne
Was singing *Stormy Weather* all alone.

xiv

Now I do not depend
     On trigger-squeeze—
     I do not need
The brassy tubes of life held out to me.
Machine-gun belt no longer leaps,
Tracked through my eager heart
Each time a charge is fired.
Link-strippers on my soul
Do not tear off the futile chain
That binds the empty cases close.

And yet, and yet
I cannot taste my ease as I would eat it.
I hold the egg-shell in my hand,

I touch the oyster with my fork,
And swallow delicate the white dessert,
And puff the rich cigar—
But taste I dreamed is never there.

I hold the fragile hand
And smell the sugar of the hair and skin—
I feel the thigh of her I love
Snuggled against my bomb-explosive body
(And fit to have the time-fuse set it off
Without the ordinary wait for arming)!
But this was not the love I sought in sleep.
In moist, monastic dream
I made a sin
Of more supreme intensity
Than I had ever known before.

Now I no longer heed, nor need to heed
The business of the crowding into line—
I do not need to fill my mouth with oaths
To say a simple thing.
      But other men
Eat at my board; I cannot order them away.
They kiss one child, and swat the other on the back,
They laugh at every joke I tell
Before the point is told;
They occupy my chair.
      And other men
Are here to purify my bed ... they would defile it
Were they of the flesh.

Sit down to eat,
My children, with the best condemned platoons
That ever met the enemy in rain and mortar spray.
Open your limbs, my love,
To half a battalion at a time.
I am forever They,
And They are I.

XV

THAT night Fred Derry was a spook,
Haunting the dark at 23rd and Pine.
He caught a bus at Grand—only because
There was no taxi near—
And rode up 23rd to Pine.
The Lorelei had twenty windows on its front
And half of them were dark,
And half were bright and loud
With people's talk, and radios'.

The vestibule
With no attendant—
The little cards beside the bells,
The boxes for the mail—
He found her name, her maiden name,
(If ever she had been a maid:
She wasn't when he met her)
Marie Lundell. He found a shock
In seeing it, so saucy, printed plain.
He wondered if she'd used the silver pen
He sent her from Miami—
Birthday, 1943.

He tried the bell. No answer.
Tried again. He knew she wasn't there,
But kept on ringing stubbornly.
A j.g. and a girl came out—
The door swung wide. Fred caught the knob
Before it could swing back.
"Thanks a lot," he said
Before the catch could lock him out.

He prowled the hall, and heard a chatter
Through thin walls. He saw the stairs
And went up to the Second.

xvi

Here it exists:
2-E. I'll ring:
I don't know why....
She isn't here;
The door is locked
Just like downstairs.
I'll ring again.
And here's her card:
Marie Lundell—
With yellow hair
That always has the shine
Of brass.
Her voice is thin—
I thought it cute
Because so shrill and round.
I said, "You've got a little voice,
Just like a mouse.
You squeak again."
She squeaked.
We lay in bed
And giggled....
"Freddy, pet,
I'm crazy for you, Fred!"
She sobbed a little—
Oh, she was fun in bed.
I whispered, "Squeak."
She was a mouse
And gave her *Eeeee* again.
I laughed
And bent my leg,
And slid it up
Across her flank.
"Oh, *babe*," she sobbed.
Her shifting lips
Were busy with my flesh again.

Love, love...
I've known a lot of love.
But I was younger, then,
And going off to war.

I had my old Observer's wings.
I had not known
So many people that I came to know:
Clark, Stein and March
And Callahan,
Gadorsky, Perkins,
Stone and Scott,
Bailey, McClintic,
PeeWee Reese....
Recite the litany
Of all the Down.

I had not known
The chilly wind of Chelveston—
The quiet road
To Rushden green—
Or Key Club far in Bedford town,
Where men who'd burn tomorrow night
Ate Spam, and drank
Their gin-and-lime
With all the Rafs.
We stood at 12 o'clock
And heard our Song,
And put our heels together—
Then the orchestra
Would play *God Save the King*.

I had not known
(When lying with Marie)
The rubble of a London waste;
I had not heard
The sirens bray,
Nor watched the searchlights
Meet and cross—
Had never run for shelter
From the flak—
I had not known
The supper clubs
And dead men's laughter
And *That Old Black Magic*
While the bombs came down
A block away.
I had not loved
With Lady Tillman
(Beatrix to me)—

Waked in a sunrise,
Thrust the blackout shade aside,
And seen her husband
Cold in Crete,
Watching us, disapproving
With his thin and scornful face,
From out a silver frame.

A chocolate fudge;
One cherry malt;
Banana split
And maple nut....
I was a soda boy
At Bullard's.
But still I'm only twenty-one—
Oh, Christ!
I'm old as God.

Marie, Marie—
I never knew
The heart of life
In chewing at your heart....
I had not seen
The sky at Kiel,
The pattern of Berlin,
The insect maze of Nantes,
And Schweinfurt flare
And Kassel dust
And fighters over Hamm,
And twenty thousand feet of smoke
Built up so high from Huls—

I had not seen
Gadorsky's Fort go down.

Come, Derry's Diamond-studded Tail,
Polish the brass
Within your hair—
Squeak like a mouse,
Scratch like a cat,
And try to harm my soul;
You can't.
I love you not;
I know no proper path of love.
But I'm between

Your legs tonight,
Or I'm unworthy of the 3-0-5th
And quite unworthy of my youth,
My age and pain,
And all I've seen—
Unworthy of
The hundred deaths I've died.

xvii

THEREFORE so ghostly, back he went,
   Walked in a dullard's road
   And smelled the damp of spring.
He stood in doorways, under glare
Of whitened light.
He watched the girls go by
With neon blue across his face.

There wasn't any sense in hunting her;
He didn't have a car;
There were a dozen places for Marie:
The Chez Rosette, the Barn, the Palace Club.
He read their ads in papers; saw the signs. . . .
One was three miles beyond Oak Park,
One was five miles the other way.

He tried the Daniel Boone:
Blue Terrace Room, they called the place.
You went down marble steps
And heard a noise
Of sour trumpets and a crooning ass.
A girlie dressed in black swished up
To flash her teeth, and say,
              "No bar.
The bar's upstairs. If you sit down,
Lieutenant, it's three dollars minimum."
He didn't stay for long. He couldn't say,
"Hon, do you know Marie?
She's Derry's Diamond-studded—"

He couldn't ask. He sat around;
Saw one man with an Air Force patch
Drunk as a skunk—from fighters—

Thick mustache—had D.S.C.
On his left breast,
And T. S. snarling in his eyes.
He saw a lot of Navy, and some Spars.
They smiled at him. He heard
The dullest orchestra in seven States.
He had his drink, two drinks;
He stayed on rye.
He paid the minimum, and left.
"Blue Ointment Room!" he sneered.
"The hell with it. . . ."
                              Go back
To 23rd and Pine, and sweat her in.

Therefore so balked and ugly, back he went,
As petulant as any *Poltergeist* in castle walls.
He haunted up the vestibule, and tried the bell.
The hours crawled like crabs. *And I am Home,
And coming Home to what?*
Fred Derry went across
The midnight-empty street,
With buds of trees above his head,
Sat down upon the steps of someone's church
And waited for Marie to come.

He smoked his last cigar, and slept,
And dreamed of coming Home—
But Home was Flight Lieutenant Grace,
And something else—a Beaufighter, head on.
They smashed the hardened sky, and people said,
"The wind-drift and the arc . . .
Go in at twenty-seven thousand.
There's a 1-0-9
At three o'clock. . . ."
He wakened cold and hating everything,
And wanting Home.
                              He started up,
Exclaimed within his throat—
Why, what was this? A church?
An ugly little church?
And sleeping on the steps . . .
Ah, yes. The Lorelei
Across the street.
His watch said one o'clock.
He didn't know it, but Marie had come.

Quick, quick he reached the Lorelei,
Prepared to ring the lobby bell. . . .
Wait, wait! said something mean and small
Within his brain. . . . He waited.
Other people came. Two older dames, a man—
He walked behind them to the stairs—
The woman whispered that he had no key,
And what was this—? The man Ahem-ed
And started: "Just a minute, please.
Do you live in this building? What's the matter?
Lose your key?"

                    "Forget it, chum,"
Said Derry quietly.
He climbed the stairs.
The people fussed and wondered, down below.

2-E. He stood beside her door
And heard another man inside.
He'd known there'd be another man;
He'd known it all along, and never recognized
The knowledge until now.
Through flimsy walls the voices chirped—
The man laughed once. Fred heard the gush
Of water in a sink. Marie squealed out—
She said, "Aw, heck.
The ginger ale's all gone."
Fred pushed upon the bell.

In later times, he counted up
The words he said, the words she said,
The words said by the other man. . . .
They rolled away like beads
From off a broken string.
He couldn't count them all.
He didn't want to count them all.

In later times he would recall
The blue pajamas which she wore—
The man stretched loose upon the couch,
A weary, hard-faced man of thirty-odd—
And this Marie, a brassy statue, gold and blue,
With cubes of ice she dropped upon the rug
The moment she had opened up the door.

The man said simply,
"Well, I never knew

A thing about it, friend.
She told me that she wasn't tied to anyone!"
He laced his shoes.
                    Looked up again:
"See, friend, I'm on the up-and-up.
I did ten months myself: the Solomons.
I wouldn't be here now if she was on the square.
She came to Carlo's, couple months ago;
He hired her. I'm not the boss—
I only work behind the bar,
And she works on the dice game—"

"Hurry up," said Fred, "and scram."
The other man got out his coat and hat,
He said, "So long," as if with no regret;
He shrugged and went away.
                              A decent guy.
Fred couldn't help but think so, even then.

"My Freddy pet! I never did a thing.
I swear to God—we never did a thing!
He's just a friend. He's got a wife
In Akron, and a kid—"

"—Which makes him out a swish."

"Fred." It was the tightest gasp.
"Fred—what are you gonna do—?"

"Me? Not a thing.
Just have a look around—"

The tiny bedroom there beyond . . .
He saw her clothes upon a chair.
The dresser held three pictures: one was his,
One a lieutenant, senior grade, in navy gray,
And one a Pfc.
"Boy," said Fred Derry,
"Quite a gallery—"

She shrieked, and wailed some words.
They weren't the nicest kind of words.
She railed, and said she wasn't anybody's fool;
She bet he'd had a hundred girls
Since he was gone—

"No," he declared, "just nine.
I've been across since April, '43—
Two years. Or don't you know?"

Marie began to cry.
She said a girl got lonely.
It was only natural. . . .
Oh, Freddy, doll—she'd never done a thing!
Those guys were only friends—
"I guess a girl can have some *friends*—"

"Yeh. Sodas down at Bullard's?" Derry asked.

He turned a knob: the closet door.
Marie flew savagely—
"You leave my things alone!"
She tried to tear his hand away;
Quite coolly Derry slapped her face,
And pushed her back across the bed.
She lay and wept.
                    The closet held
About a million dresses, seemed to him,
And most he'd never seen before.
An Army bathrobe—wool—
The kind you buy in a PX.
A set of head-phones. . . .
"Navy," said Derry, touching them.
"Say, who left these? The sailor boy?"
Some rum unopened on the bottom shelf
Among her many shoes—
A pair of Army shoes, smooth-toed—
"Size Eight. Too small for me."
                            Marie kept crying.

Then he was in the sitting room
And looking out at mystic trees and lights.
His wife crept to the door, and spoke his name.
"It's funny," Derry told her. "I've had girls,
Just like I said. Most people have.
It ought to make me feel a little different,
But it don't. See—if our wives at home
Had men, we never want to know it.
And that's not all! I couldn't take an ounce
Of this, or you . . . can't even buy a nickel's worth
Of Home. I haven't said a word

About your leaving there.
You might have told the truth
And said Hortense would drive you nuts—
Instead of sneaking back
To get your letters and your dough."

"Thought you'd be mad," she mumbled,
" 'Cause I left. I didn't want to worry you—"

"You'll never worry me again, Marie."
He wasn't watching her, but watching trees—
The bitter, chilling fuzz of spring
Against the yellow-lighted street,
And watching more than that. . . .
He saw the den from which Marie had come:
The dirty house, the mother tired of the dirt,
The poverty, the skating rink,
The older sisters with their kids,
And Dad who cut the people's hair—
A dark and silent man: he passed the plate
For the United Brethren congregation—

"Look, babe."
               Derry's voice was flat and hard.
"I guess it's funny— But the war—
I mean to say, we'd not have met, or anything,
If I had never gone down there
To take that special training—
I guess— Well, it's pretty young:
Nineteen and eighteen. That's not very old."

She didn't say a word.

"We had some fun, one time.
You got supported for two years—
Supported damn well."
He thought about those cablegrams—
The extra dough he'd sent.
Hey, listen—that's my wife—
"But I don't want you any more.
That's straight. I don't.
A pick-up in a bar—
Or, say, like someone at a supper club
In London—casual, like that.
The point is: as a wife
You're out like Flout, Marie!"

He could have said some other things:
That she was cheap and ignorant—
Well, so was he. There was so much
He didn't know— So much he'd never understand....
And anyway, she'd only cry.

"You file for the divorce," he said.
"It's easy in this State. I socked you:
That's enough. But don't you spend too much.
Look—here's a hundred bucks—"
He brought some money out
And counted off five Twenties.
"That'll be enough.
It's all you'll get from me. No alimony, babe.
And do it quick. And if you don't
I'll go myself, and file, and tell
Just what I found when I came back—"

Marie said in her tiny voice,
"I told the God's own truth.
We were just friends and—"
                              "Hell," said Fred.
"Shut up. I'm through."
A notion struck him. "Anyway," he said,
"I haven't any job. Can't send you
All that dough again. You'll get along....
Give me that Scotch. I guess the stores
Are closed."
He didn't even look at her again,
But closed the door and went away.
The thing he didn't want right then
The most of all, was any woman.

It looked like Scotch. It wasn't.
It was pale. That other guy
Had brought it.
                Derry tasted it. It stunk.
He read the label: *Neutral Spirits*—
In the lobby light.
                He broke the bottle
On the curb. Two blocks away
He found a taxi. "Listen,"
He told the sleepy driver,
"Where do I go to get a drink, this late?"

"Son, they all close at 12 and—"

"Where is it?
Don't give me that line."

The driver woke up more, and grinned.
"I'll get you into Butch's Place, Lieutenant.
But look, unless you got a card,
I'll have to give the doorman—"

"Take this Five," said Fred.
"Let's go to Butch's."
                              Thus he hummed
His lonely tune, as he was getting in.

Thick flak
Amid the Wilhelmshaven day—
He smelled the blackened tufts
And cedars of it.
                              "I have seen—
Oh, what I've seen!
That little goon—
She wouldn't know."

xviii

Tʜᴀᴛ night came Mr. Milton, telling Stephenson
The petty plots he didn't want to hear.

But first were wonderment, and happy feet
Treading the sidewalks west on Grand.

After they ate their dinner they went out,
The Stephensons, the folks who'd stayed in Boone
Because of age or sex—the softest folks
That ever hard man loved.
Al marveled at their softness . . . they were frail
And lovely as the birches on the lawn—
Even his son, for all his larking size—
As petal-pink as flowers in a pot,
As shining as a pet canary's wing.
Al's mind was cluttered, torn apart

With past and present; he could not define
The tenderness that ruled him.
These are mine,
He whispered it, a poem long extolled,
And I do not deserve . . . how long since I
Crawled craftily to hunt a sniper down?

That night came Mr. Milton from the bank;

But earlier they walked the little dog.
"MacDuff goes out," said Milly, "every night
About this time. . . . Rob, please—"
Al said, "Let's all go," and they went—
The four whose mystery now found them mute.
They went in silence. Milly held
Her husband's arm. Her fingers
Slid around and pinched him
Through his blouse. He stopped once,
Swore, caught up her face,
Pressed hard his lips on hers.
Their children turned and saw them, laughed aloud,
Made up a shrill, flirtatious jest
About a fine for necking in the street. . . .
Not very good nor very apt, the jest,
But all were clinging close to tears.

They walked the blocks.
Al saw his daughter's shape ahead
Against the street lights. . . .
"She's a woman now—no kid,"
He muttered once to Milly.
"I don't mean grown—developed physically—
She'd done that long before I left—
But I mean grown—a person—"
Milly squeezed his arm;
She shared elation, loving Margaret
The more because Al taught her revelry
The night the girl was made. . . .
"Is she engaged?" asked Al.
"That kid you wrote about—? She mentioned him
In letters once or twice. The boy from Illinois—"

"Jack Atkinson," said Milly.
"No, that's nothing much.
He's gone to China. They still write.

They're not engaged. She'd tell me."
"God!" cried Stephenson. "Imagine us—
A daughter, twenty—"
                                    "Do you feel so old?"
"Not when I look at you."
They laughed again. The tears spread thin
On Milly's cheeks. Al couldn't see them
In the dark.

They strolled, they smelled the good green juice
Of peace in spring.... Went down to Kiowa,
A street of shops one block away;
Lingered beside the drugstore. Peggy went inside,
Bought bath salts and a pack of Chesterfields.
MacDuff went too... begged for a butt of cone
Before the fountain. This was ritual
Each time he visited the store.
                                    The others waited
In the street, counted the notions,
Laughed at the cardboard ads
That filled the window.
Rob asked his father's verdict
On electric razors... thought he'd need one soon.
"Hell," said his father, "I'll give you
My Dad's banana knife! It's in a trunk somewhere."
"Listen, Pop," Rob went on. "—Wanted to ask you—
Did you have a trench knife? Are they issued,
Or do you have to get your own?"

They spoke of war again, again:
Might have been talking of
The Mayans, or the *Maine*....
Waited so docile for the lights at Grand.
They met a cocker, also strolling for his health—
MacDuff went wild, but Peggy pulled him on.
O gay—
O nature's little glee of Home and spring!

But Mr. Milton waited on a lobby seat,
Neat hat upon his knee, and thin cigar in teeth—
A powdered, shaven, oldish man
With lenses on his eyes
That shone like vital steel:
The Cornbelt Trust and Savings, twelve years president,
And cashier in the long ago

Before Boone City doubled up its size.
His suit was gray, his mouth was gray,
His eyes so sober, brown,
That many men presumed him kinder than he was
Until they learned the thorny truth.
"I simply had to come," said he,
Squeezing Al's hand. "So much to tell you
... Many matters for discussion.
You won't mind, my dear?"
He smiled at Milly from his stiffened height.
She said she wouldn't mind.
              And Milton spoke
To both the children with all dignity
And some affectionate degree,
And no imagination in his soul.
"Peggy, my niece Lorena says
You work together at the Red Cross branch....
Well, Rob. Next year you'll be as tall as Dad...."

They rode up, cramming the elevator tight.
MacDuff watched Milton with his button eyes,
And growled.
           Some folks who came
The Scotty liked, and some he didn't.
He'd bitten, slightly, one electric meter man,
One beau of Peggy's, and one minister.
Milton ignored the dog. He told just how
He'd phoned ... lucky it was
A private branch exchange. The operator said,
Why, Yes, that Mr. Stephenson was home—
She'd seen them going out.
And Milton came to wait.

A kind of dankness lay above the room.
They all sat down. Al never thought
About his manners— Only wished
That Milton wouldn't stay too long.
(What, what was this—
The president himself? He'd come to call
The minute Al got home? The president—
Old L. D. M. himself!)
He'd never called before informally, like this.
They traded dinners with the Miltons
Twice a year. They had to.
That was business. Alton Stephenson:

A roving salesman, contact man,
Golf player and ambassador-at-large,
Assistant v.p., bringing business in,
But knowing rather less of banking than he knew
About the tough approach to Number 4,
And that freak dog-lie underneath the hill
At Number 12.

Milly, the perfect hostess, held the tray.
"And brandy for you, too?"
                                        Al shook his head;
He muttered, "Just a shot of something—
Bourbon? Thanks—that'll be lovely, dear."
They drank in silence. . . .
Rob had moved politely out.
"That lousy old geometry!" he said.
And Peggy on the telephone—
Some soldier boy who called and wheedled her
The moment she came in—
"Nope. Not tonight," she told him.
Al could hear her voice
So vibrant, ringing in the hall.
"My Dad's just home— Darling, I can't,
I simply can't. Why don't you call up Sylvia?"
He heard her joviality and friendliness,
Her firmness, triviality and charm
Dissolving all together on the phone.
And suddenly he was an older man—
This peace had made him older than the war—
And mentally he shook himself, and winked his eyes,
And tried to witness Milton's face and words.

". . . Suppose," said Mr. Milton,
"You'll be giving up this furnished place
And moving back to Cherry Hill?"
And through the busy mist, were all the things
That Milly said . . . they hadn't thought;
It was too soon; they hadn't stopped to think;
The tenant didn't have a lease; they might—
She turned the eagerness of her soft eyes
On Al.
            He labored at the job of speech.
"No, frankly, Mr. Milton— No, we haven't
Talked about it yet."

"Alton, the reason that I came tonight—"
And Milton hesitated, white stone fingers
Holding up his glass.
Milly arose. "I know you'd rather be alone.
No, no! If you'll excuse me, there are dinner dishes—
We don't keep a cook, these days!"
She laughed, she hurried off
Amid their slight expostulation.
They sat down again, and Milton put aside
His glass, with slow decision.
"Alton, it's Steese—"
                            "Steese?"
"Yes, the cashier.
This business of your coming home—
I wanted to explain a thing or two
Before you walked in to the bank—"

He spoke on . . . measured syllables . . .
No warmth—but nicely simulated warmth.
No sympathy—but all the careful judgment
In the world.
Steese was ambitious. Now that Underwood
Had gone to Washington, resigned,
The other two vice-presidents would be promoted.
Steese had imagined, naturally,
He'd take the place that Prew had left
(The third vice-presidential post
In charge of loans). The Board had met,
Discussed it roundly, made its mind. . . .

"We came to this conclusion, well aware
That you would soon be back.
Alton, it's you—not Steese.
You're third v.p., as of last Tuesday afternoon."

He waited for the burst of gratitude
And proud delight. It didn't come.
He smiled, and touched the brandy to his lips again.
Of course he understood! Stephenson was
Wholly overcome. Yes, overcome.
He'd tell the Board: "By Jove,
I never saw a man so wholly overcome before
With sheer surprise. All he could do
Was sit and stare at me!"

In German street there was a burned-out tank.
"Look out," said Al.
"O.K.," said Pascowitz. "I'm looking out."
They passed the tank. . . .
"Now, Steese is hurt and disappointed,
Naturally. But, to be coldly frank,
We didn't think he'd fill the shoes so well as you.
A good cashier, but not exactly
Of the timber that we have to have.
We need someone with youth,
A man with clarity of purpose.
You've seen the world; the war has broadened you—"
Al couldn't figure what it was
He wiped from off his helmet rim—
A piece of bone?

Now, Steese is sore,
And disappointed sore.
There'll be a difference in his **attitude.**
I leave it up to you—
I leave it in your lap—
We need him in his job
But not in yours—
You've got to make him like it.
                              O the grille,
O glass, O desk, O icy door,
O name-plate made of bronze, memorial
Not to the dead, but to the walking dead;
O bars, O windows keeping robbers out,
O frightened little people seeking help.
I need two thousand badly—
For collateral, I've got—
You're overdrawn. I'm not. I'll cash a check,
I'll draw a draft, I'll cash a bond.
And how are you today. And where's the payroll
For the Midland Tin & Type?
O Undivided Profits and Reserves—
And Or Reserves—
                    O heavy sacks
Of coin, O tellers' hands,
O clicking calculator, fresh carnation, pacing guard,
O marble slab forever underfoot and overhead!

O telephone, to save me from disgrace,
(I do not know. I've got a hunch—

I think this call is mine)
To save me from embarrassment,
And Milton from the insult I could make—

"It's Corporal Annas, Dad. He's called before.
I'm sorry—I forgot to tell you . . . days ago—
I guess he called last week—"

"Annas?" said Al, and then his voice went high.
"Annas? For Christ's—"
                    He reached the hall,
Turned in the door, managed apology.
And Milton's eyebrows rose—he made adjustment—
(So nervous, coming home . . . and disconcerted,
Amazed at his advancement, filled with thanks—
We'll see a better-balanced man on Saturday)
And Milton nodded with all tolerance, and smiled.

They said Hello, Hello, again, again—
"Hi, Stephenson. That you, you dirty bum?"
"*Heil Hitler,* Annas! How you keeping, boy?"
"O.K. They couldn't keep me down— Well, what you
        say?
I called about a dozen times, I guess.
I got a sister here in town. Yeh, they had me
Down there in Louisville, at Nichols General.
Now I'm O.K. and going back to Denver. . . .
Yeh, I been here all week . . . I tell you, Sarge,
I sure remembered that you came from here.
What kind of place you live in? Jesus Christ,
That lady on the telephone— Naw, not your girl:
The one that answers first— Boy, does she lay it on!
I tried to make a date, and she got sore.
Naw, hell, I can't come out. I'm at the station now;
My train is leaving town at ten-fifteen. . . ."

"I'll make it, Annas."
                    "O.K. By the USO
Right at the door—?"

They made their date, and Al hung up.
He came back, calling to his wife; his voice was sharp.
Milly was big-eyed, Milton smiling cool.
Al talked on rapidly . . . Annas, a wounded kid—
Annas was leaving town; there wasn't any chance

For Al to see him if he didn't go at once.
"By Jove," said Milton. "Is that one
Whose life you saved? A splendid thing, old boy!
You know, no doubt—the *Courier & News*
Had nearly half a column—"

Al shook his head as they went to the hall.
"I never saved his life especially.
The way it is— A lot of people save your life,
And you save theirs, and save your own.
If you save yours, you help to save the rest—"

If Milton wasn't smiling still!
And Stephenson felt secrecy and silence
Stuck like a strip of tape across his mouth.
He couldn't say another word.
No one could understand who'd never—

Milly was watching close. He saw
A pity and a pleading in her face.
He smiled. He didn't want to yield
To her, to anyone.
                    He mumbled in the lobby:
"Mr. Milton—awfully sorry—I'll be at the bank
Tomorrow noon, if I can find some clothes to wear."
"Why, come in uniform!" said Milton, heartily.
"That's what Lou Latham did. . . . You knew
That Lou was back? Yes, splendid record—
He's major now—I mean, he was—"
"Yeh," said Al Stephenson, and mightily
He fought to keep obscenity from creeping through
His tone. "Lou was in Washington, I heard:
The Pentagon . . . a house in Falls Church.
Not so bad . . ."
                  Apologized again,
And ran to catch a cab. He whistled out
One blast between his fingers, and the cab
Jammed on its brakes and halted by the curb.
One whistle and he stopped it, just like that!
He ran across the lawn.
                        He saw them all
Mixed up and intermingled: Milly, Rob,
And Peggy, and the Cornbelt Bank
At 5th and Locust, and the people there,
And Steese's face,
And Milton like a stern professor at exams.

The cab went streaking
East on Grand,
And more than people there in Boone
Were active in the mind of Stephenson.
The memory so keen, alert:
                              The shell comes down,
The dust is blasted all around,
And boys crawl up and wipe their eyes,
And blow their noses, start to move again.
But Annas—
              Where is Annas?
                              Wheeet, says Al.
"Let's go—keep moving—don't bunch up—
Let's get our asses out of here—"
Another shell comes down.
                              And later, counting up,
They reckon piece by piece the day,
The sulfanilamide, the dusting hope,
The plasma, and just what the chances are—
Will Annas lose both legs, or only one?
They hear no more.
              A call comes in
While Milton talks about the bank,
There in the Casa Blanca.
"Corporal Annas, Dad—"

"By God," said Al
Behind imagined tape across his mouth.
"That was October. Just two days
Before Bud Rosenberg got conked.
No, it was after—"

xix

Now we will remember a cellar
     With a rampart of concrete around,
     And some children who tried to attack us
As we marched them away from their shelter—
They were ten, they were seven, with blue eyes
And the faces of little old men.
And we will remember a kitchen
With a hand grenade thrown from the window;

And a town where the Messerschmitts fropped us,
And always the rain coming down.
And why did it rain and keep raining,
And why did it snow and keep snowing
Whenever we fought in the war?
Sometimes there were gravel and cinders—
Sometimes there were ashes and pine-trees—
But mostly we think of the snow,
And mostly we think of the rain.

And also we laugh about Brownie—
He was always brown-nosing around—
After two years he got his promotion;
He got it at ten in the morning;
And the truck was upset in the evening,
And he was the only one killed,
And, believe it or not, it's part of the story—
His name it was actually Brown!

We go to the bar on the corner.
The train is reported so late. . . .
We drink, and begin to fall silent—
There is much we can never recount—
There is much that will not bear recounting
Till we're further away from the war.
And I walk with you back to the station,
You lean on your heavy new cane,
And you show me the bones in your pocket—
The pieces they took from your leg—
You have cleaned them, and chained them together,
And you claim that they'll bring you good luck;
And you talk of that Louisville girlie—
The first one you laid on your leave.

And surely your uncle in Denver
Will be tickled to see you so soon.
You'll start in to work in his lunchroom,
But not as a waiter again—
You'll sit out in front by the counter,
And gather the customers' cash.

The train is reported much later.
We talk about Brownie again,
And again we go back to the corner,
And order a couple more drinks—

You play Dinah Shore on the jook-box,
You play her and play her again....
And I think of the hour I saw you:
Pale-lipped and shot full of the stuff,
And taking the plasma they gave you,
And keeping your eyes tightly shut.

Now we talk about Maxon and Hancock,
And the lousy lieutenant we hated—
The Jerries got him on the beachhead,
And we stood up and cheered when we heard.

You are Greek, you are young, you're a bastard;
I am Harvard, an old gentleman
With stock in the Cornbelt, and station,
And a daughter you'd make if you could—
And, twice a year, dinners with Milton
(I'm a star in the Black Hawk Club flag)!
But I'd trade all that stock in the Cornbelt,
And the job that they gave me tonight,
To feel like I felt in the Army—
(I don't want to go back to the Army;
I am sick unto death of the Army.
But to feel like I felt in the Army....)
By God.
          Am I sure that I'm Out?

Yes, I'm Out. We are here. We are silent,
And what is this past that we have?
We cannot make it part of the present—
But it colors the night we are in.
We are saying goodbye when your train leaves—
I am seeing the best of me go.
You have left the weeds growing inside me,
And I have put seed in your soul,
And I have put scum on your liquor
And there's sediment you've left in mine—
We had dreamed an immortal reunion
But I'm glad when you get on the train.
For you represent something unholy
That dwells in the loneliest place—
And I fear it and love it and hate it,
And cannot repel it tonight.

Are the land and the living unworthy,
That we sit not in Grace as we should?

XX

THE train went out.
                    Al saw the face
    Of one man he had killed:
A brown and scientific visage, bent
Behind a rifle in a laboratory stance,
Within a broken window, helmet down
Low on the forehead, eyes opaque
Behind the glasses. He would kill
A boy from Oklahoma next.

He did not kill, he did not live to kill.
Al got him from atop an old manure pile:
Puk-puk-puk the carbine quacked.
Al saw the German head slide down
Behind the window ledge in slow surprise.

He thought the German ghost
Ran far and wide on a disordered tour
Across the aimless wilderness of time.
Al's own ghost met him (quite subtracted
From his living body for the nonce).
"Well, what would you have done?" requested fair
The living ghost of Stephenson, "to my boy Rob
If you had caught him? Milly's mother
Was a partial Jewess—name of Levinsohn.
Would you have mutilated Rob?"
                              All this
He asked in one imagined moment.
                              . . . German ghost
Made murmuring reply:
"*Für den Führer und das Vaterland. Sieg Heil!*"

                    The train
Exclaimed beyond two crossings: hush, hush, hush,
Its steam retreating loud.
                    "I want a drink,"
Al told the silver station-guard.

"Why, Mr. Stephenson! You back—?"
They talked awhile. Al had to talk.

This puffy saint, with one tall grandson
In the Philippines, another dead in Italy. . . .
He rambled on:
                    "I tell you, Mr. Stephenson—
There ain't no place but Butch's
After midnight. Now it's one-fifteen—"

Al went to Butch's. He remembered Butch
From long-discarded Prohibition days;
He didn't know Butch when he saw him
(Pints of gin and alcohol, delivered in a hall,
An overcoat to hide them. . . . He recalled
The bitter larceny, the fusel oil,
The silly thievery, and flouting
Of a silly law).
                    He stood alone
And drank. He didn't think of Milly.
When her spirit rose before him
He expelled it sourly.
He'd drunk a lot,
But was not drunk himself
When Derry wandered in.

Fred Derry, twenty-one, and killer of a hundred men—
But he had slain them far beneath,
Five miles away . . . anonymous the mushrooms
Of the bombs. (The barracks turns to pink,
The troop-train bursts apart
Beneath a counterpane of smoke.) O far away
The tiny gumming of the blood, the tumbled legs,
The urine running out to wet the pants.

Al Stephenson had seen the dead he made.

So odd that he and Fred should meet again
So soon! He turned around, with glass in hand,
And jook-box music smothering
The conversation of the rest who drank
Illegal potion in this troubled world.
"Hello, Lieutenant . . ."
                    Fred grinned hard;
His thin, uncertain Irish face
Displayed its pain and wrath
And fierce frustration.
                    "Hi, there, Sarge."

"So you're bad, too?"
                    "I'm bad."
There was a kind of explanation in Fred's voice,
And Stephenson declined to ask for more.
He merely said, "I'm drinking bourbon.
Will you have the same?"
                    "O.K.
I'm drinking anything, tonight."

They waited for the man to mix their drinks,
And suddenly, without reluctance, Derry said,
"That little skate I married
Just before I left— Well—"
"Something go wrong?"
                    "Yes, everything," said Fred.
"We're through. She's out like Flout.
I told her so. Somehow I feel relieved—"

"Salute," said Al. "Here's to it."
Derry raised his glass.
"I hope," he said, "that nothing's wrong for you—"
"No, nothing much," said Stephenson.
"The boss-man came—our president, to say the least.
I've got a better job . . . and all that gossip,
All the detail of the bank—it really got me down."

"You're down," asked Fred, "because he offered you
A better job?" with childish disbelief.
Al said, "I'm third vice-president,
And not so sure I like it."
                    "Oh, boy," said Derry,
"Laugh at me for thinking you might be a janitor!
A GI banker. Jesus Christ!"

"A bank," said Al, "is pretty hard to take.
I'm not a banker any more. I'm just a three-hook guy
Without a mental pot to piss in—
                    You know what I mean?
You don't. You're too damn young."

"Do you know what I mean?" asked Fred.
"You don't. You've got a wife you love to death.
A home—you've got two kids—"

"So now I'm here," said Stephenson,
"Instead of there."

"By God," said Fred. "It is to laugh, Mo'seer!
Let's have a drink. I'm buying this—"
And louder, louder rolled their talk—
Concerned no more with Milton, Annas or Marie.
Their worry made them one. And each had felt
The kiss of death so many times,
That he could only share himself
With other men whose lips still wore the damp
And pungent print of cold infinity.

"Come on, come on!"
                            They beat the bar.
A waiter sidled up and said,
"You guys sit down. Butch doesn't like
A lot of noise."
                            Fred pointed to a gang
Of folks in shadows at the other end:
Some young Marines, a girl or two.
"They're making noise. They're singing.
Listen, chum—they're singing tunes—
They're singing 'One Meat Ball' and—"

"Sure, Lieutenant. Go ahead and sing."
He took them into shadows of their own.
They had two drinks, and Butch came by,
As big as Dempsey—just as tough.
"Well, what's the word tonight?"
"You're Butch?"
                            "I'm Butch."
                                        "Say, you—
Sit down and have a drink."
Butch said, "I never drink. I'm just a bum
That runs a bar, and gets hauled up,
And pays a fine— I'm just a heel, Lieutenant."
Al said, "You heard him. He's a heel. . . .
All right, Butch, if I sing a song?"
"No, I don't mind," said Butch, and went away.
"Oh, he don't mind," said Fred.
"He'll never mind. You'll never mind—"

We are a bunch of heathen
Who do not care a rap
About the Navy's point of view
And all that sort of crap—

He pealed the song, and people laughed
Beyond the bar . . . the room was blue
And dark with smoke and shade and liquor smell.
The mirror up behind the bar was gay
With collar badges, patches, all the bright
Accumulation of the war . . . the souvenirs. . . .
Ten thousand people drinking there
Throughout the war.
                    The bar was mist.

You'll never mind, you'll never mind!
Come on and join the Air Corps,
And you will never mind!

Derry could sing, and Al could sing:
Their tenor and their baritone. . . .
They tackled "Oh, Salome"—thought it fine—
Al said, "Now, look. 'O'Riley's Daughter'—
There's a song—"
                    "Sing-song," said Fred.
"The way the British do; let's have a sing-song.
Roger! Let's sing—"

Roll me over, in the clover,
For I've 'ad it once or twice
And I thought it rather nice. . . .

. . . Take the gas-tank out of my kidneys,
Take the crank-shaft out of my brain. . . .

"Derry," cried Al. His voice was hard.
"We had a kid; his name was Armstrong;
He had a voice. You never heard a voice
Like Armstrong's. Crosby wasn't in it—
He could sing—"
                    "Well, where's he now?
Why isn't Armstrong here to sing—
If he's so bloody good?"

"Say, that's just what I want to know!
Quick—just like that— Just lots of pine-cones
Blowing up. And where is Armstrong?"
                    "Under here!"
Said Fred, and pounded on the table top.
They drank again. They drank an extra drink
For Armstrong—him who sang.

There's a blackbird in the sky,
Singing Auralee.
There's a blackbird in the sky,
Sing Auralee....

"There's a sailor in the sky...."
Fred roared it long and pointed far,
And Homer Wermels came from distances.
He wore a pea-coat (he had sent his things
Ahead, when he was in the hospital).
But even in that jacket: quite the same.
If he had worn a beard: oh, surely, surely
Quite the same.

The funny thing was: Butch was helping him,
Walking with him, and welcoming.
Derry and Al—they couldn't understand;
They were too tight to understand,
To worry, wonder ... they could only care.
Homer was theirs, and they were glad
Because he'd come.
                    He flew with them
One afternoon a hundred years ago....
Al helped him in the bomb-bay.
He had fought a war, and so had they.

They greeted him with yip and yowl—
Now they could sing, now they could drink!
"Listen, you—we were waiting for you—"
And the boy doubted, knowing it untrue—
Grinning and babbling with his twisted face
But grateful none the less.
He tried to tell how it had happened:
Butch was a neighbor—Engle was his name—
Lived almost right across the street—
The black sheep son of a devoted dame—
He'd gone to sea—the other war—
He used to gamble, too,
And bootlegged through the age
Of mid-west drouth.
                    Now he ran "Butch's,"
Paid a fine sometimes, and made a lot of dough.
Homer's folks had gossiped readily,
Telling their tales about the neighborhood,
Talking to keep their spirits up;

While Homer spilled his supper on the tablecloth,
Upset his milk, and sent his Wilma home in tears.

But Homer heard just what his people said
Of *Butch's, after midnight.*
He remembered later
When he needed to.
                    Tiptoe in darkness
(One toe tipped, at least, and fervently
He tried to keep his left foot civilized)
He found the stairpit, clattering
And dripping curses underneath his breath.

His mother switched the light.
"Oh, Homer—what?—"
                    "I thought
I'd take a walk," he said;
And watched the shock he slapped
Against her pale-lined face
With every word he uttered.
                    What a thing—
To say I *hawt* instead of *thought*—
And what a lousy way to walk!
"Oh, honey—Homer—
Don't go out—
You'll fall and hurt yourself—"
Her whisper whistled in the hall.
She wound her hands within the nightdress folds.

"No . . . got to go.
Sometimes it's hard to sleep—
I get up, walk around
An hour, maybe—then I sleep."

Her face was scrolled and tearful
As she tried to understand him.
"I'll call Father—"
                    "No! I'm going out."

His father heard him then,
And Aunt Sade called a question,
Shrill and so startled, from her room.
And Homer kept on, wrenching down the stairs,
And making noise enough for ten.

His father followed.... "Homer—
What's all this—you going out—"

"I'll be back after while,
Pa. Go to sleep."
And then his mutilated patience ripped apart—
He cried with spume upon his chin:
"I ain't no kid. I've been around—
You got to let me go!"

They had to let him go. He went.
They burned the lights behind him
In the living room and hall.
"Ma," said the father, "go to bed.
I'll wait around for Homer.
Guess he's kind of nervous;
You know—used to hospitals
And all those other folks—"
He sent her to her room to weep,
And knowing well how Homer must have wept.
He sat, did Mr. Wermels, in the dining room;
Tried to read comics left by Luella there,
Tried to discuss a business problem with himself
(He was freight agent: the Rock Island Lines)
Couldn't half think of it....
He was now middle-aged
And more. He'd married late.
He'd had a lot of troubles, different times.
He hadn't ever felt like this before.

xxi

AT THREE, when Milly wakened on the couch,
She found herself soft-covered with a puff—
A comforter they'd brought from Cherry Hill
(The bedding in this furnished place was cheap
And meager).... Milly lingered sleepily,
The satin at her chin.
                                    "Peggy," she called.
Her daughter came in dream-walk from the dining room,
Her hair neat, brushed, ashine—her figure slim
Wrapped in a flannel robe. "Hi, there!" she said,

Her little chuckle warming all
The broken, cold disturbance in her mother's heart.

"Peggy-weg, you covered me.
How very kind of you!"
      "I'm kind," her daughter said,
"To cats and dogs, and wives bereft of husbands."
"What time, now?"
     "It's three—
Five minutes after. Probably you heard
A clock somewhere. It must have wakened you."

"Oh, darling," Milly yawned,
"Why didn't you get into bed—?"

"Nonsense, my love. I had a million
Forms to fill. The Red Cross dearly loves its forms.
Septuplicate? Is that how you say seven forms?
Good grief—imagine if one were prolific
In multiple maternity— Just imagine if one had
Sep*tup*lets! You know, Mom, like the Quints—?"
She knelt beside the couch, and put her face
Against her mother's. "I'm afraid,"
She whispered, "that, as a substitute,
I simply stink."

They loved, they understood, they were two women—
Not merely mother, child; but women who
Might lay a comfort each upon the other
More daintily than any satin puff.

And Al had called. He called at twenty after twelve.
He sounded just a little tight, perhaps. . . .
(Poor Milly didn't know. So long since Al
Was tight with her! Perhaps his voice was different
After drinking, in the Army.)
Annas's train was yet to leave. All trains
Were late this year. All trains were late
Forever, always, all the years since Stephenson
Had gone away to be another kind of man.

And so he was another man. They didn't know him now.
Husband and father— Any Alton Stephenson they knew
Would never seek an ugly joy
Apart from them.
     Alone, alone—

The women who had loved him pricelessly:
The one with body reminiscent of his own,
("Oh, Peggy, when you laugh like that—
Just like your father! Honestly—")
And she who'd yield her face and brain
And every tender feminine device
And rich endowment in her soul and body—
Who'd yield them cheerful to a torture
And a death, for sake of him.
She loved like that:
A clear pink love. He was her passion
And her pet.

"Darling, I'm worried." Milly's voice
Had all the private plea
Of *Now-I-lay-me*
As she whispered by her daughter's ear.

"My child," said Peggy, young and bright,
"I fear that Corporal Annas is an influence
To be combatted.... Let us go
And seek him out. I'll wear a ragged gown,
And stand barefoot, and whimper,
While you wear a shawl.
We both must sing a gentle song:
'Father, dear father, the clock in the steeple
Strikes—' All of three-forty, by the time
We get there!
            Come on, my poor deserted dear,
I'll ferry you the best I know—"

She tossed the comforter away
And took her mother's hands
And drew her up....
"*Look* at that dress—
One *mass* of wrinkles!
Mildred Stephenson, you'll pay the pressing service
Out of your *own* allowance—"

Cajoling, luring wearily,
She stood her mother on her feet,
Lifted the shoes—
                "Here, put them on
Like a good girl. We'll go and get
That nasty man."
                "But, Peg.

Just where on earth—?"
                              "Nonsense.
There's only one place in this town
Where they could be, this late.
I rather think that big Butch Engle
Has taken Daddy for a ride!
                              Unless, perhaps—"
Her voice was shrill, and close to tears
As she shared hot
Her mother's bafflement and pain.
"Unless perhaps your boy friend has picked up
A fondness for the gals in red kimonas. . . .
Don't they wear red? I've always heard they did."

"Butch's," said Milly plaintively,
"That awful place. So stuffy—full of smoke—
Peg, do you really think—?"

"You didn't think it was so bad, my love,
When you went there last New Year's
With Commander Leffingwell.
He brought you home at five.
Tut, tut! Should I tell Daddy?"

"Oh, pooh," said Milly feebly.
"Wilmer Leffingwell: why, he's just like his name!
Peggy, your mother loves the sergeants best—"

"I know one sergeant I should like to scalp,"
Said Peggy, honest as a dog.
She growled like one—said *Grrrr,*
And made her mother fix her hair,
And fix her face before they went.

She brought their coats
From out the hallway closet;
Jingled her car keys. . . . A sleepy night man
Took them humming to the ground—
Another sleepy youth moved cars in the garage
So Peg could back the Buick out.
She drove deserted streets
In wind to tear her hair.
The traffic lights flashed yellow, yellow,
As they went. And Milly huddled close
With coat around her shoulders.

This wasn't what she'd dreamed—
The husband, lover, coming to her arms,
The bright light burning on the hearth. . . .
(When Mr. Milton came, the light went out.
When Corporal Annas called, it was as if
An angry bugle blew. And grim feet marched away
Before they'd barely halted by her door.)

In German street there was a burned-out tank.
"Look out," said Al.
"O.K.," said Pascowitz. "I'm looking out—"

She couldn't know a fury Al had never told her.
But she felt its coarsened breath—
Because the wounded soul of Stephenson
Lived like a child in womb of hers.

xxii

"AND THEN this general," Fred Derry said,
      "He used to be our Group commander
      Before he was a general—
When he was only colonel—
The boys all called him Iron Tail—"
"Not to his face?" asked big Butch Engle,
Watching him.
                  "Not to his face," said Fred.
"This general—
But what I started in to tell
About the neckties:
At a party after 2 a.m., at Chelveston,
You can't wear neckties; not a single tie,
Because the guys will pull them off,
Or cut them off—"

"Say, look at me," said Homer, praying,
Holding out his glass so proud,
And staring glad as he beheld
That fewer drops spilled past the rim.
"Say, look at him," said Stephenson.
"He's drinking with his left hand!
Look at Homer."

"Don't you take another drink," said Butch.

"I guess I'll take a million drinks,"
Said Homer,
"With my left hand!
What you got to say about it, anyhow?"

"All right," Butch told him, soothing him,
"You take that drink;
You take as many as you want;
Just don't mind me."
"O.K.," said Homer, loftily,
And feeling he had won a war.

"And so this general," said Derry,
"Here he comes, at 2 a.m.
He's come a long ways—
Clear from the 4th Wing.
Our colonel asked him
Because he was our Group commander, see—
Before they put a star on him.
And up comes Oakley—
He's a guy from Alabama; quite a guy;
And up comes Oak—
He's got a pair of tin shears in his hand
He got some place, for cutting off those ties.
And then our colonel, and the officers,
Are talking to the general—
But here comes Oakley. Says,
'Why, look at this! He's got a necktie.
Look at this. He's got a tie on—' "

"Look at this," said Homer,
Holding out his glass.
"Say, look at him," said Al.
"He's hardly spilling anything!"
"I'm hardly spilling anything," said Homer Wermels.

"The general is wearing his," said Derry.
"See, Butch, just like this:
He's got a necktie on.
And Jimmy Oakley cuts it off!
He takes those big shears, just like this,
And cuts it off."

"Now, listen, Butch," said Homer,
Speaking plain, and scarcely holding any lip
Against his teeth.... His mouth was loose.
Spasticity is overcome by alcohol;
And jungle poison does it too.
You take too much of jungle poison
And you die;
You take too much of alcohol and—

"Just like this," said Derry,
Waving wild his hand, and pulling at the tie of Al.
"Old Oak he cuts it off, right here!"
"I bet the general was sore," said Butch.
"No, sir!" said Fred.
"I've seen sad apples in my time,
But not old Iron Tail!
He just said something ... maybe ...
That he shouldn't wear a tie,
Or things like that.
The other guys took Oak away;
He never knew he'd cut that tie
Until we told him in the afternoon."

"I want to sing," said Al.
"I want to sing that song you sang
About a bunch of heathen.
I like that song
Because it's good."

Come on and get promoted.
As high as you desire—
You're riding on the gravy train
When you're an Army flier—

And they were all alone with Butch;
The door was locked at three;
The bouncer slept upon a leather seat;
The bartender was gone.
A few lights gleamed;
The bar was clear and clean.
And Engle sat so soberly
Beside the men who drank—
He hadn't let them buy a drink since three,
But he had poured a few for them.

He never drank, himself:
He hadn't had a drink
In eighteen years;
And now he marveled at the way
These three could handle it.
And even little Homer....
He remembered Homer
On his tricycle,
Pretending he was engineer
Of the Rock Island Lines,
Who towed a wagon after him,
Containing nameless cargoes of his toys.
Now— He was not a man to tell the boy
He couldn't drink, when surely
What he needed was respite
Inside the door his disability had closed to him....
Butch couldn't reason out the words,
But this was current in his mind....
He wished that he had gone himself. He tried.
They said he was too old. They said
His teeth weren't right,
Nor were his pulse, the pressure of his blood.
He looked at Homer, wistfully....
"Say, listen, Homer—
Tell about the South Pacific."

"They all were bad," said Al.
"You heard him say so.
Every one had sores:
A white man couldn't even look
At anything like that!
And Africa is lousy too—
You ought to see those Arabs—
They were foul! But every now and then
Some guy would make a pass:
And if the other Arabs found it out,
Well, it was just too bad!
We had a guy. I used to know his name,
I can't recall it now:
I've had too much to drink....
He made a pass;
I guess the Arabs saw him,
And they waited till he went on guard....
First thing, when it was light,

We found him.
Boy, he was sure a mess!
They had his mouth sewed up;
I guess they sewed it after he was dead.
We cut it open, and just guess—
Guess what we found inside? . . . .
By God, that's right. They cut them off
And put them in his mouth
And sewed it up. . . .
Believe me, all that regiment
Were pretty well behaved.
The passes, after that, were noted
By their absence."

"Say, I heard that," said Derry,
"Many times.
Some fellows from the 15th Air Force told me—
What you call—I bet you never saw it!
What you call—"
"Apocryphal?" said Al.
"Well, maybe so.
But how you like?"
"I like," said Fred.

"Yes, sir," said Homer, speaking plain.
"I like to have another drink."
"No, listen, boy," said Butch.
"It's almost 4 o'clock."
                    And then the women came.

Butch went, annoyed
At the insistent rapping on the door:
The buzzer and the knocker sounding both.
And through the dimmest distances
Al Stephenson heard Peggy's voice;
He heard her laughing, telling Butch
She knew just where to come.
And Butch was sheepish, all apology:
"My gosh," he said, "Miss Stephenson,
I sure am sorry!
Guess it's all my fault.
I thought they ought to have a couple on the house,
And then we got to talking—"

"Look at this!" said Homer Wermels,
Facing both the women when they came,

Not knowing them,
But thrice-accomplished,
Standing strong and nerveless
On a thrice-exalted peak
With smoke and silver clouds around.
"See, I can drink! I'll hold this glass
With my left hand—"

"It's done with mirrors," Derry said,
And nearly fell against the table as he stood
For introduction.

Oh, this is wonderful, said Stephenson,
Within his swaddled brain.
Oh, what a bold and happy world!
She comes to me—
And is she beautiful? Oh, boy!
Oh, look at this: my wife, my dove,
My angel child, my love,
My spirit bright,
My mistress of a thousand fragrant dreams. . . .
"Oh, look at this," he said, quite thickly,
With an arm around the shoulder of his wife,
And leaning hard on her.
He introduced:
"Now, this is Fred—
This Fred— And he was in the war.
And this is Homer. Homer—in the war—"
"Of course," said Milly, twenty thousand miles away.
"Of course! How glad I am
To meet you both!"
"Let's all go home," said Stephenson,
"And have another drink."
"Why, certainly," said Milly.
"That's the reason that we came."

Al bellowed with his heavy voice,
"You hear that? This is wonderful!
We'll all go home
And have another drink."

"No, no, not Homer," Butch implored.
"I'll take him home.
He lives almost across the street:
That's Homer Wermels.

Say, I knew his folks
Before they ever had a kid."
Al said, "You heard me.
We'll go out to our place—
Isn't really home—
That's Cherry Hill—
We're going to the Casa Blanca—
Have another drink.
Because these guys— We flew together coming home,
Flew here from Welburn in a 24."

"A 17!" said Derry,
Though he could not lift the lids
That hung like lead above his eyes.
"A 17," said Al. "We flew."

They couldn't hear when Peggy
Whispered close to Butch:
"No, they're too drunk.
Now, please don't worry;
We'll just put them all to bed.
If you know that boy's parents,
Tell them he's all right—
We'll take them home.
We've got the car.
Heavens and earth, it's nothing!
I'd much rather face this
Than some amorous lieutenant
When I'm out alone!"
And Engle nodded—
"Maybe that's the best.
I sure am sorry,
But what's a guy to do,
If they insist on coming in
And getting crocked?"

"Just help us get them in the car. . . ."

Debauched they went—all leaning, staggering.
As bad as ever, Homer flopped,
An object lesson for the Drys
Who would have been delighted
If they could have seen.
All hoisted, boosted, helped, persuaded:
The age-old problem of the Drunk—

Three Drunks this time,
And singing lustily
Amid the blankness of the 5th Street dark.
"Pipe down!" said Butch. "Pipe down!
We don't want every cop in town—"
"O.K.," yelled Al.
"Pipe down, you guys!"
And Peggy drove them home.

Homer and Fred were both asleep
Before they came to 34th and Grand.
Nobody knew where Derry lived;
Butch wasn't there to tell them
What to do with Homer.
"Nothing to do but that, my dear," said **Milly**,
Soft voice splintering
The while she tried to keep it calm.
"Just as you say—
We'll put them all to bed."

They did.
They moved Rob out; and sleepily
He tramped to Peggy's room
And bedded down upon the *longue* couch
By the window.
This was no bitter pill for him:
He grinned, still half asleep.
He thought it fun.
So did MacDuff
Beside him on the quilt.
Rob was asleep before they even
Led the others to his room.

Peggy and Milly pulled off Homer's shoes....
The big one with the sole. They gasped;
How much did that shoe weigh?
They got him into bed;
He didn't know what they were doing.
He mumbled: "Look at me. Say, look at this,"
And then he snored
With mouth sagged open,
Water running down his chin, and yellow hair
That pointed forty different ways.

Derry sat sotted on the other bed.
His head drooped low —

He couldn't hold it up.
"... I guess I'd better go.
I sure am sorry—making all this trouble."
"For heaven's sake, Lieutenant," said the girl,
In her clear voice,
"It's not a bit of trouble!
You're a friend of Dad's.
You'd do as much for him.
Now, wouldn't you?"
Derry observed her mistily.
"I'd do as much," he said. "I'd do—"
His chin dropped down again.
"Now, lie back," Milly said,
"And let's take off your shoes...."
They pulled them off;
They dragged the spread and blanket
From beneath his nerveless shape
And put the blanket over him;
He slept.
"Open the window wide—"
And Peggy moved to do it,
Disarranging all Rob's things
Upon the window ledge inside:
The racquet, models, books and soldier toys:
Mementos of the childhood
He was shedding all too fast.
"What about towels?" asked Milly, whispering.
"Good Lord," said Peggy.
"... Much too drunk to use them
If they had them!
                    Here—
I'll switch the bathroom light
And leave the door ajar,
Hoping they'll find it if they need to.
Let us pray!" she said.
"And now, Mom dear, please go and see
What's happened to my sire,
And I will go to bed,
And you go too,
And take your boy friend with you."

Then Milly found him,
Hunting drinks.
He'd blundered to the shelves
Within the tiny butler's pantry...

Broken one tall glass,
Spilled some soda,
Trying to mix up the drinks.
"By God," Al whispered, wistfully,
"I'm awfully sorry I got tight.
I stayed away too long. . . ."

He let her lead him to her room.
He let her hang his blouse upon a chair.
He sat down heavily
With Milly turning down the spread.
"Let me undress you," Milly said.

"No, I'll undress myself.
I'm not that tight. I tell you—
Mr. Milton. L.D.M.—"
"Yes, he was here," said Milly,
With a gaiety she did not feel.
"Remember that?"
"Oh sure," said Al.

A million things he hoped to say. . . .
He wanted them; he wanted her;
He wanted all the things
That occupied his consciousness
When he was far from her.
He wanted music, and the flute
Of her soft voice.
He wanted food he hadn't had.
He wanted—

"L.D.M.," he said again. "You didn't hear—
I'm third vice-president."
"You're what?" she gasped.
"That's right." He nodded loosely.
"What you heard—
I'm third vice-president
Instead of Steese.
The Board—the Board—"
And Milly sighed
And, drawing in her breath, she cried,
"That's wonderful!
Oh, Al, that's—"
"Well, I am not so sure," said Al.
"Now you lie down," said Milly. "Please!"

She stripped him of his clothes.

He lay sedate
And tried to keep his lids from sinking shut.
"What—what—" he asked,
"About those kids?"
"They're in Rob's room.
Now go to sleep."
"I can't," he whispered, "watching you...."
And then she gave the only sob she gave:
"You're much too drunk to think of *that*!
No. I'll turn off the light."
She pushed the switch.
But there was light
That drifted in: soft, yellow,
From the bath next door....
He heard the rustle of her slip,
He heard the sounds he had not heard
In legal process of a love,
For all those thirty months—
In decent process of a love,
That any man'd prefer
To any paltry substitute he got.

He saw the nightgown billowing—
The lace went high;
She put her arms within the folds,
She slid it down.
"Oh, Milly," whispered Al.

"Now go to sleep."

"I can't. I want to tell you—
Listen: kids like these,
They make me think—
We had the best kids in the world.
I tell you— Our platoon—
Bud Rosenberg. You should have seen—
We had a kid named Armstrong:
He could sing.
By God. I guess that sometimes I was tough—
I had to be.
But when I got them into shape,
I tell you—kids like that—
Give me a squad of kids like that—

I'd take them anywhere—
And, sister, would they go!"
"I'm sure they would," said Milly,
Climbing in beneath the sheet.

He felt her knee.
It was unreal. He couldn't move.
His ears resounded
Like a windy sea;
And suddenly, clean-cut and menacing,
He heard the riveting machines
That tore the smoke, and sent
Their angry haze of death
From every pine-tree and ravine
He had to pass. . . .
He'd passed them all. He'd come to this,
And he was here,
And this was it,
And he was Home.

Oh, Milly.
   And he touched her skin.
"I guess I stink. My breath is bad.
I'll try to turn my face away.
I hadn't thought—"

"Now, darling, if you'll go to sleep—"

"No, no," he said,
And fearing well his future in the darkness
That surrounded them—
And all that noisy fog within his ears,
And mortar shells that crumped within the mud—
"No, no," he gasped. "Forget those kids.
Oh, let's forget just everything!
I couldn't love another soul;
I couldn't!
Listen. You—you're . . ."
He drew her, unresisting,
Mad, intent and smothering
With her warm mouth. . . .
And smothering each protest, explanation,
Angry dream he might have had.
His ears still rang. He lay entranced

And yielded up the pulsing joy
Which, drunk or sober,
He could always give to her.

xxiii

So DRY my throat, so full my head
Of swollen hurt and broken fancy—
Raw my eyes, and walloping my pulse—
(I heard an ocean, saw a feast of lights
And planes up-ended in the colored rain
Of rough-resounding guns).

Now I will creep
An unfamiliar course
To do the things I need to do
For this deceptive body:
                              I will drink
One glass, another, other—
Splashing half the water
On my clothes.

How long like this?
How many years
To watch in envy worthless men
And children walk the way I used to walk?
To see them vault the fences,
Climb the steps, pilot the cars,
Assuredly dispatch their food,
And wrap their arms around ... the girls
Recoiling never at their touch,
As if a mauling dog
Had slobbered all too close—?

I know a gun;
And once I hung behind an Oerlikon
And felt its rigor in my arms.
I never got the Junkers 88,
For I am not the sort who gets a plane;
For I am of the breed that fires fervently
And dies in some disordered state—

So ludicrous and pitiful, my kind of death—
That I will never understand
Why it did never claim me in entirety.

These words I muddle in my mind,
Or part of them: attendant thoughts
That are not given able voice
By men so young as I.
I feel the power of my helplessness,
And recognize that I'd be dumb
To quite express it, were my tongue unloosed
And all my motors turning properly.

But still, despite the morning-after agony,
I cherish recollection of the night.
I held my hand more steadily than any time
Since Off Oran....
The taste of liquor on my lips,
And swallowing—
Oh, it was inspiration to a hardihood!
I'll drink again, and often.

Let them deplore it:
Pa and Ma, who cannot understand
That men with ribbons colorful as mine
Can seldom be subdued to childishness again.
If Wilma doesn't like it
She can go to hell—
With all her crying, and her baby platitudes
(This thought I soundly set in force
In simpler words,
Within my aching brain).

Who are these people? Do they pity me?
Why lie I in a foreign bed,
And see the unfamiliar stuff around—
The intimate effects
Of people who are strange to me?
Oh, I must run away
Before those women overcome my soul
With any kind solicitation—

Yes, dress, by Jesus Christ!
I'm not a baby...dress myself...
They do not recognize

That I have seen the stars explode,
And felt the angry decks descend
Across more oceans than the pirates sailed.

Nineteen years old, but twenty soon—
(And not so long since I cried out my heart
Because my kitten ran away).
Ah, let me slip in silence—
Best as I can manage—
Find a taxicab to take me Home.
But where is Home,
When no one in my life
Can gain my understanding
Or give theirs?

xxiv

WHEN Derry woke he saw an empty bed
Quite disarranged, and standing next to his.
At first he didn't know just where he was.
So many times he'd wakened
In a house unknown to him. . . .
(And usually through act of romance.
Romance?
Maybe use another word.)

This might have been the flat of Lady Tillman,
But it wasn't. . . .
Might have been that place in Kent
Where he spent two days with a buxom blonde,
Whose husband served the King
Five thousand miles away,
While Derry served the husband's wife. . . .
The homespun spreads,
The figured carpet on the floor,
The sum of little decencies
To which a house on Brighton Drive
Might not pretend; and might not even wish to own.

And then he knew just where he was.
He had a vague remembrance
Of the women pulling off his shoes.

He thought of Al; he heard the songs;
And where was Homer?

Derry bathed. His head was like a can
In which some metal clattered when he moved.
He found his shoes. He found his blouse,
He carried it; and tottered to the kitchen,
Interloping none too comfortably,
And there was Peggy all alone.

He didn't know her name . . . the vague remembrance,
And the spots before his eyes. . . .
"Hello," he said.
                    "Good morning," and she smiled.
"I'm Peggy," and she gave her hand to him.
He shook her hand, and it was cool,
And his was hot and weak and dry.
He said, "My name's Fred Derry."
"Yes, I know. Dad introduced us,
Down at Butch's. Or don't you remember?"
"I guess I do," Fred Derry said.
"There was a little matter of some shoes—"
"We took them off," she told him.
"Hope you didn't mind!
It's quite traditional, I guess,
For drunken musketeers
To perish with their boots on."

He shook his head and felt forlorn;
And all that ringing in his ears. . . .
"Well, thanks a lot. I'm sorry to have caused
Such trouble."
                    "Oh," she said,
"I wouldn't call it trouble.
But it would have been, if we had never hunted Dad.
Imagine that old villain going out with you,
And getting drunk, the first night he came home!"
"Gosh," said Fred Derry.
"What a head!"

She laughed again,
But not with sympathy.
She thought he had it coming.
"Here," she said, with tall and frothing glass,
"Drink this. Now, down it quick,

While it's still foaming!"
Fred drank and made a fearful face.
She offered him a paper towel to wipe his mouth.
She said, "Suppose I make a prairie oyster
With tomato juice?"
                  "What's that?"
"Raw egg. Don't tell me
That you never had one—
An old soak like you?"
"Well, thanks," he said,
"I'm not so crazy for raw eggs—"

"Come, come. It's therapeutic—
Good for you," said Peggy Stephenson.

He drank the egg. . . . She'd beaten it
With condiments, with lemon juice and pepper;
Mixed it with tomato juice.
The glass seethed high,
And Derry drank it to the dregs.
"Now," said the girl. "You'll live, I guess."

"Say, where's your dad?"
"He's still asleep."
"Where's Homer?"
                "Homer?
That's the crippled boy?
Why, wasn't he in there with you?"

"He's gone, I guess."

She made a sound, and shook her head,
And looked at him with pity.
Neither said a word just then
About the case of Homer.
Neither could have said a word
To match what they were thinking.
"Yes," said Fred, "I guess he's gone."

"I thought I heard the door—
I thought that it was Rob, my brother,
Going out. He's got a job on Saturdays.
I guess he must have gone before. . . .
One moment, while I call downstairs."

She went away and called.
And then came back; her face was grave.
Yes, Homer'd gone. The doorman called a Yellow Cab
And Homer went. "Oh, dear!" said Peggy.
"Well, I guess there's nothing we can do.
And so, Lieutenant Derry,
What about some breakfast?"
"You bet!" said Fred.
The bromide burst within his throat,
And he excused himself; but Peggy only laughed,
And asked him what he'd like to have.
She hadn't eaten breakfast yet, herself.

They huddled opposite, inside the breakfast nook,
Like children playing house,
When she had set the breakfast down:
The bacon, toast, the berry jam,
The coffee dripping hot inside its orb.
They ate and talked; or Derry talked.
She made him talk. Somehow she knew
The kind of things he'd like to tell.
She didn't say,
"I know you're sick and tired of the war,
So let's not talk about it, shall we?"
.... Didn't ask him how he felt
When he was wounded;
Nor how many Jerry planes he'd got.
(He had got four. He thought he'd like
To tell her that, but didn't.)
Little things ...
He liked to hear her laugh.
She didn't laugh too daintily;
But bright amusement occupied her body
And her spirit, all at once.
She'd lift her pointed chin—
Her eyes would nearly close—
The messy curls around her ears would shine—
She'd laugh.

And so he told again,
About the necktie Oakley cut;
About the time when Major Price
Arrested Dris and Spring
Because they'd crept along a path behind their site,
And stayed away too long;

And how they rode up merrily;
The MP stopped them—said:
"Lieutenant Driscoll?"
                              "Yes."
"Lieutenant Springstun?"
                              "Yes."
"Well, much as I regret it, sir,
You're both arrested here and now!"
Or something like that:
Quite a formal speech, the MP made.

Fred told about the time
The trucks went over Rushden way,
To gather girls. There was a party planned.
The ladies who had charge of things like that—
The Voluntary Services:
They'd picked some girls so carefully,
And passed upon them—morals, mainly,
If they hadn't passed upon their charm!
Girls waited with their chaperons;
But all the trucks stopped right in town,
Right on the main drag . . .
Let the tailboards down. The guys got out,
And started propositioning the girls along the street:
"Hey, girls, you want to dance?
You want a party? Listen, girls—"
"At Poddington?" "Hell, no! The 3-0-5th."
It took about five minutes, and the trucks were full.
Then they went back to Chelveston.
"We didn't like the hand-picked girls," said Fred.
"They looked about like this—"
He made imaginary spectacles around his eyes,
And made his teeth stick out;
And Peggy squealed again.

They sat and smoked when they had fed themselves.
The little kitchen clock ticked on,
And Derry sighed (his headache gone)—
He sipped the coffee that was left
And settled down in comfort, dreaminess.
And thus he found:
This wasn't any girl you had to talk to
All the time. He found her quite content
To sit and smoke, and drink her coffee too.
The warmth of domesticity

Was golden all around them.

Each could feel
The sly and simple current run,
The juice between them, flicking forth,
The anode-cathode of themselves—
The mighty earnestness so small
They couldn't see it—might not even
Speak of it. And yet it lived, would always live
Between them, day or dark.

She thought,
"I like his face. I like
The way he grins ... oh, surely
He has seen a lot, been hurt a lot,
Been tossed around in those old bombers,
Shot at, frightened, frozen, driven, iced.
He's got a fierce maturity.... His tone
Is lower-class. His humor isn't.
Somewhere he has been exposed
To some sophistication. I wonder just
How old he is?
And is he married? He's not on the make;
He doesn't try to flirt, to sell himself.
I wonder ... honestly, he's awfully nice...."

She said, "Perhaps you've speculated
Why I'm not in uniform—"
                                    "The hell!"
He answered quickly. "I like girls
In dresses better than in uniforms!"
"Yes, most men do," she said.
"But it's a total war. The women
Should have had to go, just like the men.
I criticized our President for that;
I think he should have simply *made*
The Congress back him up: a full conscription,
Like they had in Britain—"
                                    "Look," said Derry,
"I don't think that—"

"Just the same, I tried—
As soon as I was old enough.
And honestly, the whole bunch turned me down!

Wacs, Waves, Marines and everything.
I'm 4-F, honestly."
                              She pointed.
"Punctured ear-drum! We don't know
Just how it happened. Isn't that too grim?
And I can hear as well as anyone—
I'm not the slightest bit inclined to deafness—
Still, I can't get in.... And so, in after years,
When all my grandchildren come round
To grandma's knee, and ask about the war,
I won't be able to recite a thing
Except how Mrs. Huttner wrote the records wrong,
And Mrs. Everleigh had heart attacks
Whenever things got rough
Down at the Red Cross rooms."

And then appeared MacDuff,
Fresh come from long mid-morning snooze,
And scenting grease and toast and jam
And other things he liked.
He sat up like a furry post
And begged, and barked when Fred
Neglected him too long.
He swallowed down illegal bits
While Peggy ordered Fred to quit,
And Fred said, "Heck, he's hungry.
Let him have another piece.
Just one more piece?"
                              He said,
"Say, he's a dandy. Gee, he's—
Where on earth did you get him?
He looks just like a champion."
(Fred couldn't tell a champion
From any beat-up mutt he ever met.
But still he thought MacDuff was—)

"Certainly, his blood is blue as ink!
He's got— Let's see—" She counted.
"Fourteen champions in just four generations.
We've never shown him, though;
We're not the dog-show kind.
We just like dogs, that's all. I think MacDuff
Cost Daddy some ungodly sum;
But Wiggles—that we had before—he was a stray
And never cost a cent. We just like dogs."

Fred listened as she jested on;
She told of Wiggles and his darling ways,
And how he died beneath a passing truck—
But all the time those words played hob with him.
Ungodly sum ... and only for a dog.
Fred Derry's dogs had always been—
Like Wiggles—those you pick up free.
We're not the dog-show kind. Well, maybe not;
But still he thought of laughing families
Displayed informally in double-page accounts
He'd seen sometimes in magazines
Like *Country Life* or *Spur*. Oh, years ago
He used to poach off magazines like that,
In hateful secret sessions at the store—
Alive with fascination, dark with gloom—
Resenting every ounce of wealth such people had
Because he didn't have a single grain.

So now he thought
With fierce unworthiness that rose inside
As bitter as an acid in his throat:

"Look here, what's this?
Why am I here?
I don't belong. I'm not the kind.
How could I manage anything like this?
How could I hope to manage it?
I've got a little money, and no job.
I don't know how to do a single thing
But set the hairlines where they need to go—
And how much bombing will they want in Boone?
And who will pay me for it?
How's about the drugstore, Derry?
How's about banana splits?
And how much salary will Bullard's pay you now?

"These easy little things—
They seem so much a part of life
When you have been exposed to them:
The petty luxuries,
The taxicabs, the dinners just for two,
The drinks at every bar you come across;
The tailored pinks, the custom-ordered shoes;
The flight pay you will never get,

The overseas allowance that is gone,
The basic pay that is not yours.
A soda-jerk you were—
And maybe are again.
So what's the score on **this?**

"This girl—she's had
The lovely things of life.
She's had them all the time.
She doesn't know what it would be
To stand in line with tray in hand,
Except perhaps—a school-girl lark.
She doesn't even buy her things—
Her clothes (the sweater that she has,
The little shoes,
The ribbons in her hair)—
She doesn't get those things at Oppenheimer-Stern's,
Or any such department store.
She goes in to Chicago shops.
She's not above a breakfast job like this,
When someone comes, as company—
She isn't anybody's snob—
Or anybody's fool.
But everything is nice around her;
Everything must cost a lot.
It always has, it always will.

"Say, she is cute!
I guess I haven't really looked at her that way:
Can't tell you what her legs are like,
Not even now.
Because this table in the breakfast nook,
It keeps them covered up.
But all I know—I like her voice,
I like her eyes, I like her laugh,
I like the things she says,
And all the things she doesn't say.
But—what the hell!
Let one of those smart boys—
Nice boys—young college boys—
Let some young j.g. come—
Some guy she danced with at the country club.
Just let him come!
A guy like me— Well, he'd be out.
Yes, really out—

So fast his head would swim.
Imagine if she met Hortense?
Imagine if she knew about Marie?
Oh, God! I guess I'm lost in this—
So how's about a Q.D.M.?"

He stood abruptly, saying,
"Well, I have to go."

"Oh, wait for Dad!" cried Peggy.
"You all had your fun last night;
I think that he'll be hurt
If no one sticks around
To help him with *his* head."
And Derry grinned. He forced himself to grin.
He said, "I'd like to stay—
But there's a lot that I should do.
I've got to travel, Hon.
You certainly— Well, you have been—
I sure appreciate it. Thanks a lot."

She went with him, out to the hall.
They found his cap. He buttoned up his blouse.
She saw his ribbons. "Oh, I wish," she said,
"You'd tell me more. Perhaps sometime you will?"
There was important question in her voice.
"Perhaps," said Derry.
"Thanks a lot."

He went away.
He knew that she would think him crude
And suddenly abrupt,
Without a worthwhile reason in the world....
But still he had to go.
She wasn't anything for him—
Nor he for her!

XXV

AL STEPHENSON tried on a suit:
 The one he thought would fit him best.
 Milly had given many of his things away;
But several suits she had, all brushed, awaiting him.
He tried on one—another—
Tried the tweed.
It was the same in every case.
He'd changed his body
As he'd changed his soul
He weighed around two hundred when he left
And now he weighed one-eighty-two.
His hips were thin, his belly flat,
And there was room he needed now
Throughout his shoulder surface
That he didn't need before.
                          With aching head
He thought about his soul—
How it had undergone a change.
He couldn't tell how much:
He didn't know the weight.

The chalk-stripe, blue, the Scottish twist:
They'd need to be set right again
Before he wore them any more.
("Why, come in uniform," said L.D.M.
"Just like Lou Latham did!")
"By God," said Al, "I won't—
Just like Lou Latham did."
And Milly watched him quizzically.
"You're making such a face," she said.
"Most certainly you're not ashamed
To wear a uniform?"
"You know," said Al, "I'm not ashamed!
As for the face—I look like that
Because I've got some adders in my brain:
The bromide didn't kill them all.
I don't care how I look," he said.
"I'll wear this flannel. Here we go!"
He dressed again.
The flannel hung so loose in front

And bound the movement of his arms.
"You wear a white shirt, and a tartan tie.
At least," said Milly,
"I am sure the necktie fits you perfectly!"
His shoes, unwrapped from paper,
With the trees removed, would fit him very well;
Though seeming stiff and tight at first.

This blessed world,
This world of Boone,
Was very stiff and tight at first.
He'd better wear it soft,
As soon as well he could.

"Mama," said Peggy in the hall,
"Just who's that man?
A perfect picture of a third vice-president?"

Al stood before the mirror, fascinated still
By the strange object that he made
Within the mirror's depths.
And Milly laughed in tremolo:
Thought it advantage of a sort
That he'd removed his uniform so soon.
That outward gesture—it might mean
That "Butch's" was an accident along the way
(The stubborn way he'd have to tread
If, like poor Homer, he was ever right again).
She said he was the best civilian type
She'd entertained beside her bed,
In—certainly—six months or more.
"*Upon* your bed," said Al,
And slapped her on the rear.
"Look, Dad!" said Peggy,
"Hurry up. It's nearly twelve.
They close at twelve—or don't you know?
I rather think they're all expecting you....
Come on, I'll drive you down.
I'm late at the Red Cross.
But where's your badge?"
                              "What badge?"
"Your button—showing Honorable Discharge."

He looked at it a moment, weighing loose
Its gold metallic weight within his hand.

"Oh, hell," he said,
And put the button in a drawer.

He couldn't quite elaborate
The way he wanted to.
He couldn't say
That he'd seen dozens of those things
Already since he landed in the States.
Of course it wasn't shame. . . .
No man could be ashamed
Who'd done his job the best he could—
Even the little orderly at Omaha
Who didn't get to go and kill the Japs
He thought that he could kill.
Even the actors in Long Island studios,
The MP's strolling on their posts
At Union Station terminals,
Even the doctors, tired of Sawtelle,
Even the war-room men who hung the maps
Upon a wall in Washington. . . .
The toiling engineers in Tennessee—
The boys with transits, tractors, fountain pens—
The drivers of the garbage trucks—
The rabbis, priests—
The people on the proving-ground at Aberdeen—
The menials unsung in any war:
The people who repaired latrines at home.

It wasn't shame—
You couldn't call it that;
But only dumb reluctance to accept
A single brand, and let it burn your hide,
And then to let some beaming dunce
Who'd struggled to keep Out—
Who'd struggled to get Out
The whole time he was In—
And let that fellow clap you on the back
And call you Pal, and call himself a veteran.

A proud and private brand. . . .
Al vaguely wished
That he might wear a patch upon civilian clothes,
A regimental button, possibly—
An emblem telling all that he had lain with Death,
Had kissed her clammy teats

Until her bony arms relaxed
And let him rise,
And leave the awful love they'd had.
"I know some guys," he said to Milly,
"At the Separation Center. . . . Well,
They said they didn't give a damn:
They'd take the buttons, if they had to.
But they dropped them down a grating in the street.
I won't do that.
But I don't want to wear it.
Funny. Thought I would."

And turning quick to look at her,
Because she hadn't said a word,
He found her standing by the dresser.
She had something in her hand—
Her jewel-box lid ajar,
And she had something—
                    "I don't know," she said,
"Just how they do it. . . . Come here, sweet,
I never decorated anyone before.
Do I get kissed?"
She tacked it bold upon his coat:
The single ribbon of the Silver Star.
She pinned it on his left breast,
Where it ought to go if he were wearing uniform.
"I do recall," she said, "in England
Long before the war—
And you remember too—Maybe they do it still.
But all the men— So many used to wear
Their ribbons from the other war,
Sometimes in miniature, and sometimes of this size."

She kissed the ribbon on his coat.
He stood and kissed her hair.
"Come *on*," yelled Peggy from the hall.

xxvi

THEY'D locked the doors before he reached the bank,
The blinds drawn down, all blank behind their panes.
The clock showed seven minutes after twelve
When Stephenson knocked on the glass.
He knocked again. He waited; then
Tapped tough his knuckles on the door again.
At last a guard appeared and pushed the shade aside,
Smiled grimly, shook his head, and waved Al on. . . .
A face he didn't know. It wasn't Wade's—
Who'd stood in sober uniform beside a lobby desk
Through all the years that Al worked in the bank.

He rapped again. The guard came back, annoyed,
Unlocked the door—
"I'm Mr. Stephenson," said Al.
The guard exclaimed, and let him in.
"I'm sorry, Mr. Stephenson!
I thought you'd be in soldier clothes.
I'm kind of new; I took Wade's place.
My name is Jensen, sir."

That *sir* felt funny, too.
You didn't call a sergeant *sir.* . . .
"That's quite all right. But what became of Wade?"
"He went to war, sir, and—"
                              The people spotted Al.

They came from past the polished fence;
They got up from their desks and came;
They rose from black-upholstered chairs;
They said, "Well, well!" and put their pens aside,
Left off their conversations on the phone,
And let their secretaries stare.
Prew, Wilson, Steese, and Mr. Mulendorff—
They said, "Well, well! I'm glad to see you.
Hail the Conquering—"
                         They all wore smiles.
Steese wore a smile a trapper might have worn
When Winnebagos tied him to a stake.

They came around him, racketing
With tiny praise and welcoming;
They made their jolly pleasantries;
(They thought them jolly)
They called Stephenson, "Old Boy."
And he was dumbly glad that he'd delayed
Till customers were gone from off the floor.
Only a few left, now, in chairs
Behind the sacred rail, the holy place.

"We're very glad that you are back," said Steese.
The dreadful words that he'd rehearsed
A hundred times within his mind
Since Tuesday afternoon.
"Congratulations, Mr. Stephenson!"
"Thanks, Will," said Al. He called him by his name,
And hoped that Steese would take the hint.
He didn't. Still the eyes looked frightened, sad,
Beneath the spectacles.
Al thought of Steese's wife—an invalid;
And Steese's daughter—thin, afraid of life,
But not so old as Peggy yet. . . .

The kind of man who married late and sadly,
With no juice exhilarated in his veins,
No lover's song,
No understanding of a laugh he might have made
At even this existence here in Boone.
Worked like a dog, chained like a slave—
A nervous little slave in paper chains
That he had forged himself.
　　　　　　　　　　"Oh, what's the joy,"
Thought Al, "in any such promotion,
When I know his soul is sick,
And mine is not revivified?"

He went the rounds, the others leading on
And shepherding behind.
Above his head the giant service flag hung down.
Al stopped and counted stars;
He counted forty-six; and two were gold.
"Look here," he said, while people pointed out
That young Miss Mutzell waited to be introduced.
"Look here," he said, and indicated stars of gold,
"Who's dead?"

"Why, let me see," said Milton.
"First, there's Wade."
                   "Wade? The old guard?"
"Yes. Wade—he went in '43."

Al said, "He didn't have to go!"
"Oh, he was dying to get in.
He'd made some trips across—the Navy—
Back in World War I.
They wouldn't take him, though,
And finally he made the Coast Guard.
He was on a boat in port somewhere
Out on the West Coast; and there was an explosion.
Wade was killed."
         "And who's the other one?"
They grinned a little; shrugged, and rolled their eyes.
They said, with depreciation,
"You remember Johnny?"
           "Johnny?"
                  "Yes—
The little messenger?"
"He wasn't what I'd call a lad of promise," Milton said.
"Not quite reliable. What was his name?"
And Al remembered. "Johnny Dyke."
"He ran away," somebody said.
"He wasn't really old enough."
"He thought he was," said Prew, in solemn tones.
"I found him smoking in the washroom;
Gave him quite a lecture. That was Friday.
Saturday he went away."
"But he was killed?" persisted Al.
"Oh, yes, he was. The South Pacific somewhere.
We weren't notified.
We read it in the *Courier & News*.
He had a mother here in town, I think."
"No," said somebody else, "a sister."
And Stephenson desired to know more
Of Johnny Dyke, and how he died.
He asked again: the Army or Marines, or Navy? . . .
People drew him on. They were not proud of Johnny
    Dyke;
He used to tell bad stories to stenographers.

Al went the rounds,
And Milton had him by the arm awhile.

They went past glass partitions....
"You will find a much more pretty staff
Than those we used to have!"
A woman teller showed her teeth and laughed.
She wasn't pretty...what a laugh!

"And this is Miss O'Connor.
She took it over— Let's see, Miss O'Connor—?"
"Eighteen months," she said.
"I came when Mr. Barlow left."

They passed comptometers and files,
And mighty ledgers spread;
They came to vaults.
And other guards who waited there...
The baskets carried in, the money bags...
The beaming smile that hid suspicion not too well.
They'd heard of Al so many times—
Even the ones who didn't know Al's face.
And Milton left his side, called to the phone;
Another took his place.
The man named Prew was prowling close behind—
Vice-president, relieved of his third post
To move one step above,
And planning even now
The rich advice he'd give to Al.
Prew hadn't thought this course was wise:
He spoke objection to the Board—
Was sure that Steese would do much better—
But the Board had ruled him down.
Prew was a Methodist, an elder of the church,
A leader in the drives and charities—
He had *Y.M.C.A.* tattooed upon his heart—
And owlish sons who fought their war
Without a drink, without a vagrant sin.
So grimly pure, the Prews, and fleshy-faced,
And hating vice,
And seeing vice
In every course that they did not pursue;
Embittered, honest; each Prew holding in his mind
A portrait that he called by God's own name,
And made to look like Grandpa Prew
Each time he thought of it.

They came to tall Lou Latham, mortgage manager:
Bald, blond, and poker-grim.

He looked about the same:
The Army hadn't done a thing to him,
Nor had the war he'd fought.
He'd fought his war
With requisitions, stamps and telephones.
He was the beau ideal of those bureaucracies
That distant soldiers dreamed,
And hated most obscenely
When they thought of Washington.
He shook Al's hand, still conscious of his rank,
But quite judicious, knowing he was Out.
"Well, Sergeant Stephenson," he said,
And made a smile. "I guess you'll let
A poor ex-major shake your hand?"
His eyes went down.
He saw the ribbon of the Silver Star,
And disapproved, because Al wore civilian clothes.
"Well, well. That's nice," said Lou.
"I see you've got a ribbon on.
Congratulations, Al."

Remotely, Stephenson could hear himself say Thanks.
Across a desk, a grinning girl that knew him When,
She squealed and beamed—said,
"Tell us all about the war!"

xxvii

YES, I will tell you all about the war,
   Said Stephenson within his heart....
   It isn't fought with currency,
Though people say it is.
It isn't fought with rank, or any guns;
It isn't made with cannon—that's a lie.
Now, I will tell you all about the war:
It only has one sad consistency:
It's made of youth, it's made of boys
With staring baffled eyes,
With hair upon their chests
Or bodies smooth as silk.
If still you want to know the final truth:

It isn't even made of boys like that,
But of the stuff inside—
The wet and greasy parts you never see
When any man strips down.

If I must tell you all about the war
I'll tell you how the corrugations swell
Inside a shell-pink skull.
The little piece lies pressed on ground,
Like garbage scattered there.
Somebody lifts it up. He takes a shovel tip,
Unless he's in a hurry—then he uses hands.
He lifts the broken bit of drying pink,
(And printed by the mark of someone's heel,
Who stepped upon it, as it lay forlorn and loose,
And wholly unprotected)
Tosses it away, away; he throws it in a ditch,
Or digs a hole with his own shoe,
And puts the thing inside,
Treads down the earth above
In burial for any piece of him
Who died dismembered there.

And war is made of gassy, oily bowel—
A nasty looseness that they call GI's.
Sweat, blood and tears?
The surgeons have a name
For all the yellow stuff that men must wear inside,
And never know it's there
Until they see it dripping out,
And running down ... and watch their bodies
Shudder as it drips.

Oh, call it protoplasm if you must—
And name the veins and clavicles,
And tell just where the bullet went,
And what the bursting shell has done!
But still you won't identify
Each poor distressed and wettened bit—

Because they mark the end of youth:
A picture puzzle that the very angels couldn't place
In nice array again.

That's all about the war, Al swore a hundred times
Before he left the bank, on this triumphal tour. . . .

That's all about the war.
You said that I should tell;
So I have told.

xxviii

THE WAY Fred felt, he couldn't stand their house
Nor all the smelly little tired life they led,
Nor gray (it seemed to him) the wintry look
Of empty-hearted lower middle-class.

That weekend, Derry entertained
His father and Hortense;
He took them out on Saturday,
Prepared to ease the shock his dad might feel
When told that Fred had taken quarters
At the Daniel Boone.
The way it was, his father didn't seem to care,
And Hortense felt relieved—
Fred saw it in her face . . .
And knew he'd be an exile, always,
From his own house.

His father said, "The Daniel Boone?
That costs a lot!"
"Five bucks a night," said Fred;
And didn't tell him he had paid
Eight pounds for two-room suites at the Savoy.
He used to gamble overseas. He didn't gamble here.
If you were broke when overseas
You didn't mind too much;
If you were broke in Boone, you'd mind a lot.
And Derry knew that he'd be busted soon;
His roll was getting thin.
So, with a mind he'd manacled before,
He closed an iron door against the thought
And screwed the hatches down.

They went to Olson's, where you went for steaks:
A walnut-ceilinged room with steins upon the wall,
And hunting prints—
A phony rathskeller, and equally
A phony British pub—

But New York cuts were pretty good.
And Hortense wore her rope of imitation pearls,
And she had washed her neck, and done her nails;
She didn't look so bad.
Fred Derry's dad was proud;
And he was drunk by nine o'clock.
He left the table often, walking stern and proper,
As if with cares and much responsibility,
But strutting just the same.
He'd stand beside the bar that occupied
The inner room, and tell all strangers
That his son was Home—
And point Fred out across the tables—
Endow him with some medals he had never earned.

Pat Derry met two fellows from the *Courier & News*
And brought them bold to introduce to Fred,
And Hortense squealed at jokes they told.
The jokes were tired, tough and poor.
Fred Derry set his jaw, and told a few himself,
And watched the others howl.
Long, long before the clock struck ten
His father went to sleep, his black-nailed hand
Extended in ice-cream.
"I'd better take him home," the woman said.

"I'll go, if you need help."

"Oh, not a bit. Why, I can handle him just fine;
I guess I weigh just twice as much!"
Fred took them to a cab, and stowed them in,
And paid the cab, and waved them off.
He walked a block or two,
And breathed the light rain that came down.
The thing was done—the Welcome Home—
The festival.

That weekend,
Sunday afternoon
With Milly, Al went out to Cherry Hill.
He met the tenant, sat with him and made a deal.
Al saw that money talked to any man like this.
He said that he'd remit the April rent
If Mr. Buck would move before the tenth of May.
And Buck agreed. He had to go back East, he thought,

Before the summer.
He told them how the Midland Tin & Type
Was reconverting fast to make civilian goods;
He offered them a drink.
They thanked him. . . . No,
They'd rather walk around the grounds.

They moved in sunset.
Light came through the branches, wet
And dripping from the rain.
And little patches of the sun
Were pasted red on sodden earth.
A robin made its water sound.

They stopped within the row of oaks,
Looked back and saw their own white house:
Tall columns at the door,
The portico in need of paint,
The shrubs so badly trimmed,
The pool with waste of winter leaves. . . .
They saw it all, and loved the place.
They'd bought it when their little girl was five;
And Rob had never known another house but this.
Depression price . . . the house was all run down;
A rotting barn still stood, and there was no garage.
So, through the years, remodeled bit by bit . . .
They'd put their thousands here and there
When they could find the cash.
They'd planted fertilizer of themselves
In mystic gardening beneath the lawn,
And built the good red bricks of their young life
Inside the chimney crests.
"Well, here we are," said Milly.
"Here we'll be again. Oh, baby!"
And she bit his coat lapel.

And then Al heard a scratching in the woods;
He turned; he didn't have an M-1 in his hands;
He couldn't shoot, if enemies
Should trail and kill him,
Kill the men he led. . . .
He felt a sweat that sprang with suddenness
Inside the leather in his hat.
"Why, what on earth?" said Milly.
"What did you think? That we were chased by bears?

See—that's the setter from the Somervilles.
You know, Al—Dick and Mayme?
See—it's their setter. *Yup, yup, yup—*"
She whistled to the dog.

O sweet security of happy Home!
An enemy behind each maple tree,
And ghost machine guns threatening
Before you'd smelled the sauce of your own dirt!
(But his Division clung within those woods so long—
Within those other woods he'd left—
The frightened wold where skeletons might march
In column with the foggy Goths
Who first invaded there.)

"It's growing dark," said Milly.

                              That weekend
The boy named Homer went to Butch's place again—
On Saturday; and Sunday he was sick.
His parents were alarmed ... they talked it over.
Mr. Wermels walked across the street to Engles'—
Waited there for Butch.
Butch stopped his car before the house at five,
And Wermels rose to meet him.
"Listen here," the older man said heavily,
"I'm asking that you keep my son away from—
Well, I mean— I don't want Homer drinking there."

Butch Engle sighed. . . .
"O.K.," he said, "I'll do the best I can.
But, Mr. Wermels, take a tip from me:
There's plenty other places he can get a drink.
I don't sell all the booze in town—
But just the best!
That kid, he's having quite a time—
It's plenty tough on him.
And if it makes him feel
A little better when he drinks—
If he can use his arm, and use his leg
A little better, why—"
"I guess," said Wermels, showing cold
The whites of both his eyes,
"I've thought of that as much as you!
Good God. He's my boy, ain't he?"

"Sure, he's yours," said Butch.
"Please don't get sore. I only tried
To help the kid the best I could,
And see he didn't fall and hurt himself.
I put him on the sofa in my office,
Let him sleep, and brought him home
When I was through."

The father blinked, and couldn't say a word—
And moisture rising hot within his eyes.
He moved his mouth. He tried to speak,
He shook his head and turned away.
Butch Engle watched him go.
He thought, "I'd like to meet the guy
Who fired that torpedo.
... Like to take just one good poke ...
The German bastard."
                Engle, Mueller,
Romerheim and Rach: these were the bastard blood
That filled Butch Engle's frame.

                  That weekend
Derry sat with people in the Daniel Boone.
They called it *tea dansant* on Sunday afternoon.
You couldn't buy a drink;
(The miracle was made—the water turned to wine—
In country places, not in town).
But still the terrace room resounded ...
Dull guitars ... a vacant voice
That mauled the microphone.
And dancers crowded on the floor;
The people huddled close
And touched their hands or knees,
And made their timid try at love
Without a drink to tempt them on.

Fred found some guys from 29's:
A pilot and a navigator, and their girls,
And one girl's sister, extra—
That was why they wanted him.
They'd met across a pin-ball game upstairs.
The marbles clicked, the lights went on,
A red-haired wench stood close, and breathed,
"Lieutenant, you got Number Three!
How marvelous! I tried and tried—

And Number Three's the one I never get."
So in ten minutes they were drinking cokes.

The ETO seemed very far away.
These other guys had newer, fresher war,
But not so tough, it seemed to Fred.
A Zero went to pieces if you got him in your sights;
They didn't carry armor like the German planes
(Ah, you could hammer 50-calibre for half an afternoon
Against a Focke-Wulf. Still his belly swallowed it.)
The landing gear on 29's:
A tricycle, like 24's—
No one from Forts could ever trust
A landing gear like that!
                              But it was good
To sit, and see familiar wings
On other fellows' chests.
It felt like life was looking up again.

He hauled the red-head round the floor.
She said her name was Bob....
Roberta. But they called her Bob.
She had a mane of crinkly, pinkish hair,
And when he stood above her, dancing,
He could see the darkened line along the part.
Her shape was good.... She talked too much.
She gave him tiny pressure of her hand
When they were dancing.
Therefore he said, within his heart:
"I've been beguiled
By experts. Leave my hand alone,
Unless you mean The Works,
And I don't think you do!"

He saw another head across the floor,
Revealed in sheen ... the low blue lights
On hair he knew,
On hair he'd like to touch....
Maneuvered close and circled slow again;
He saw her: Peggy Stephenson ...
And with the style of man he thought she'd have—
Young, dark and calm—
A Princeton fellow, probably,
With two gold stripes upon his sleeve.
Fred thought. "I underestimated.

I just said j.g., and he's a Senior Grade!"
But Peggy's gaze tied into his;
He saw her eyes declare
She'd give him warmest welcoming.

He couldn't wait till he was by her side.
He stood beside the table, looking down.
She introduced him to the Navy guy.
Fred asked if she would dance.
They moved together to the floor,
They didn't say a word until they'd circled,
Far removed from bleating brass and strings.
He said, "You're wearing black. I like to see
A girl in black."
                              "It doesn't put
A gloom upon your soul—
Like mourning? Some men say it does."
"Well, I don't know," Fred Derry said.
"Somehow I think a girl is prettier in black.
I'm glad you came down to the Daniel Boone today."

"You might have asked me if I'd come."
"I know," he said. "I might, but I'm afraid."
"Afraid of what?"
"Oh, just afraid of lots of things."
The Navy fellow tapped him on the arm
And cut the girl away from him.
He watched her when he could.
The red-head acted rather sore.
He had to talk to her a while;
And when he looked up, Peggy and the Navy man
Were going out.
He didn't get to say goodbye.

These girls possessed a car. They drove
Five miles beyond the town.
Fred didn't know where they were going— Didn't care.
He thought of Peggy . . . fallen hard.
"But this won't do," he told himself.
"I guess you'd get to First—
You wouldn't get to Second Base!
You haven't got the dough;
You haven't got a job;
You haven't got a thing to offer
But the D.F.C., some oak-leaf clusters

And a Purple Heart.
And boy, they're drugging up the market nowadays!"

"Now, tell me all about the war!" Roberta cried.
"Yeah," said the pilot from the 29's.
"Get him to tell you all about the time
They grounded him for sinus."
Three boys laughed.
They didn't tell the girls just what was meant.

And this was Carlo's:
Yellow glare inside and out,
And booths along the wall,
And private dining rooms upstairs.
The bar was filled.
Fred saw the cold and weary face
Of one man he had seen before. . . .
He heard the thud of dice within a green baize bin,
He watched the men, four-deep around,
And small and smooth, the brassy head of his Marie,
Bent down and rising high,
And moving as she laughed.
He heard her thin voice
Reading off the dice.

"Oh, not tonight," he thought.
"I couldn't take it; couldn't buy
A nickel's worth of Home, or you!
No longer Derry's Diamond-studded—"

He turned and drew the navigator to the hall.
"Sorry," he said. "I've got to go.
There's plenty Air Force all around,
And other guys. You'll get a man for Bob."
"Roger," the navigator said. "But why the hell
Did you ride all the way out here?"
"I'm sorry, chum. But when you gotta go,
You gotta go," said Fred. "So long."
He flagged a bus, and rode to town.
He held his empty evening in his hand.

He stood with open window high;
He stood undressed with darkness in his room,
And watched Boone City's bitter lights.
And I am Home,

And coming Home to what?
He thought of Peggy—
Wondered just what Al would say.
No. No, he wouldn't try a thing.
He wouldn't call her, wouldn't dance again.

Fred lay upon the bed, and smoked his pipe.
He watched the raw coals sputter in the gloom.
He sucked the smoke and blew it out,
And tried to suck as well
The atmosphere of this new life
On which he'd need to feed.
He thought of London midnights . . .
In a job for Air Force P.R.O.,
He'd lived some months in town,
And heard the raids resounding, night on night.
He'd open windows at the Atheneaum Court
And see the colored flash of doom in Shepherd's Bush,
And hear the wistful women in the street below.
Their voices . . . "Taxi, taxi!" plaintively.
You'd hear them farther than the men.

He scorched the sheet. He put the fire out.
He tried to pray;
He couldn't say the Latin any more;
He couldn't even utter English for his prayers.
He couldn't press a bead, because he had
No beads to say.

He stared at dark. The old war
Had him in its clutch . . . not new,
Not recent months when everyone came back
Intact from Kiel—when rare the Forts fell down—
When flak pooped up in sickly little puffs—
The last black gargle of a dying Reich—
Not recent. Old, mean war.

And so, he slept. The *Black Swan*
Quivered over Nantes.
It lost its altitude;
The chutes broke out,
And Bailey died, and Stone,
And King.
              That night
Gadorsky burned again.

xxix

THIS is the limit of security:
Unarmed with hand grenade
Or metal gun
Or knife for cutting flesh.
No carbine,
Nor a pouch for shells,
Nor weapon of a lethal kind
Except two pens
Set slanted up
Like pointed A-A guns
Upon my desk.
(The ink in one is red—
A thinner red than blood.)

And three initials—*A.M.S.*—
That carry weight and certain power.
Curling, rapid, and concise—
The signature so notable
That gives one man
Just what he wants,
And slays the hope
Within another heart.

The gloss on wood,
The calendar,
The telephones,
The switches on the box,
And marble ash-tray
With a silver base.
The little box for cigarettes.
The lighter with its flame.
The chair with leather seat
That does not squeak or creak.
The wooden basket
Where the sheets of paper go.

Here by this desk
Another chair will wait
Through hours and the days,
And hold the men

Who come to talk
Of that commodity they need—
Commodity of all the earth desired:
Meat and bread,
All certified
By entry in a book,
By check with nasty little names.

For this I fought.
For this I suffered cold.
For this I dreamed
In dark and loneliness.
For this I tussled,
Hungered, sought.
For this I let myself be killed
In awful fancy
(Never killed in fact).
For this I sped the bullets out,
And pulled the pin,
And threw the charge.
For this I hated, sniped and crawled;
For this they put the colored tape
Upon my blouse.
For this I took the needled shots,
And felt the prophylactic burn.

And now, enduring calm,
I hear the talking tongues,
With all their notion, prophecy,
Opinion whetted sharp
To say the wrong words
That assault my ears.
I cannot make my mind embrace
The trivial, the arrogant,
The mean....
I cannot be intent
On saving dollars for one man,
Or guarding well the wealth
With which they let me play.
The little ciphers on the slip,
The digits, numerals, the signs
Are only hieroglyphics ...
Cannot tempt my wits
Nor now excite the thrill
I used to feel.

I guard my voice,
And measure it
And bring it up
And keep it cool and low—
Each moment that I want to yell,
And cry my charge
Against insensitivity....
My fellow men!
The friends I had in part—
No longer fellows,
As I see them now—
No longer men
Of any kind I value high.

Sometimes, in these first days,
I see an eye
That reaches into mine:
A GI tool
That cuts away
The difference between.
I see a face,
And hear a word
I'll always understand.
If men like that
Will let me know
The things they need,
I'll sign a deed to them.

The fussy wife,
The matriarch
So worried by her wealth....
The merry fool,
Who thinks he knows
The answers I will give....
The threat of angry mind,
The avaricious plea,
The frightened, whining dolt
Who does not sell
Such substances
As I might wish to own:
From these I turn away,
To these I give rebuff.

And all about me
Are the watching eyes—

The eager spies,
The whisperers,
Who cannot yet decide
How dangerous I am,
Nor estimate the hate
They'd give to what I represent,
If but allowed to give.

O marble bar!
O desks behind—
O people sitting there!
O holy place—
So sacred to unholy deed,
And sacrilegious thought!
O praise that falls
On selfish men!
O praise that will not fall on me,
Because, in grim unselfishness,
I have supremely selfish thoughts
Within my soul.

And, one by one, they will escape,
And bring an end to this.
They will explode
Their demolition charge
To let me loose,
And let me wander in the wind
Of savage freedom once again.

XXX

FRED DERRY didn't have a suit to wear;
He'd given all his things away
One time when he came home on leave,
And marveled at the inches he had grown
In height, in girth and swelling chest.

Now he was thinner than he used to be
Before he went across.
But still he didn't have a rag to wear
Except a high school sweater, sweat shirts,

Socks and handkerchiefs,
Some neckties he was fond of....
Never walk
Boone City streets
In neckties and in handkerchiefs!
Fred had to have a suit.
He thought of London, and the tailors there
In premises upset by bombs—and tidied up again—
Upset once more—and tidied up:
Some doll's-house windows in blank walls of brick
Set thickly round, where big show-windows used to
    be....
The scuffled din of Oxford Street and Bond,
The regimental ties, the riding crops;
The ribbon counters where, amazingly,
The green-and-yellow of a Border Service bar
Looked like the green-and-yellow of the Territorials.
Fred thought of tailors he had known:
The tired voices, the aloof respect;
And tea they brewed at four, out by the closets
Where you tried your trousers on.
No, not on Monday, sir.
I'm sorry—we're a bit short-handed now.
Suppose we say on Friday week?
I'm sure we'll have it ready
When you're up on Leave again.

He thought of tailors in Boone City—
Didn't know a one.
He used to buy his things in upstairs clothing stores:
"Walk up ten steps and save ten dollars."
....There was a place called Merman's.
He had heard that richer folks
Had all their clothes made there.

He felt afraid, and shy with poverty.
He thought of bragging: "Look,
These clothes I've got—
This uniform I'm wearing now—
Well, it was made for me by tailors
Who make clothes for Raf Air Commodores!"
And that was silly. Merman's wouldn't know
Just what Air Commodores might be.

One guy at Merman's had a pansy face;
He wore a button showing he'd been In.

He came from folding neckties, with a winning smile.
"Yes, yes, Lieutenant. What can we—?"
Fred said, "I'd like to have a suit.
Civilian clothes."
                    "Yes.
Do we have your measurements?
Have you been buying clothes from us—?"
He laughed with girlish glee.
"I mean—before the war?"
And Derry answered, "No."
He chose a sample—took him quite a while—
He couldn't quite decide—
He chose a brownish check.
"Oh, lovely—double breasted!" said the man.
"Suppose we use this style, right over here."
The tailor came; they measured Fred.

"Now what about
A single-breasted stripe?
Perhaps of flannel? It'll soon be warm, you know."
"No," Derry told him. "Just the one."
And after that the fellow seemed to freeze
Politely: ice that filmed
Across the sweetened water of his smile.
He spoke about a check—a small deposit?—
Derry couldn't write a check.
He had his dough in cash,
And not too much of that. Let's see:
He'd get a hundred from the government in thirty days,
Another hundred in another month, and that was all.

He paid the fifty bucks that Merman's asked,
Planned for a fitting, made his date.
He went away. He guessed he'd been extravagant.
He saw some suits in Oppenheimer-Stern's display:
At thirty-seven-ninety. . . . Be yourself.
You haven't got a job.
You've got a little wad of bills, and nothing else.
Who cares if you're the best—the very best—
To touch the toggle-knobs in your whole Squadron?
What's the union scale for bombardiers?

He went with ambled pace;
Tried to observe
Which girls were best, of all that flock

That ran before the traffic lights.
He thought the green-coat beauty best,
But couldn't keep his mind on her.
He knew his feet should take him
Only two short blocks away,
Where Bullard's waited.

Derry didn't want to go.

But still he went, to Sixth and Maple,
Where he had not passed
Since he came back to Boone,
And someone should have told him what he'd find.
No one had told. He saw it glaring now;
The red light quavering unseemly through the day,
The white light baking hot
And all strewn round the low façade
In script with letters four feet tall:
The Midway Drugs.

Well, it had been
Just "Bullard's" in the long ago
When Derry knew it—
When he hoisted soggy sack from out the coffee urn,
And shoveled garbage down a hole,
And cut the edge of cartons
That the toilet tissue came in.
So here it was, the Midway Drugs—
A chain of them from coast to coast,
And called by other names in East and West;
But yet the labels on the bottles on the shelves
Were shaped the same as those you'd find
In San Francisco, Boston and Mobile.

At first Fred stared and then he was amused.
Why had nobody told him? Well, he hadn't asked.
He hadn't talked about the store—
He hadn't walked to Sixth and Maple
On that night when he went wandering,
Awaiting his Marie.
He hadn't come that far downtown.
But here he was; and here was Bullard's,
Where it used to be.
Show-windows changed, the entrance changed,
Another entrance cut along the Sixth Street side,
And misery of toys and lamps,

And flasks, and plastic gimcracks
Crowding up the window space.

The lighted ceiling rang with buzz and hum
And shuffle, and the fountain din.
All surplus space was bargain squares,
And booths were built—red-cushioned, shining,
Modernistic—where they'd never been before.
Fred stood beside the Pocket Books
And watched the people paying checks.
He looked around. He saw a man
With spectacles as thick as china plates—
A man who'd lost some hair and gained some weight
While Derry twisted rate and drift knobs
Over Oschersleben.
                         That was Bullard.

They stood, ten minutes later, in an office space
Behind the bright prescription room.
And pharmacists were busy there—
Fred heard the clink of glass,
The buzz of phones, the rapid steps;
And Bullard smoked a cigarette, and sighed.
The lenses magnified his eyes a dozen times.
"Yes, Freddy. Since you went—
Let's see: it's twenty months ago:
You must have been in England at the time. . . .
And I was always strong for home-owned stores.
I held out to the last. But it was hard
To get the merchandise.
I couldn't get it half the time—
The things I needed. Nothing I could do.
And they've been pretty fair with me.
I made a deal. I guess you'd call it good.
And here I am: the manager.
Well, that's the way it goes:
We've got to change. And son, you sure have changed!
I hardly knew you. You don't look
Like any kid that used to be in here!"

He tapped his shiny fingernail
Against the wings that Derry wore.
"Good stuff," he said. "I wish I could have gone.
You know, I put in sixteen months last time
At Camp Pike, Arkansas.

Well, that's the way it goes....
So how about the Midway Drugs?"

"You've got a lot of store," said Fred.
The druggist nodded.
"Quite a lot of store.
Of course, it might seem pretty tame
To any fellow like yourself, who'd been across,
And flying all around, and chasing Huns—"

"And being chased sometimes," said Derry;
He grinned, but Mr. Bullard didn't give it back,
For this was business to the hilt.

The neon hurt Fred's eyes when he went out.
But he was all agreed—he'd shaken hands—
The thing was done. He had a job.
It wasn't any job he wanted ... couldn't hang
Around without a thing to do.
And how much bombing will they want in Boone?

The job was his. He had to get a suit.
A dark suit, Bullard said.
And certainly he'd have to have a couple—
Just suppose he tore his pants.
                    Oh, Christ!

He walked in Maple Street
And never felt the concrete underneath his feet.
He drifted with the crowd,
He fought with fresh new crowds at crossings;
Still he walked.
                    He saw a bar,
And went inside and bought a beer,
And watched the bubbles melting in his glass.
He'd start at forty bucks—
And that was generous enough, the druggist said.
He had a chance to be assistant manager
In ten or twenty years.
(Oh, what the hell? He had to have a suit—
A plain suit, Bullard said.)

He'd be a floor man—
Forty bucks a week. Let's see:
About a hundred seventy a month...

And fifty hours every week. No, fifty-four:
Six days: nine hours every day.
He'd be a floor man for the Midway Drugs.
A manager— A manager's assistant
In another ten or twenty years.
And always neon marching, throbbing
Up above the window panes,
And always soda-water gushing loud,
And all those faces, faces ... people in and out.
He had to make them buy.
He had to keep things going well.
"You will have responsibility," said Bullard.
"You know what it is
To lead a lot of men!"
And so the 3-0-5th became the Light Brigade...
To lead a lot of men!
"Just get your suit and put it on,
And come to work."
And how much bombing
Will they want in Boone?

The beer
Was tepid in his glass.
The froth had shriveled down; it lay like soap
Upon the stuff inside.
Fred Derry paid and went away.
He walked another block,
And then he let his feet go back;
He turned the proper course;
He crossed the streets,
He came to Merman's where he'd put
His fifty dollars down.
(He'd work a week. He'd serve
The Midway Drugs a week and more,
To earn another fifty bucks).
"I'm sorry," Derry said.
The pink face looked at him, and leered.
"I'm sorry if I've caused you trouble.
But, if you don't mind,
I'd like to just forget about that suit."

The pansy bowed, and pushed his eyebrows up.
He went away, consulted with the boss.
They both returned. They acted hurt and bored;
They paid the fifty dollars back.

They hardly said a word.
And Derry thanked them once again.
They said, "It's quite all right."
They might as well have said,
"Don't come to Merman's any more,
But go where you belong."
He went. In this bedraggled mood
He knew where he belonged.
He mounted to an upstairs store.
A nice old man sold him a suit,
Cheap, trim and blue,
For twenty-seven-ninety-five . . .
The single-breasted brown
Cost thirty-two.

They scratched their chalk marks on the cuffs,
They marked the sleeves,
They rubbed the chalk beneath Fred's arms.
He dressed again, put on his uniform.
They told him he could have the suits
On Friday afternoon.

xxxi

ONCE, on a Saturday,
        A boy named Homer sat
        There in the big wide swing upon the porch.
The slatted wood was smooth,
The cushion on the seat was new,
So were the pillows—some.
He placed one underneath his thigh:
An old one made by Great-aunt Em;
The little stitches, pink and greenish silk,
Of her old hands, had run the patches through.
And Homer liked that pillow.
He remembered times
When he was tired after supper . . .
Went to sleep upon the floor.
He'd take that cushion,
Plant it underneath his head. . . .
His mother called a dozen times:

"Now, Homer, go to bed. Now, Homer, dear—
Don't go to sleep there on the floor.
It's hard to wake you up!"
But still he'd turn his face away and sigh
Reluctant wakefulness at hearing her;
He'd sigh, and try to sleep again.

They had this pillow on the porch,
Because the cover was all frayed;
And there were new ones in the living room:
The bright new spread his mother fashioned,
While he lay in distant hospitals,
To keep her spirits up.
The little blocks of painted yarn
With afghan roses bright in every block:
She thought that he might want it in the hospital.
He didn't. . . . Told her not to send it.
But he liked the colors from the first time
When he saw them after coming home.

He swung and swung. His head no longer ached.
He'd had some lunch: tomato soup, home-made,
And cabbage slaw he asked for;
There were chicken, creamed, and candied sweets.
Aunt Sade said tartly, "Well, you eat enough, my boy,
For anyone who's dissipated half to death!"
And Mrs. Wermels made a sound and shook her head
At poor Aunt Sade, who'd never touched
A drink in all her life;
Who'd been too cross and virginal
For any man to ever ask to have a drink.
But Homer wasn't mad. He only grinned his grin,
That showed more teeth
Than any grin he'd ever worn before,
And twisted one eye shut, each time.
He told his aunt that drinking gave him appetite—
He'd drink some more.

She gave a sniff of rank disgust,
And sniffed again some minutes later
When his shaking fork strewed cream and chicken
On the doilie at his place.
"You see," Aunt Sade rejoiced,
"I told you all along, it wasn't good for you!
All cocktails are a drug. I guess the doctors know."

"Sade," said the mother, weakly, and Luella coughed.
The father wasn't there; he never lunched at home.
But Homer merely said, "Aw, you don't know—
Say, tell me, did you ever have a date, Aunt Sade?"
And then he laughed.
It wasn't nice, the way he laughed;
But only half his words were clear to her.

She went with stiff back to the library,
Five blocks away, where she held solitary court
Among the children's books;
And Homer sat and swung.
He smoked a couple cigarettes;
He watched the street.
He saw some kids with bicycles,
And he remembered times he'd gone
With straining legs, on his old bike,
Along the shady course.
Out all the way, far west on Grand,
He'd found the hills
And sunny valleys where spring beauties grew.
He'd gone with old brown knapsack on his back,
And slouch hat on his head;
He'd ridden far with other kids.
And once he had an accident:
He rode too close—a truck swung round,
And Homer jumped;
(The truck had only crushed his wheel—
The front wheel rim)
And he remembered what it cost
To get that bike wheel fixed.

He'd ride and ride—
With wind that cut his ears—

And now some boys appeared on trodden turf
That lay beside the Engle house,
A vacant lot, where once a house had stood,
But now reserved content for boys—
A playground of the happy kind
They always found in such a neighborhood.
There were the marks of bases there.
If you looked in the grass you'd find some marbles . . .
Long-abandoned toys, all brown with rust.

The boys prepared to play baseball;
They wrangled, choosing sides.
And every size of boy was there
From five to fifteen, all the way.
The little ones performed their solitary tricks
When they were scorned by all the rest.
They yelled and wrestled.
                      People called
Across the gardens they had dug;
And robins flirted down from trees, and up again;
And dogs were there, to roll and whine,
And sniff the limbs of boys they loved.

So Homer watched and smoked upon his swing.
He heard the clink of chains above his head:
The thick corroded chains from ceiling hooks
That squeaked like Home...
The sound of Home in every squeak.
He shut his eyes awhile, and thought of shelving
    bunks—
The million men who lay at night
On narrow shelves at sea.
He thought of winches, and the blat of guns,
The engine moan of seaplanes overhead,
Fat Catalinas that patrolled the dawn.
He tried to think
Just how they sounded— Couldn't think.
He heard the chain. He felt it crunch
Against the curving hook.

At length a foul ball cracked across the street
And bounded on the concrete steps.
A boy ran close to pick it up
(A kid about the age of Scouts,
In overalls and tennis shoes
And polo shirt).
              He looked at Homer,
Saw the bars upon his chest. . . .
"Oh, boy," he said.
"You seen a lot of service, Mister!"
Homer grinned, and spoke a word or two.
The boy came closer—climbed the steps,
And others came—the dogs came too.

Their ball game waited while they talked.
They asked if Homer'd been to France,
To Africa, to Solomons;
They asked about the Philippines,
Pearl Harbor, and the submarines.
He couldn't tell them much.
                    He tried to tell.

Sometimes he'd dreamt of this, so long before—
Of coming back—a hero—make a talk at school.
Miss Emerson would say,
"And we are very fortunate
To have, right in this classroom,
One who served his country
On the foreign seas.
I ask for Homer Wermels
To address the class!"
He'd talk and talk (that's what he thought)
And see their eyes grow wide.
He'd tell some jokes: some things that happened—
Things quite fit for girls to hear.
He'd see the girls exclaim,
And whisper back and forth;
And always Wilma ... white-blonde hair
And round green eyes that watched in solemn faith ...
And with his Navy pin upon her dress.

He wouldn't tell them he was tough;
He wouldn't frighten Wilma. No, not he.
He wouldn't tell the things he did with other guys
(That time on L.A.'s Main Street, back in '42,
When he was sixteen, nearly seventeen)
But he'd recite the kind of war that they should hear,
And not detract from his own stature
In the telling.
                    Foolish, simple dream ...
He'd talk at Sunday School, perhaps,
And to the Scouts as well.
And he'd take Wilma to a dance down at the USO,
Or maybe in the high school gym.
On graduation night he'd wait for her....
Somehow he'd still wear uniform—
He'd wear his blues—
He'd wait supreme as she came from her graduation,
Her young face holding cool the mystery

Of this great night; and with
A kiss for him upon her lips . . .
And slim the bosom beating close to his.
Because, when she had graduated—
Ah, surely she was grown,
And they could be engaged.

These little dreams he'd owned
And nibbled tenderly from time to time
Like candy, to assuage
The toothache twinge that any man might feel
Ten thousand miles away from home.
He hadn't laid them consciously aside;
Just hadn't nibbled lately on the dreams.
And here he was reciting peril to these boys:

"Right Off Oran," he said.
"We hadn't flushed our tanks at Liverpool.
The skipper said, 'We'll miss the convoy if we do,'
And everybody said, 'Let's go.' "
He talked of JU 88's,
And stood himself again upon a deck,
And put himself again behind the cannon there,
And sped his greasy 20-millimeter shells
Upon their fatal course.
"We got a few," he said with deprecation.
"88's are hard to get."

But still, no matter how he fired guns,
No matter how he sketched
The grayish oil of savage seas,
No matter what he said—
He saw his audience go drifting off.

He couldn't understand why they should go.
When he was young, he would have been quite glad
To sit or stand, and listen to a soldier tell of wars,
Or listen to a sailor tell of wounds.
He would have been as glad as he could be;
He would have asked for souvenirs!

But all he heard . . .
The whisper, and the mutter all around:
"Hey, Chuck, come on."
"Hey, Ray, let's go."

"Come on, we got to finish up the game,"
And then they went, the dogs and all.
They crossed the street in caravan,
They filled the vacant lot again.
And shrill their voices rose
When once they thought the distance safe—
And shrill and clear he heard the words
They hadn't meant for him to hear—
Because they all were reared
In charity of some small kind,
No matter how unlaundered
By the moral soap of years.

"Hey, listen," with a giggle under breath,
"I couldn't understand a word that that guy said!"
"Well, I could understand...."
"Boy, he could talk Chinese
For all of me!"
"I guess he's wounded in the mouth."
"No, in the leg—I saw him walk."
"My sister said his arm is hurt."
"And Mrs. Jacobson, she told my aunt
He always spilled his stuff
Right on the table when he ate or drank."

He heard it all. He heard the curse and plaint;
He heard the ruin of his life displayed.
They hadn't meant for him to hear....
A Scout is kind—a Scout is courteous.
The little ones would be as kind and courteous
When they were Scouts.
But still he heard.
                    He hated them.
He hated specks that burst
Like baby bombs before his eyes;
He hated all the smell of spring;
He hated days when frogs were vocal in a marsh,
When luncheon tasted good on any warming hill.

Fleet as a tom-cat
In those other springs not long ago,
With deft and able leg, he flew.
He shot, like any varnished fish,
Across the silver breadth of time.
He had more speed and purpose

Than a cottontail.
                    He bicycled,
He fled, he danced and scampered,
Playing Run-Sheep-Run
With infants he had played with in the past—
With infants who might populate his dream—
But Homer ran with better zest than they.
The races that they ran:
He won them all.

O shafting arrow, straining kite,
O flicker soaring out against a tree—
(And Homer Wermels acted each of these
Within his mad hypnotic spell)
O butterfly alive above the bridal wreath,
And moth assaulting flowers in the dusk!
He'd set a record better than the bugs,
If only he could loose the little cords
That bound him down.

Traumatic said the doctors over charts;
Spasticity. They checked the case away.
They didn't know that he could beat
The thinnest children, sparrow-fast,
At Hide-and-Seek
Or any games they'd play.

The porch swing sounded in the afternoon,
And Homer smoked some other cigarettes,
And burnt a lot of matches lighting them,
And nearly set the cushioned seat aflame.
Across the street on Engles' vacant lot
The boys smote hard their mitts in One-o'-Cat.

And Homer waited for a girl to come,
To visit him, from Jacobsons' next door.
She didn't come; so Homer hated her.
He hated all the little kids who ran—
Began to hate Luella, as she pranced
Down to the corner, buying him ice-cream.
"I don't want any, Sis," he said,
And nastily he slapped the dish away.
Luella squawked at him, appalled,
And flounced off. She had thought to please him.
Homer didn't have to act like that!

In vibrant panoramas of the past
He ran as easy as a wolf.
In motion uninhibited
He flew.

xxxii

F RED DERRY didn't have the merchant's soul,
Shopkeeper's eye, or vendor's hand.
　　Tense, nervous and immaculate
He stalked the noisy aisles,
And trying hard to hold a pompous smile
And dignity within a proper face.
He worked from ten till two.
He worked five hours after that
Each day except his holiday.
He alternated with a tall assistant manager—
Who lorded sternly over Fred.
(It seemed that Mr. Luce had not been In;
But he was pleased to show his power
Over one who'd been an officer.)

Three days Fred walked from three till eight;
Three days from seven until twelve.
He punched the brown cash registers,
He warned the counter boys to keep the marble clean.
He set the Kotex boxes true when they had tumbled
　　down.
He stood behind a waitress who was giggling too long;
With ominous import, he made her feel authority;
He bullied her with silence.
Bullard said he must, because he'd led a lot of men.

Fred Derry picked the nickels up
When they were dropped;
He guided shoppers past the carpenters
Who built the bigger, better bargain squares.
He opened doors for women loaded down with parcels
When the queer electric eye
No longer opened doors by elfin means—
No longer did the job it should have done....
He called the men who come

To fix electric eyes.
He spied against the new tobacco girl;
Politely he advanced to soothe the soul
Of any customer whom she misunderstood.
The little goon who came with frightened voice,
And ergot's old prescription in her hand—
He took her back to Mr. Daggett,
Cautioned him to serve the Lady first—
This was emergency!

He watched and peered; he concentrated—
Sold the aspirin, the Agarol, the BiSoDol,
The other things, when other clerks were busy.
But he was not a clerk; he was an ugly minor god,
Who walked on rubber toes
And made employees all detest his guts.

And thirty-seven-fifty every week:
The chain had said that was the maximum to start,
In such a job. So Bullard had to break his word.
He promised Fred the forty later—
After ninety days. That was the rule.
And in the office Fred saw forms prepared,
Quadruplicate: one for the National,
One for the Regional, and one for District,
And one for their own files. . . .
(You had to know the rules, if you would be
A profit-making part of Midway Drugs.)

They paid the drug side on each Saturday;
They paid the soda help on Mondays,
In the principle that soda help
Would incapacitate themselves
Through reckless living, if you gave them cash
On Saturdays. (And it was true.)
The soda help looked up and hated drugs;
The drugs looked down on sodas.

In grim back room, the cartons stacked,
The stock room shelves,
The elevator and the basement hatch,
And rats that came at night to peek and chirp
Like brown and furry birds. . . .
Fred thought he'd have some fun.
He and the Negro porter got a .22

And sat up late at night, assassinating rats.
The second night, a bullet spattered off a pipe
And ricocheted, and broke a flask
Of rare expensive drugs—some kind or other.
No more .22.
And Bullard said to set some traps,
To use some poison. Poison wasn't fun:
The rats went off and died forlorn in dark.
They didn't use the poison any more;
And new rats came to chirp and peep.

Upstairs there wasn't any hint of rats.
You'd never think a single rat could live
Among the Midway Drugs ... the gassy glare,
The anesthetic tiles, the leather seats
In luncheon booths, the sanitary smell,
And clink and tinkle of the registers,
And push of crowds ... the people grim
Who fought for empty soda chairs from twelve to two.
Fred Derry marched the aisles.

He wore his neat blue suit—
His cheap blue suit, with proper tie.
He alternated with the brown he'd bought.
And Bullard frowned: brown wasn't good.
The Midway Drugs said blue or back.
The Regional Inspector came to peer and nod,
And whisper estimates on this or that.
He criticized Fred Derry's suit.
"Listen, pal," Fred Derry said,
"You'll get the Midway Drugs
To blow me to another suit?"
"Look here—" the Regional Inspector cried,
And flushing angrily— But Bullard laughed
And led the man away. He warned Fred Derry
Not to speak like that again.

Sometimes Fred saw a girl or man he knew
From high school days. He'd slink away
And never meet them face to face.
He was ashamed of this disgraceful little job
(It is not good for you,
When you work daily in disgrace).
He lost some weight; his stomach acted up.
It hadn't acted up before,

Except when he got in some combat time
Too often and too hard: too many ops in too few days.
He went down to the flak-house for a rest. . . .
Boone City didn't have a place
Where you might fish and snore, and stroll and eat,
And play gin-rummy—swim and lounge,
And play croquet, the English kind—
They didn't have a flak-house for your nerves
If you became flak-happy at the Midway Drugs.

He lived down at the Hotel Seneca
For thirteen bucks a week.
He didn't like to share the bathroom.
That was funny, when he'd shared a bathroom
With a hundred other guys;
But it was different, at the Hotel Seneca.
He paid a little more and got another room.
He had a private bath.
He didn't have much dough to spend on girls.
Three different nights he'd stepped around:
Each time a different girl.
He quarreled with Shirley;
Fay and Lena liked him very well;
They called him at the Hotel Seneca; they left
Their names and numbers.
                              Derry didn't call them back.

He walked a lot, on nights he didn't work
(In better mileage than he made within the store).
He walked and watched the lights.
Sometimes it seemed he'd never get enough
Of lights at night. He liked the sound
Of busses; liked the smell of flowers
Filling thick the yards on residential streets.
He wished he had a dog,
But couldn't keep one at the Seneca.
But he did have a cat—three days—a big gray tom.
Tom wandered up the iron stairs,
The fire stairs that climbed in rust
Through prison of an air shaft, just outside.
The cat came up . . . no telling why he came . . .
He mewed and mewed;
And Derry baited him along the ledge
To haven in his room. He went down to the Greek's
And got some milk. He fixed a box with paper.

All night long the cat lay snug
Upon Fred's bed, and purred.
But three days later Tom was gone.
He'd vanished down the iron stairs.
"So what?" said Fred. "He couldn't take the Seneca."

And how much bombing will they want in Boone?
They didn't want a bit.
They only wanted you to glide attentively
From place to place, from counter to the soda booth,
Back to the front, to Anacin, to Kleenex hoard,
To drugs and sundries, back to toys,
And to the soda lunch again.

In Britain there was discipline
That you might put upon yourself
To take you off the ground sometimes
When you were scared to go.
You didn't need to discipline yourself
When you were over targets; then you knew
Just what to do. You did the best you could.

But, day by day,
In this pathetic, shopworn, buying, selling dance
Of smiling when you didn't want to smile,
And soothing men you didn't want to soothe—
But daily
In this travesty of peace—
Fred Derry felt the landing-lights
Wink harder, hotter in his brain.

In times like that
You felt the oxygen was out;
You couldn't get your breath.
Well, what's the score on this, Gadorsky?
At least you didn't finish at the Midway Drugs.

...
xxxiii

THE lilac bushes ranked along the lawn
Full-bodied, Persian, white and blue.
They'd put them in from year to year. . . .
"More lilacs, Dad?" the daughter cried.
"Yes, more," Al said devout a dozen times.

With soil upon his hands, and pipe in mouth,
He watched the gardener, he watched the planting;
He saw that it was rich.

He worshipped lilacs, for they meant to him
A charm of childhood, charm of legend,
Miracle profound.
"Perhaps," he thought, "it's Whitman."
Still he couldn't quote
The lines that wandered in his mind.
And thus one night,
When lying on a hard Italian hill,
And hearing shells tear up the mud,
And feeling raw the wet black cold
That gnawed his toes—
He nursed on Whitman,
Lilacs and the rest.

Sing on, O singer in the swamp—
No, that was not the way it went;
He couldn't be quite sure.
O strong, bright fallen evening star . . .
To lay upon the grave of him I love.
He didn't know it now;
He'd never known it, never kept the words
In ordered nicety within his mind.
He only held the thought and found it good
And somehow warming to his toes.
He put his helmet half across his face, and smiled.
On one ripe middle-western ridge
The sun was newly down,
And this was early May;
And lilacs wore their weight of rain,
And rain brought out the smell—

A crushing attar—sweetness
That seduced your sense
And made you love the world.
And, with that mist of lilac smell
Before your eyes, you could not see
A fragment of the world
Save any part that men might wish to love.

A shy and hidden bird . . . and once again
He tuned his hermit song, for once again
The awful Actor crept in bitterness—
The awful Actor Death, to take a life,
To plunge a war-wet nation into night
And let the Negroes weep in Washington.
"He's dead, he's gone . . . I loved him so. . . ."
They printed out the plaint in *Life* and *Time*;
Men made a god of him they hated most;
And soldiers sobbed across a bullet-bitten world;
And men like Stephenson looked up at stars
And found no answer—only emptiness.

Now, moving back to Cherry Hill,
Al lived among full-hearted green;
But in remembrance wandered through
The young years of the century
To honor elder burials.
He paced beside his father in the pines;
(A thousand other people silent there).
The G.A.R. came sainted with their flag
And trilling fifes of cocoa-wood,
And tanned skin of the mighty drums
To roar their story of a war in Tennessee.
Outlandish tufts of whisker, peeling scalp,
They caught the patriotic sun,
And purple bloomed in recollection of the day
A bearded man came sorrowing
To lay his flower soft on Lincoln's bier.

This was the tender past of all America.
The Southern women wept in story,
Offered wreaths and garlands to the graves
Of those who lay
In warm sequestered battlefields . . .
The Shiloh bloom, the swelling turf
At Murfreesboro . . .

O proudest war we ever fought!
Because we learned an equal pride
In friend and enemy.

No chivalry
In tainted provinces
Where children planned amid the mess
Of their spoiled homes
How one day they would live to cut you down.
The brag, the sneer, the swastika;
The boiling water poured from windows as you passed;
The dark warehouse where once the victims screamed,
Oh please Oh don't Oh don't Not that again!
Until Gestapo men wiped off their hands,
And drove away in trucks.
                    Thus dwelt a memory
To last you in a nightmare till you died.

But you might love the lilacs,
For the war was noble that they knew.

With thanks they came, the Stephensons,
To shingled roof and spreading bush
And cock-crow wailing in the morning dusk
Across green counties of the east,
Across the fields where corn and oats
Would soon make tinder for the blaze of dawn.
The roosters talked, they took it up
From farm to farm as light progressed ...
The silver little clarion
And signal of a feathered host.

Half, half asleep in this new home,
This old home now redeemed—
Half, half asleep
With Milly docile in the bed beside him,
Al Stephenson might open fair his eyes,
Release the sleep that crusted ...
See the room, disordered, dim,
With bags strewn open on the floor.
He still pursued
The mystery and turmoil of his night,
But heard the roosters crow.
He stirred and turned,
He hugged the woman's body up to his.

She sighed, she wakened,
Kissed his shoulder solemnly.
He said, "I had an awful dream about you...
Dreamed that you were dead!"
"Dead?" she murmured, waking more.
"I dreamed a lot of times that *you* were dead,"
And then she went to sleep again,
Calm, blissful in acceptance of a treasure.
They were Home.

Al lay and listened
To the song of sunrise.
                    Lilacs,
Blissful, dusty, wet and orchid wall...
Oh, once again to dress the native lawn
When early May had come!
The soreness of the brogans he had worn
Through galling interlude—
The cobbler's hammer, hammering at peace—
And petty penny-changing life he'd come to lead—
These uglinesses fell away
In hope of flowers growing in a better year,
In echo of the chicken cry.
Half, half awake, Al loved the dead
Whom he had known amid the bullet hum...
Imagined them in GI battle dress
Come up to wade the leafy scrub,
Walt Whitman strolling as a guide,
And holding delicate a spray within his hand.
And on a portico, awaiting them,
Abe Lincoln sat beside a brave and crippled man.

The roosters sang, the light grew wiser.

Sergeant, sleep again
In knowledge of your bride,
In worship of your dream
Like lilac odor near.

xxxiv

FRED saw her by the perfume counter, bending down.
The blue-gray of her uniform ...
He didn't know that it was she.
Sometimes the Red Cross women came in there
For other things than perfume.
He said, "Have you been waited on?"
And then she looked up, laughing;
Hair turned live and bright and curly
Underneath the slanting cap.
He mumbled something, stood and grinned.
He flushed; he felt embarrassed,
Like a boy in school when he is waiting with a note
To hand to some small girl.

Hello ... Hello ... they said it back and forth.
And how are you?
Your dad comes in sometimes.
I know, he said he saw you.
Once in a while I see him at the bank;
He's usually quite busy ...

Fred feebly mentioned perfume—
Said he'd get a girl to wait on her.
And then, before the girl could come,
He saw the staring Western Union clock
Above a wall of bottles opposite.
"One fifty-five." He blurted out the words;
He couldn't help it. Said,
"I'm through at two. That is, till seven;
That's on Tuesdays. Usually—
Well— Other days, I mean—
When I work afternoons, I eat in here.
But how about it— I mean, have you had lunch?"
She said with ease, "I'd love to lunch with you."

They walked in sun on Sixth Street, down and down.
They went past Walnut, Mulberry, the rest.
They didn't know where they were walking.
"Say," he said, "I think it's funny:
Here you are in uniform. And look—

I've got civilian clothes."
She told him she had signed to take the early shift
Up at the Red Cross rooms that day,
And now her day was done.
"It's just begun," Fred Derry said. They laughed.

They walked and walked. They found a dark cafe
From which delectable a smell came forth.
"Oh, *Mexicano!*" Peggy said. "Let's go in here."
Fred shook his head and followed doubtfully.
She ordered—used the words of Spanish that she knew.
A little man in apron damp with grease—
He laughed at her. He brought the soup,
The enchiladas, beans and tacos.
"Gosh," said Fred. "I didn't know that Mexicans
Had stuff like this! I thought it all was chili."
They drank intoxicating coffee, made their glee
Of tiny things, the way the young can do....
A little dog came up
To sniff around their chairs.
Perrita, Peggy called the dog.
She told about a summer she had spent
The year before her father went to war:
Wild mountains turning blue; the rocky hills;
The bright *serapes* dusty in the street;
And dirty children laughing
With their eyes as bright as pepper pods;
And statue of a hero in the plaza,
Throwing off historic chains.
She told Fred tales.... He loved to hear her talk.
She told things, sharp and honest
As another man.

And yet, when on they went
Along the warehouse streets,
And angled past a railroad track,
And stepped among the broken crates,
And dodged the tail-boards of the trucks,
And on they went, down to the river bank—
He knew that she was Woman.

Oh, surely he had missed the best of all!
For even in that uniform—and low-heeled shoes—
He liked the little bones he saw:
They bulged enticing in her ankle skin.

He liked the curve that swelled below her knee.
He liked the strong young hips within their cloth.
Again he dreamed of her in cocktail dress
And dancing at the Daniel Boone.
He wondered how she'd look in negligee,
In nightgown ... brushing hair, her breasts displayed ...
(If she might see his face grow hot again
She wouldn't know the reason why.)

But angrily as sex proclaimed
Its summons unto him, suspicion grew and flared.
His sensitivity was rubbed by presence of this girl.
He thought, "Now look, why did we go
Down Sixth Street?
Why did she pick out that place? Now look—
That Navy guy she had last month—
Would she have steered a guy like that
Down Sixth Street, to a crumby joint?
No. Luncheon at the Black Hawk Club
Or at the Daniel Boone!"

He could not squeal his private wrath aloud,
But only feel a sullen gag within his mouth.
He couldn't talk awhile. He followed Peggy—
Walked beside the river flow,
Along the concrete stairs and stone embankments.
There was a feeling of the Thames,
And windows looking out from the Savoy;
And how the mighty bridges, Parliament,
And Abbey beauty loomed above the tide ...
Westminster.
                    Derry's voice was hushed.
He said, "You know, a lot of those old folks
They buried in the Abbey—
I don't know just who they were ...
I went to high school, never more than that;
I didn't care a lot for English history;
I didn't learn so much. I wish I had.
But I remember Pitt and Fox—the way they fought.
And now they're buried fifteen feet apart,
Maybe a little more, or less. They're buddies now."

She said, "I wish that I could go
To England. Tell me more."

They sat on grass, and soon they lay
On grass above the river bank,
And heard the trucks resounding on the bridge,
The busses swishing half a block
And all a world away.
An old tramp came to gather up
A paper. Was it theirs?
No, no, not theirs . . . they blinked at him.
And maybe he was God; he beamed benign;
He went away to walk the universe again.

Soon Derry found his voice released;
He said the things that crowded in his mind,
The angry residue of war.
He told of empty beds left by the boys
Who took their last cold bath off Beachy Head;
And other boys who argued, wrangled, rolled the dice
To see who got the radios and kodaks left behind,
The brand new flying-jackets. . . .
(What the hell? The guy can't use them now!)
Who spoke with tough tone of the Messerschmitts
That danced in to the kill, like eager bees—
The hard guys, seldom crying tears,
Who went away to cover up their heads on cots
Sometimes, and never speak when people
Knocked upon the door.

"And coal strikes, rail strikes back at home—
The workers making parts for fighter planes—
If we'd had John L. Lewis over there
In 1943, we'd dropped him through the bomb-bay. . . .
Used to lie in bed and talk about it;
We wondered if he was too big to go!
And I'm not kidding. Plenty fellows
Would have pushed him off the edge.
We thought that men like that
Were killing us, and killing better men than us,
Because we didn't have the fighter-cover
That we should have had."

He told about Gadorsky's Fort,
And of the day the *Black Swan* fell.
He talked of Second Schweinfurt:
Thirteen Forts they dropped that day,
And two came home.

It wasn't trivial, the stuff he told;
It wasn't Oakley cutting ties—
Nor nights when he and Hark
Sang loud their songs of mountaineers
And dying cowboys, in a club in Kensington.
It wasn't stuff like that.

He told about the planes which bumped,
The ones which overshot the field;
He told about a load of guys
Who'd finished up, who'd done their missions,
Started off for Home,
For Scotland, and the road to Home,
And how they piled up at the runway's end
And how they stewed in their own juice
Amid the sizzled flames.
"They killed the fatted calf
For them, all right;
And guess just who
The fatted calf was?"
                    Peggy hid
Her face against the grass.
She held Fred Derry's hand.

The light fell longer;
Shadows touched the cool embankment.
"Growing late," said Derry.
"Look—we've spent the afternoon!
I guess you had a million things to do."
She smiled at him. "I didn't have a thing
That I'd call half so good as this, to do.
Did you?"
                    "Why, no," he lamely said,
And helped her rise.

Back through the afternoon they went
To brighter streets, to brighter stores.
They carried sound of river in their minds.
She heard his voice, and he heard hers.
She held his arm;
When they were crowded in the street
Between the cars, he felt her leg against his own.
He thought it wrong to feel the way he did.
He was so young, despite the women he had had:
He didn't know that no young love is worthy of itself

Unless it's painted with a torrid blush
That silly men describe by baser names.

They parted on the corner, Sixth and Maple.
"Well," he said, "I'll have to thank you for—"
And Peggy told him quickly, "I'm the one
Who should say thanks."
                              "Well—
It's been quite a day."
                              "It has.
You told me many things."

He looked at her. "I didn't tell you
Other things I should have told.
I didn't tell you what my home was like,
Or how my mother died—a rotten death—
Or how we got along, or didn't get along,
The year my father went away to take the Cure.
And, I might add, it never cured him!
I wonder if my grandmother
Did washings for the Stephensons?
I know she did them
For a lot of folks on Grand.
I used to go and get the baskets
With my wagon. . . .
Lots of things I haven't told you:
Haven't said a word about Marie.
I married her before I went across.
She's not the kind you'd want to know.
She's—"
          "Fred," said Peggy Stephenson,
And put her hand on his.
"A lot of things you haven't told me, I can guess.
Now, you won't mind if I—just guess?
And let me tell you this:
I didn't want to buy an ounce of perfume;
I've got loads. I didn't want a thing.
Except, when Daddy told me you were at the Midway,
I thought— Never mind.
I don't know why I'm saying this!"

And Derry couldn't watch her face.
He saw the sign across the street;
The script went flashing, crawling up
Above the window panes.

"Well, it was swell," said Derry. "Thanks.
Goodbye."
    "Goodbye," she whispered softly.
Then she went. He didn't watch her go.
He turned to cross the street;
He swore between his stiffened jaws.
This wasn't right!
He hadn't meant to do a thing like this!
He was in love. The first time in his life
He really knew what it was all about.

It wouldn't do him any good—or her.
He'd only bitch things up if he kept on.
If they kept on like this, they'd sleep together
Very soon. They'd marry. Have a stinking flat
Somewhere upon a side street....
Thirty-seven-fifty.
    "Hell," he thought.
"Those shoes of hers cost half of that,
Or maybe more."
And how much bombing
Will they want in Boone?

XXXV

Iⁿ June, the month of brides and lace,
 And clover cut on prairie meadowland,
 And warm, wet dusk when tree-toads talked,
And plentiful the leaves hung rich ...
In June when insects flirted, lost their dust,
And lost their lives at night, electric death ...
Intoxicating, pungent month
Before the hot, dry hand
Of summer squeezed too tight ...
Through all this husky, musky June
Poor Mrs. Wermels tried to do her best,
And minister to him who occupied
The weak and overflowing pity of her heart:

Her son, her baby boy, her only boy—
The tow-head yellow on the pillow top.

All slavish, querulous and syrup-sweet
The rearing she had given him before;
And now she tried to furnish therapy
Devoted as her hands and mind could make it.
This and that: the little treat—
Which muffins would he have?
What kind of dressing wound in veal
Or gushing up from out the chicken breast?
The milk and cookies on the table top—
He'd find them there when home he came
At some wild black and awful hour,
Scraping on the steps
And smashing out the screen he leaned against
To get his bearings;
For liquor and the war had made him walk
Too many ways at once.
His mother left the cookies and the milk,
But Homer saw them seldom—
Was too drunk to know or care.
He'd gobbled hot dogs in some greasy place;
So rancid, undercooked or overcooked,
The things that he would eat—
So poison, acid, all the drinks he'd guzzle down
(Oh, Homer, Homer, in your tender belly!
Happy, hungry, boyish pouch
I warmed against my own when you were small . . .
And now to think the ruin you are making!)
Still, she wouldn't say a word.
It did him good, she tried to think.
It did him good to lead
The stumble-bum existence that he led.

In June, the graduation festivals,
The gowns that made young girls exult,
The pins they got as presents from their aunts,
The watches from their dads,
The new pink garter-belts, the brassières,
The emblems of maturity
Investing fresh soft bodies of the young.
These things were happening to Wilma Jacobson;
And far and wide, across the town,
A male equivalent befell the boys.

A lot of them forswore new suits.
They said that Uncle Sam would give them

Better garb when once they graduated.
They spoke their wise, awakening discourse
In washrooms, backyards, stores and streets;
When mowing lawns or stacking crates
Or pulling radishes at home
They'd meet and talk.
Their eyes would shine, their ears turn pink.
"The Coast Guard, yeh...
But listen, boy: my cousin told me that...
Now if I go and take my training at the U...
My brother got his bars;
It only took him seven months...
Say, if I just—"
And still, no matter how
The half-tracks clattered in their minds,
No matter how propellers turned, or Hellcats flew,
They bit with eagerness the flavored pulp
Of man's good fruit; they saw themselves
Well dramatized and fledging forth,
In youngest season of their ripeness...
Felt their manhood muscular between their legs.
They loved to shave, they loved to smoke.
The tricks that older people called
An indication of their Youth—
These things were Age to them,
And glad they were to have it.

But all such pulsing, nervous plan and push,
Such galloping in garb of citizens—
Such festival should be her boy's.
This Mrs. Wermels knew,
Quite inarticulate, and never speaking
Sharp her recognition to a soul.
The knowledge only turned to sponge
Each matronly resolve that she had made.
Her voice grew softer, whining, rising, questioning
Each time she mentioned Homer's name.
He couldn't have this salty life;
He needed it; it wasn't his;
He'd never sniff the scent of it,
For he had run away to war
Before he reached the age of seventeen,
And—God in Heaven—
She had let him run.

The only medicine that she might mix
Was every toy and tidbit that she knew.
She tendered them
Upon the neat pale platter of her life;
She made her husband lug the platter in
And offer it in salutation to the boy.
Some Chinese checkers? Anagrams? Or croquinole?
(He used to like that years ago.
He'd snap the little wooden discs across the board
And crack his finger black-and-blue,
And beat his Uncle Alf.)
Some hot potato salad—jellies, jams?
The choicest pickled pears
Old Grandma Haverstraw might make?
Some fudge, ice cream or pie?

"Let's play croquet!"
And Mr. Wermels found a set,
And put it up behind the house.
A croquet set was hard to find; apparently
They didn't make them any more.
Poor Homer knocked the balls around,
And hit his shin-bone with the mallet—
Cursed aloud and fluently.
This time his Aunt Sade understood each word;
She let her gasp of horror go aloft;
So Homer turned and bleated other words at her.

He didn't like to play croquet. . . .
The rain sank into varnished wood,
And angry sun destroyed the gloss
Of colored rings upon the stakes:
The scarlet turned to pink,
The grass-green faded gray.

Well, try the double feature
At the Hollywood tonight.
Resort to limpid curatives:
Deanna, Danny, Disney, Dunne.
Fill up a spoon with physic of the celluloid!
Perhaps Bob Hope can chill a fever-flush,
Or Judy Garland do the job of opium,
Or Betty Grable make medicament!
                                        Bleed, bleed,
Ye leeches of the silver sheet,

And drain a laugh from him we love;
And we will call ye blessed evermore.

O radio,
O Hit Parade, O Information Please,
O Burns and Allen, Benny, Bergen, Charlie Chan,
O Lum and Abner, Answer Man and Major Bowes—
Resound within his brain and stuff his ears,
Until he cannot hear the weeping of his soul.
And let him like the ice-box cake,
And munch meat-loaf and cabbage slaw,
Divinity and popcorn, salted nuts—
Before we fetch the cribbage board again.

O checkers, jig-saw puzzles...
What's the thing Dick Tracy did today?
And what about a car ride?
Father has some gas. We'll drive
To Rock Springs Park.
And would you like to try these new cigars?
And would you like— What would you like to own?

Oh, tell me, tell me honestly and avidly—
Tell me the thing you wish to have.
For I will buy it, steal it, make it,
Shape it, garner,
Cook and press it,
Season it—the thing you want.
I'll put the jolly juices in,
And salt it proper with my tears.
For this I know: I cannot drive the devils out
That make unhappy holiday
Within your body and your brain.

xxxvi

OR better holiday than that,
For balm and fresh forgetfulness
She chose a Sunday noon. She chose a woodland
On a farm that Mr. Wermels owned
Halfway to Sperryville.

They sacrificed their coupons, bought their gas—
The tires checked, the oil put in,
The car washed clean,
And baskets, cartons, far too many things
Stowed, balanced, hoisted loose on top,
To make the car trunk smell of deviled eggs
And chicken-legs for many weeks.
Luella baked a cake herself,
The way they'd taught her at her school,
And she was proud . . .
And in the driveway next to theirs
The Jacobsons filled up their car as well.

When Homer came to breakfast
(They'd cajoled him, petulant, from out his bed)
He found some little gifts beside his plate;
And he pretended not to know a thing.
"What's all this junk?" he cried.
His left hand did absurdities with string
And paper . . . so he read the cards.
He saw the Happy Birthday signs.
He liked the V-neck sweater, put it on;
He liked the pipe his father bought.
He said, "Gee. Thanks, Aunt Sade!"
And mentally resolved that he would never read
A book called *Moby Dick*;
It looked too thick—old-fashioned—
All too many words.
He thought Luella's gift the best of all:
She'd got a Varga calendar.
The hussies, month by month,
Had thighs too thick for normalcy
And legs just twice as long as most girls had.
But Homer waved the calendar, and crowed,

And Aunt Sade made her clucking sounds,
And Mr. Wermels turned away to smile.

The sun was bright outside.
The sun was gold and winsome in their hearts,
And covered all their hopes
In momentary gleam.

And Wilma Jacobson appeared;
And modestly she gave to him
The box she'd wrapped.
He opened it; he flushed. . . . Three neckties:
Horseshoes, purple cobwebs, polka-dots.
He muttered thanks. He said,
"It's sure a nice day for a picnic."
Wilma laughed.
                    Her eyes
Looked clear and round and penetrating, sad,
The way they often looked, these days.
But still she laughed. "I've got to put
Wax paper on the sandwiches," she said.
She hurried off.

And Mrs. Engle crossed the street;
A little witch with fluffy hair
And hatchet-sharpened face,
And birdlike body wrapped within
The cleanest, brightest starchy print
On all that street. She limped around
To the back door, in neighbor fashion,
Holding proud a covered dish.
"Why, look at this!" cried Homer's mother.
"Homer, come and see. She knew it was your birthday;
Mrs. Engle heard! Just look—
She's brought a lemon pie!"
Old Mrs. Engle cooed and prattled.
No—the crust—it wasn't quite her best,
She'd got the crust too short!
But she had thought: a lemon pie. . . .
When Harley (that was Butch)
When Harley was a little boy,
He'd always been a fiend for lemon pies.

The Wermels women cried that she must come.
"There's plenty room. Now, Mrs. Engle, please!"

A picnic on the farm—
Why, it would do her good.
And Homer grinned. His eyes were bright,
His lip hung loose.
                    "Say, Mrs. Engle—
You ask Butch if he won't come.
Say. Ask old Butch!"
And everybody gasped; the silence fell.
No one had ever asked Butch Engle
To a feast of families . . . with sandwiches,
And brownies, celery
And olives on a paper plate.
"Yes, yes," they chattered, horrified.
"Why, Mrs. Engle, ask your son!"
But Homer went instead.

He scraped his way across the street.
"Huh?" said Butch Engle.
"Picnic? What the hell!"
Within the open window
He stood motionless, and watched
The twisted, red-eyed vagabond
Upon the lawn outside.
Butch glowered with his roughest gaze
And put the razor to his chin again.
The blade rolled up the heavy cream.
Butch spoke again. "O.K. That's swell.
Sure: count me in."

They drove intent, they filled two cars;
And fifteen miles away they made their track
Across the pasture-grass.
A gate swung wide, admitting all
To glory of this June,
To sorrel, thistle, tumble-bug,
To basswood shade and bottom land,
And running gopher, warbler song,
To smell of middle-western woods,
To mouse and cottonwood and elm,
And clam shells in the river mud,
To wild phlox blossom, musk of moths—
Strong green persistence of the woods,
No matter who'd turned spastic in the war,
Or who was blown aloft
And hurt beside the coast of Africa.

Bold Butch went shooing cows away;
And Mr. Jacobson drove deep a stake
And Mr. Wermels spaded unoffending earth.
The women talked and twittered; Wilma wove
A flower diadem to crown Luella's hair.

An hour long the horseshoes tossed and rang.

"Look out, look out!" Butch Engle bellowed.
"Look out for Homer! Hey—he's got a horseshoe—
Ladies, move away!" And Homer glared ferocious,
Threatened Butch, and made him flee.
The rest sat silent, dreading such a joke.
They couldn't take it. Homer could.
He made three ringers in the game.
His father tried to let him win.
(He couldn't win, he knew. He didn't wish
To have his father try to let him win.)
The lunch was spread, the hammock swung,
And Mrs. Engle told Aunt Sade
Good gossip of the neighborhood:
How Elma Aiken's child was due September first,
And she and that young Coast Guard boy of hers
Were only married February fourth!

The flies fed thick, the greedy flies;
And ice-cubes melted in the jugs;
And fondest inclination bloomed again
With Homer and his Wilma strolling far.
So slow they walked (uneven ground,
And sticks and berry vines and cow manure
To make obstruction in their path).
But on they went. They stood beside
A muddy creek. They stood and talked.
And it was good a while,
But only for a while.

She said her awful words,
Inviting him:
                    The senior prom
Next Friday night.

But Homer saw the prom—imagined it—
The filmy gowns, the boys who danced—
Tall smarties, debonair of limb.

And Homer saw himself grotesque
Upon a folding chair,
And watching Wilma dance with other boys.
Or worse than that: he saw her nursing him,
A martyr of renunciation at his side.
Not that, not that!

He said with cool brutality,
"No, I won't go.
The hell with any senior prom."

She turned her face so white away;
She didn't want to let him see her cry.
He went on, having no control of things he said,
Or manner of his utterance.
"The hell with that. Not there in that old gym.
Say. I'd look pretty, dancing. Wouldn't I?"
He acted it, with sweat upon his face,
With awful leer, pretending in a pantomime
To show her what a Caliban he'd be.
He hopped and tottered, like a Bottom
In an ass's mask—a wound-up monkey
On a stick.
"Say, I'd look pretty, dancing, wouldn't I?
I'd walk all over you.
They'd kick me off the floor, I guess!"
He stamped the turf, a troglodyte;
He brutalized himself.

She cried. She ran away,
She fled away between the trees.
Then Homer hoped to follow, but he couldn't run.
He stammered, "Wilma— Hey, come back!"
She couldn't hear him now.
The trees and bushes swallowed her.

He watched the water burbling
Across the little stones.

Then from his pocket (secret vice
Encased in heavy glass:
The half-pint bottle that he'd bought
And hidden sly from any gaze)
He brought it out. He drank.
The liquor tasted hot and raw.

He didn't care . . . these swallows brown
To burble, belch like water in the stream—
They'd do more good for him, he swore,
Than any water in a stream.
He sat and drank. He poured it down.
He shook the stinging tears from out his eyes,
And hiccoughed once,
And threw the empty thing away.
He threw it well.
He threw it with his left hand.
                                        Glass
Went spattered over rocks
Where he had aimed.

"For Christ's sake!" brayed Butch Engle,
Coming up behind the cottonwoods.
"Can't you lay off that stuff for just one day?
I'm sorry that I ever let you in
That joint of mine.
I guess it didn't do you any good.
Look here!" he said to Homer,
Standing giant-like and glaring grim.
"Look here, old cookie.
What you say about your getting wise, and laying off?
You look like hell. Your eyes are pink.
You're going to be a drunk, that's all—
A bum nobody wants around."

"So what?" snarled Homer. "It's my dough.
A hundred-fifty every month:
A hundred-fifteen total disability,
And thirty-five because this leg and arm—"

"O.K. O.K.," said Butch.
"I guess you ain't the first.
But how's about the guys who haven't any legs? . . .
Well, I don't know just who they are,
But lots of guys you read about . . .
They make themselves a decent life somehow.
Sure, it takes lots of guts to straighten out.
I guess that maybe I could never do it.
But look—I'm just a bum. I run a joint.
Take you: you're young—you got a lot ahead.
That girl of Jacobson's—
I guess she likes you pretty well—"

"Yeh? Yeh?" said Homer,
Liquor singing in his ears
And coloring his wizened face.
"You know a lot about it, don't you, guy?
I'm spastic-athetoid. I guess I know
The score! I know what gives.
A hemiplegiac: that means one side. . . .
God damn it, in those hospitals
They did the best they could.
I turned a wheel—like this—
I turned it all the time!
I did my exercises, went to walking class—
The nurses— Sure, they did their stuff.
So what's the score?
I'm back at home. I'm Out.
I get a hundred-fifty every month,
And I'm like this.
They fed me quite a line of crap;
They said that I'd get better soon.
By God, I do get better.
Every time I take a drink
I get a little better.
Look, I threw that bottle;
Hit those rocks—that's where I aimed.
And if I want to take a drink,
Nobody's man enough to stop me, see?"

All this he chattered like a squirrel—
His glare so bloodshot, frightened,
Fervid, rash and wet—
His mouth distorted as he talked.
His frenzy wouldn't let him see
The face of Butch lamenting
Like the face of Wilma Jacobson . . .
And Butch's callous voice
Becoming suddenly as courteous as hers.
"Homer," said Butch,
"Forget I ever said a word."

Long, long sat Homer Wermels by the creek
An hour after Butch had gone.
There must have been some talk;
Butch must have talked to Mr. Wermels—
Anyway, he came at last—the father—
Spoke about the fish:

There used to be some bass right in this creek;
He'd caught some years ago;
He guessed the bass were gone, these days;
Perhaps the catfish too were gone.
He mentioned youthful wanderings
In these same woods
(Resorting to the painful measured speech
Of one whom life had never made
Articulate to any point of ease).
Elaborate and fulsome, Mr. Wermels
Skirted round the talk of disability.

At last it had to come:
The curse of liquor. This was just too much.
He'd have to take some steps:
Yes, even to impounding all that money
Homer got each month: the hundred-fifty bucks.
A minor child— Well, Mr. Wermels knew the law,
And he'd invoke it if he had to.

Homer looked at him
With bitter eyes and fallen jaw,
And water seeping down his chin.
"You think you'll get that dough?
Two bits you won't!
I bet a hundred bucks you won't! Just try it.
Talk to anyone down in that office
In the Federal Block. Sure, go ahead!
You'd never get away with that.
The money's *mine*. It comes to *me*.
You charge me for my board and room.
I'm willing. Go ahead and charge—
And if you charge too much I'll move away!
But listen. You can't ever take the money
From a man disabled in this war.
I'm not a kid, not any longer. Say—
I've been around. I know the score.
You'll never get that dough!"

The father cried in mercy, "Listen, Bub.
I mentioned it as just a possibility.
I didn't mean—"

"You didn't mean a thing," said Homer.
"Sure, I know. A bluff."

He made himself get up and stand;
He saw the ripples running past.
They turned him dizzy as he watched.
He slid his shaking hand to anchorage
Along the trouser seam, and felt a fold
Of money there beneath the cloth.
This night at Patsy's or the Bon Ton Bar
He'd find his rollicking release again.
"What time we going home?" he growled.

They crawled the long green pasture-land.
They drove in silence. Homer didn't ride
With Jacobsons this time.
The sun went down in pretty haze of June
As when the Pottawatomies were there.

xxxvii

AL Stephenson and gawky Rob
And L.D.M., and Latham, mortgage manager—
They stepped in sober pace
Along the tight-mown grass.
They walked as solemnly as any men
Might ever wander in a search for joy.
They'd talked their game across the barbered greens
Of every hole they played.
They didn't have a word to utter any more.
The straps of heavy golf bags creaked.

(O raw and red
The sun above—
The sun of empty afternoon.
O creased my skin
Beneath the russet strap.
What, only one—?
One simple toy so heavy as I go?
And what's become of weight of walnut,
Webbing, mask and gear of mess,
And brass and wool and lead and grimy belt?
How is it that I am out of uniform
With easy leather on my feet,

And purple pigment in my sodden shirt?)

They played the 18th hole. Rob won.
He took a Four, and four was par.
He grinned in sunburn ... freckles on his face
Like pepper. Al and L.D.M.
Had five apiece, and Latham took one more.
They picked the balls from out the cup.
"Good boy!" said Mr. Milton. "Good boy, Rob."
He stood stiff-shouldered, green across his eyes
Where light came through
The patent hat-rim which he wore.
"Al, I'll bet you fifty dollars now
That Rob will win his Flight in August
If he straightens out that hook he's got....
I tell you, son,
You'll beat the breeches off your dad
Before the summer's over!"
                              "Heck,"
Said Rob in modest joy,
"I blew up on the 3rd and 9th."

He blew up. Yes,
But not the way some boys had blown.
The primer never plunged from out the sky,
The cap did not discharge a metal wind
To paste him harmless over yards of earth and air.
No bomb exploded him, no rifle butt
Released the friendly brains he carried in his skull.

He blew up on the 3rd.
That must have been the day—
October day when Rosenberg flew wide
And wet the trees on either side of him....
Al didn't know just what it was
He wiped from off his helmet rim:
A piece of bone?
                    Rob blew up
On the 3rd and 9th....

And later, later when the showers drilled
Their freshened spray and density
Against the skin where sweat had stood—
When childish rang their whistles, grunts,
Their sighs and humming in the shower room,

Al saw the bodies of the rest:
Old Mr. Milton, shoulder sagging down,
And chest hair turning gray.
He saw the pillowed paunch of Louis Latham,
And the knobs and crockets of his son.

Oh, fragile, never tanned
Or disciplined by dust and mud,
By coal and frost and cordite smell—
These were too old and prim,
Too dull and comfortable—
Or young, as in the case of Rob—
Too young; and bashful as a girl.
The boy turned quick away, to hide
His private nakedness when anyone came near.
He wore a towel to the locker room;
He got his clothes. Lou Latham slapped him
On the back. "So you blew up?
The hell you did!" And Rob grinned,
Glad to find himself grown into this,
To find his person recognized,
To be a male adult among the other males.

And later, later still, with sun
Turned milder on the awning overhead,
Each banker sat and held his glass.
They lived in flannel, linen, cleanliness;
And Mr. Milton, Latham took their luxury
Not as in contrast to a pain,
But as the common thing
Decree of all the gods awarded them.
They sat, they sighed; each held
His thin Martini glass and drank his drink.

Beyond the tennis courts, beyond the trees
Al saw his son disport with other kids
Around an old jalopy in the road.
He heard the coarse squawk of a changing voice,
He saw the slim legs of a girl
Who'd changed herself not long before.
He saw this skinny flock of fowl
Go cackling, crowing in the grove.

"—Or like a bunch of pups," he thought
With love and sadness. "Just as waggy-tailed

And beautiful. Oh, Jesus Christ,
I guess they're just as doomed:
A short life—and a merry one, perhaps.
God give them plenty bones to chew,
So long as they can chew them. . . .
Give them plenty balls to chase."
He offered liberalities
And blessed Boone City's *Jugendbund.*

He heard Lou Latham's voice:
"So that's the kid
That blew up on the 3rd and 9th!
I bet you fifty, Al, he'll never blow—
Not in the tournament this year."
"Oh, no, he won't," Al Stephenson agreed.
Once more he spoke the thing he shouldn't say.
"No, Rob won't blow—
Until he blows up in the war to come."

The war to come.
                    They looked at him,
And L. D. Milton froze his face and eyes,
For Al had uttered words like that before.
"If you don't mind my saying it," said L.D.M.
"I think it's in bad taste
To keep on harping on a theme like that."
Lou Latham held his heavy silence:
Applause for Mr. Milton, scorn for Al,
All tinctured with the jealousy that dripped
Forever in his soul. . . . *If I had only gone,*
He thought. *If they had only let me go—*
Go overseas . . . fat chance . . . I never had
A chance. By God, I could have done as well as—

"What the hell, sir!" Al was telling L.D.M.
"I'm not an ostrich. Couldn't hold my head
In sand for more than seconds at a time!
I'm not a dope. I just can see
The things to come; and anyone can see them."

Mr. Milton spoke benign
And soothing. (He was still annoyed.)
"I'm older, Al. I've seen three wars.
And if you ask for my opinion, I'm inclined
To think we'll never see another war.

Not on important scale. We can't afford it;
And the other nations can't."

"That's quite correct," said Lou. "We can't.
I'm with you, L.D.M., on that.
It's talking war that makes men want to fight.
Good heavens, Stephenson, I'd think
That you would never want to see another—"

Al shot out a word
That struck them like a club.
You didn't holler words like that
In any place where women-folks might hear.

They looked around in guilty shame:
Ashamed of Stephenson and what he'd said.
Good luck there were no ladies near!
"Look out," said Mr. Milton,
With an icy little laugh. "Look out.
The house committee—they'll remove your scalp
And hang it up to dry,
If you go shouting words like that!"

Al Stephenson put down his glass
So hard he broke the stem.
He shook a gem of blood from off his fingertip.
"I could have said," he told them,
"Things much worse than that.
It isn't that I want a war. It's just—"

He shook his head. And Milton waited—
Judge behind the bar—and Latham was a bailiff
Guarding him.

"Sometimes we used to dream,
And have a theory that this was all—
The last, the very last, the end of wars.
I guess a hundred times I listened
When the boys were talking:
                              'Never want
My kid to go through anything like this.'
So what? We worked together:
England, Russia, U.S.A. We could have done it,
Could have worked from scratch,
And built a decent structure...."

Hell. We didn't. Now we're watching them.
They're watching us.
We're spying or resenting. So are they.
We're human . . . all the damn United Nations:
Mean and selfish. We're afraid.
And where's the thing to end?—I ask you that—
When we have let the Germans live
To hate united guts of our united tribe,
And pray with tinny voices for *der Tag*?
When we know all the nastiness of Greece,
Trieste, Syria? . . . Oh, name the land
Where we have done the thing we should have done,
And done it right! And Roosevelt
Is dead. We might as well
Declare that God and Hope
Died Thursday, April twelfth, in 1945;
And now there'll never be dependable
A sun or moon to look upon.
Who blows up? Boys like Rob?
Sure—ten or twenty years from now.
They'll have a better way to blow them, then."

"Ah, what's the matter with this man?"
Thought Mr. Milton, president,
And prophet, planner, boss of people's lives.
"Now, what's it called?
Yes. Disillusionment."
                         For he had heard
That men came back from war all disillusioned.
He was wrong: they came illusioned,
Having learned a faith they never held before.
The tepid water dripping from the faucets—
Clammy plumbing of their life at home—
Would wash their fair illusions all away.

So Milton spoke his piece:
"I don't see why you talk like that.
It can't be very pleasant,
Thinking that your son will die
To try to do the job you left undone!"

Al Stephenson arose and never said a word.
He didn't speak the insult in his mind—
The combat-word to slap this monster with.
He went away; he took his car and drove.

And once he grinned an impish grin
To think of how Lou Latham must have stared,
And Mr. Milton must have felt
A bullet darting through his dignity.

But only once he grinned
(He drove and drove; he wasted gas;
The corn-leaves rustled for a million miles).
His knowledge wouldn't let him grin again.

"The dream I had one time
Was just as wrong as theirs.
But still it seems I had excuse
For holding it. And now I have much less excuse
For never speaking out the things I want to say,
When there is need to say them."

He had fought in Africa; he'd heard
The shock of disillusionment that rang
Among the Frenchmen there. He'd fought in Italy,
And seen the famine of a liberated land.
He'd fought in Germany... sometimes he thought
Of words attributed to mad John Brown,
Explaining carnage he had made
In Kansas: "Nits breed lice."
Yes, maybe so. And little Germans grow
In time to big ones.... Little ones
Would grow again; the marching songs
Would echo in the roof-trees that were left;
Some other day this ardent, stupid race
Would strut impassioned on their neighbors' soil—
Some day again the boots would beat
A Wagner chorus. Valkyries would ride.
The *Nibelungenlied* would whip its dragons out.

Al didn't doubt. He knew.
And more than that were casualty:
The brotherhood, the honest plea—
The fearful questions asked by fearful voice—
The matters talked to other men
In darkness—cold and wet in straw—
Not with articulation such as poems gave
Or odd-imagined plays in which the players spoke
Their souls aloud—
                    But broken, brief:

The obscene word that told a million tales
Untold by men who never might command
Such simple force of language.
                                   "Atlantic Charter!"
Cries the spokesman in the Book of Miracles;
And, instantly responding,
Twenty million other men cry, "Scrap of paper!"
Paper of a certain kind. And tell the stuff
That's smeared upon it—tell it in one word.

And so, demise: the union, love and sacrifice
All massacred by motives older than their dream.

Al thought of Spits. He'd had them come, one time,
To save him and some more who lay in fright,
Half buried under sand and rocks:
The bombers whining down, the brown and awful birds
Releasing hot excreta as they fell.
Here come the Spits! a boy cried out
In hoarsened voice.

They saw them when the dust had cleared:
The round wings turning up against the sky,
The RAF rondels, the patter of their guns . . .
Dive-bombers swept away; the Spits were biting
As they fled.
                    A man might stand
And now draw in the breath of life again,
And say within his heart that Britain was a pool
Where angels spawned.
                              The cherubim
Sang, "Rule, Britannia" with a flint
Of desert dust upon their feathers;
And grenadiers were fed upon the fish and chips
Of London legend, and the ale was good.

Here come the Spits! It took a year or two
For pilots to put on their horns and tails.
Calm-voiced, calm-faced, and deprecating fact—
"Bad show, bad show," they muttered. "Jolly bad."
They snapped their harnesses around, and climbed
     aboard.
The wind-screws turned, the jet went out, the 3-0-3's
Began again; the cannon coughed.
Bewildered little Greeks

Sprawled on the temple-steps of better centuries.
O Solon, Solon!
           Sickened cry
Above the slash of tracer-streams
That touched the ragged, running crowd.
O Solon, Solon!
           In the heat
Of Marathon, we well believe
No Spitfires came down. But still Pheidippides
Could never fly so fast as they.

xxxviii

ON AFTERNOONS like this, in 1942,
    Fred Derry wandered fast the skies
    Of Florida and Texas in uncertainty,
In fevered hope, in doubt and dread.
A million other boys
Held then the selfsame fright:
Not terror of the combat yet to come,
And flak, and freezing blue, blue, blue—
But fear of failure, fear of washing out.

In 1943, Fred dwelt in long dismay
At what awaited him above the cirrus clouds
Surmounting St. Nazaire and Hamm.

In 1944, on such an afternoon as this,
He left Victoria, got off in Surrey,
Found the bicycle his friends had left for him.
The hedges flew along—
The little church of Norman stone—
The bus he passed—
The lorries parked beyond.
He came in greenest shade to Hedding Beech;
An old maidservant let him in.
A Waaf with long legs (Sylvia:
The girl with whom he'd sleep that night)
Put down her glass and cried in glee,
"I say, here's Derry!
Darling, awfully good of you to come.

We're playing bridge—it's stupid.
What about a stroll
As soon as we've another beer?
There's time . . . oh darling,
Have a sardine sandwich, do! . . .
How stupid of me! I'm so sorry:
Squadron Leader Margetson—
You haven't met before—?"

In 1945, upon this afternoon,
With sunshine heavy on the awnings,
Motor traffic squealing at the 6th Street light—
Amid electric humming, gush of taps,
And moaning of the malted milk machines,
Amid the cheapjack clang and clatter
Of the Midway Drugs, Fred Derry stood precise,
While Miss Kovardis checked cosmetics
On a yellow sheet.

"Yes, here it is. This must be it.
I'm sorry, Mr. Derry!
See—I marked a dozen Rubensteins right here.
See—here's the mark. And all the time
I meant the Ardens. Here they are.
I've got them on the shelf down here.
See. Here. 'Elizabeth—' These must have been
The ones that Mr. Bullard meant."

Fred thanked her, warned her,
Gave the sheet to Mr. Luce . . .
Went over to the side and changed a nickel
For a woman; gave her pennies for the weight machine.
He found two air-mail stamps for one old customer. . . .
A foreign woman tried to tell a clerk
Just what she wanted. She was a German Jewess—
She couldn't speak to make them understand.
Fred fetched a pharmacist—a Mr. Finklestein—
And thus they found just what was wanted.
Fred waited on one man; he sold him batteries.
He waited on another; sold an eye-cup. . . .
"I'm sorry. No, I'm sure that you're mistaken.
We haven't had cigars like that in weeks—"

And far beyond the shiny tops of booths
He saw a halting shape

Come twitch-and-scrape-and-scuffle through the door:
Contorted boy, mad-eyed and bare of head,
And needing Nazarene to put His hands on him
(But Nazarenes were few and far between;
Boone City didn't have a one to spare).
Fred watched, while stacking up the honey-almond
    cream,
Saw Homer Wermels hunting for a booth;
And Homer found a booth
With two young sailors drinking malted milks.
He sat supreme, preparing now
To show the ribbon bars he carried in his pocket—
Eager and intent to tell about the convoy
Steaming down from Liverpool.

A saucy girl flounced up to wait on him,
And still Fred Derry watched.
He didn't like that girl;
She'd worked there just six days;
Her name was Bunny, and her cheeks were fat,
Her mouth was pulpy, pettish, squeezed,
Her black eyes sullen, sharp.
She said a word, and Homer spoke,
He looked at her—
The girl said something else,
She said it angrily, and other people looked.
She turned to walk away.

Fred Derry came,
A bottle of the almond cream still in his hand.
"Hi, Homer."
        Homer's eyes flashed wet,
But there was smoky anger in his face.
He tried to talk. Fred didn't wait.
He called the girl by name.
She turned.
      "I won't serve him.
No. I don't have to wait on him!
He's drunk."

And still the people all around:
The people by cigars,
The folks on fountain stools,
The gabbling crowd of bobby-soxers...
Everybody looked.

"Look, Bunny," Derry said.
"This fellow isn't drunk. Come here."

She came. Her mouth
Was pouting more. She glared.
"Now, Homer?" Derry asked.
"A chocolate soda? Sure."
He told the girl, "He wants a chocolate soda."
"All right," the waitress snarled.
"But I can smell the liquor.
Still I say he's drunk!"
She went to have the soda made.

Fred Derry talked to Homer just a moment more
(So hard to talk to him
With gush of conversation,
Gush of soda in his ears).
"So long," Fred said. "Be seeing you."

A woman tried to use a booth to telephone;
The door was stuck, and Derry helped.
A sliding door ... she'd pulled it off its track.
He put it on again. The woman thanked him.
Derry turned; and he saw Bunny coming back,
The soda balanced on her tray,
And clear and fair, as all the mob turned mute,
He heard the hate that Homer Wermels hurled
In one fast phrase:
"I'll show you if I'm drunk!"

He tried to lift the soda off the tray.
He used his left hand ...
Athetoid, unmanageable, flopping like a fish.
A brown wave flew on high,
The glass fell, broke,
And ruddy brown the chocolate froth
Stained wet the uniform that Bunny wore.

"You dirty little drunken bum!"
Her strong fat hand swept round
And slapped the boy across the face
As hard as she could slap.

Fred Derry, twenty-one, and killer of a hundred men.
(And how much bombing will they want in Boone?

And what's the union scale for bombardiers?)
He had the waitress by her wrist;
He swung her rude—
He took his other hand
And pushed the tottering and outraged boy—
He pushed him back upon his seat.
"Just look," screamed Bunny.
"Just you look!
He threw it on my skirt. Just look!"
And fifty people stared,
And made their way as close as they might come,
And others seemed to come behind.

Fred Derry's voice was vicious.
"You're a bitch
To slap a guy like this,
You dumbell! Can't you see this fellow's hurt?
He's paralyzed; he isn't drunk.
I'll tell you where he got it; off Oran.
He used to wear a uniform just like these sailors here.
Yeh. Girls like you—
You see a guy in uniform;
You think he's pretty cute;
Those pants, those sailor collars—
Yeh, you think they're cute.
Shut up! Don't say another word.
This fellow's got the Purple Heart.
And now you slap his face.
Your precious little skirt—
It isn't even yours.
It's furnished to you by the store!"

"Aw, shut your mouth," the waitress yelled.
"I don't care if that guy's got
A dozen Purple Hearts!
He's fresh, he's drunk—
I guess I know a drunk!
He doesn't have to pour his soda over *me*."

The whispered agony of Mr. Luce
Drove into Derry's ears:
"For Lord's sake, Derry, have you lost your mind?
What is this? Look— The customers!
Miss Holt," Luce told the snarling girl,
"You go back to the locker room at once."

Fred Derry got a cloth;
He wiped the floor;
He wiped the table top.
The sailors stared and stared.
"I'm going," Homer said, and tried to rise.
"No, wait," Fred Derry told him,
"I'll be back."

In office space behind prescriptions
Bullard looked at him, and rubbed his chin
As Luce described the scene.
The thin voice rattled on in horror, telling all,
And telling more than all.
"He grabbed that waitress, Mr. Bullard—
Made a scene, manhandled her!
I tell you, she might sue the store—"

Said Derry wearily,
"I'll never make a scene like that again;
Not in the Midway Drugs.
I'm through."

"Well, I should guess you are," cried Luce,
With triumph in his tone.
But Bullard said, "O.K. Just let
Me talk to Mr. Derry privately."
And Bullard talked and talked.
It didn't do a bit of good.
"It's not my dish," Fred Derry said.
"I'm much obliged to you;
You've certainly been decent to me—
All a guy could ask.
But— Well, I guess I know
I'm piss-poor in a job like this.
It's trivial, it's dull:
I hate it more and more each day.
It's not your fault.
I'd rather go."

"Freddy, I guess you know what's best.
I'm sorry, sure as hell.
Say, let me help you get another job?"

"No, thanks," said Fred, "I'll manage.
I'll try something else."

"Say, look," said Bullard.
"If it's dough— I mean—
You haven't got much money saved,
Not if I know you. Anyway
You can't save much on what you get.
Say, wait a minute—
I've got plenty cash on hand;
My own, I mean.
So, just a little loan? O.K.?"
He turned, he tried to open up
The small drawer in his desk
Where he kept matters personal to him.

"No, thanks," said Fred.
His throat felt stuffed.
Old Bullard blinked and blinked
Behind his heavy spectacles. . . .
"Well, let me know what gives."
They pressed their hands together.
Derry went.

He went with Homer, dragging him
Down to the Hotel Seneca.
They had a drink in Derry's room;
They cursed the girl, the store, the world;
They said Boone City stunk.
The hell with people like that slut!
They finished up the bourbon. At the desk,
When Homer left, Fred told the clerk: "Here.
This is Mr. Wermels. He's a pal of mine. And any time
He wants to use my room, when I'm not in,
It's perfectly all right. You let him have the key.
Sometimes he's tight—"
He jabbed his elbow into Homer's ribs,
And Homer leered, and jabbed him back.
"Sometimes he's tight and needs a place to rest,
You let him have my key, just any time,
And tell the night man too.
But if he comes up with a blonde, no go.
A brunette either. Red-heads only.
He can only have a red-head when he comes."
The old clerk sniffed, and laughed at such a thought
(He hadn't made a sin like that
In nearly fourteen years). . . .

And Homer went to waste five dollars
In the Bon Ton bar.

An hour earlier than that,
Down at the Midway Drugs, a girl
Rose quietly from off her soda stool
Far, far down at the end,
Beyond the soda straws, beyond
The menu stacks.
               She'd seen it all;
She'd heard what other folks had heard,
She'd listened to the bobby-soxers—
Heard them bleat and giggle,
Heard the shock and wonder they expressed. . . .
Pale girl, young girl,
So neat and Nordic in her walk—
Her name was Wilma Jacobson.
She'd seen it all. She went away.
She walked among the crowds of Walnut Street.
She tried to think what she might do.
She didn't know a thing to do.
She was too young. And so was he,
And so was he!

XXXIX

A MAN named Novak came and sat by Al,
    Flat-headed, broadjawed, staid of face;
    He was Bohemian. He wore a globe and anchor pin.

Al didn't wear his ribbon any more—
The ribbon of the Silver Star—
Not very often. People asked
Too many questions; and he saw covert
The smile of other men who'd also served,
Who had no Silver Star
Or any other kind of star.
               John Novak sat
And held his hat upon his knee.
His plain green eyes looked solemn into Al's;
And when John Novak spoke,
His voice was like a cricket-song.

"I've got a little nursery.
I guess you know it?
Out where 52nd Street runs blind
Right north of Black Hawk Boulevard?
The Novak Nursery, we call it.
My Pop—he used to have the place.
I helped him there, and then I went to war.
My Poppa died while I was in the South Pacific.
I guess you don't remember ... years ago
We used to sell you lilacs, sir.
My Pop and I—we set them out for you."
Al Stephenson sat close
And said the words he should have said.
He spoke the thought within his mind,
And that was quite enough.
The bond was soldered hard between.

The picture Novak reconstructed of himself,
The flowers that he grew,
The life that he distilled
From earth and offal, muck and guano, lime—
The war he'd seen, which had contributed
Such talent to the soil in other places—
All these things he told.
His flat strong hands, so cleanly brown,
Impassive ... new black shoes that squeaked,
And thick and fuzzy socks you'd see
Because he'd pulled his trousers high
To save the creases at his knees.

And—"Were you in the South Pacific, ever?"
"No. The ETO. In Africa
And Italy and Germany."
"I guess that that was pretty tough."
"You must have had it worse out there."
"Well, food was pretty bad sometimes. And bugs—
Say, what were you? A major, maybe?"
"Sergeant. What were you with? Marines?"
"Yes, I was in the Corps."

He talked of tropic verdure, trees ...
John Novak thought in terms of growing things.
The chlorophyl of this green world—
He had it in his eyes:

A pigmentation of the lushest leaves.
He talked of grass.

They took a strip one time. (Ah, grass
Would grow so rapidly, he said, in lands like that!
He couldn't quite get over it.)
They took a strip. The place was pocked
And pounded by the guns of ships
Before they went ashore.
He didn't recapitulate each detail—
How they snaked across the hummocks, inch by inch—
He didn't tell about the heat
Combusted from their angry pipes
And sending little dark half-naked men
In squealing, chatting mirth of greasy flame
To curl and kick,
To try to throw their hand grenades,
And try to bite,
Until the ash of their own burning made them stiff.

But still Al knew
Just what the Gyrenes did.
They took the strip. They painted every yard
With frightened sweat, with dying fat
That emptied from their bodies
When the bullets sighed and struck.
They took the strip. The blaze burned wide
And fried the weeds and Zeros into black,
To dry and smoldered emptiness.
"The place," John Novak said,
"Was empty." Hard and hot as any concrete floor.

That afternoon, while he patrolled along the edge,
And while the tanks still banged and coughed across
    the beach,
And while the landing barges splashed against the shore,
And people emptied out, in hot and tired tonnage—
He said that he patrolled the strip,
With cinders crunching underneath his feet.
"It never looked like anything would grow again."

And someone killed a Jap,
A sniper in the torn and plastered palms beyond.
The man came charging, wounded,
Dripping blood, and making strange and birdlike cries.

John Novak said, "One of our fellows shot a Jap."
He didn't say that it was he;
But Stephenson might know.

The gargoyle sprang a hundred yards or so,
Until collapsing, limp and weak, he died,
A toy tan mound amid the dust and embers.
Thus the miracle began.

"We saw him,
Turned him over, looked at him,
And he was dead. . . . We didn't bother for a while.
There were an awful lot of Japs around,
And lots of our guys dead.
The medics gathered up our own,
We let the others lie.
We had a lot to do right then.
That night it rained like hell."

And Novak walked beside his private little Jap. . . .
The sun the second day came cooking down.
Rain hammered hard once more
Against the blackened oily sod.
The next time Novak looked, he said,
He saw a fuzz of green.
Examining his Jap again,
He saw the outstretched swollen hand,
And there was weedy richness shown
Between the fingers.

Sun and rain . . . the hours' chemistry . . .
The wonder of the heat and wet.
John Novak went and looked.
And this was grass, and growing tall,
Extending wide and emerald
Between the swollen fingers
Where the flesh was still too raw
For certain worms to feed.
And so, the pullulating green . . .
With birds to bugle mystery
In jungle wet around.

"You won't believe it, Mr. Stephenson:
In four more days that grass was high enough
To cover up the Jap. It blew and blew;

You couldn't see him laying there.
You won't believe it. Still I can't believe it.
That grass, it just exploded—
Vines and tendrils tangled up,
And pretty soon the flowers too.
That's how it grows down there;
That's what the vegetation's like.
It's hard to make yourself believe it
Even when you see."

xl

FOUR THOUSAND DOLLARS loaned
To Novak, John, the ex-Marine
Who owned a nursery, and sold the lilac trees—
Who had a herbage in his eyes.

John Novak brought his papers, deeds,
Methodical and wise.
                    He had a little candy box,
And all these things, the evidences of his life—
He'd put them in the candy box, and tied a string
    around.

An hour ticked away.
They filled the forms, the questionaires.
The details once so cumbersome and fearful—
These were clear as Al explained them.
The government would guarantee
Just half the loan: two thousand dollars.
Other risk was taken by the bank:
Two thousand more, at four per cent.

"That's subject," said Al Stephenson,
"To government O.K. I'm sure you'll get it.
Certainly you'll get it
Insofar as we're concerned.
I wouldn't let it worry you:
Perhaps a week, two weeks or maybe more.
I'll make a side-bet. Do you smoke cigars?"
So they bet one cigar. John Novak bet against himself.

He laughed, pretending to believe, for one cigar,
That no administrator of the government
Would think it wise to guarantee his loan.

Al Stephenson was proud. He thought of how his father
Managed banking, in his other time.
The loans of character...the bright-eyed immigrant,
Who earned his first hard silver in a new community,
And sought to bury it, to plant it in the soil,
And make his crop more bountiful.
Al'd heard his father tell about the time
He loaned one thousand dollars to a man
On just his given word. The note
Would be signed later. Then the man was killed—
Gored by a bull that very afternoon.
The months went by. The man's tall sons
Walked in the bank. They straggled up;
They made their halting speech;
They paid the thousand back,
With interest at six per cent.

Such sturdy, simple banking, when the smell
Of fresh-shelled corn was in the air;
When strong the good brown apples of manure
Were heaped in roadways; when the land,
The clean untarnished sky,
And new-sprung cottonwoods were joy.
And this was it again. John Novak had
The color of a prairie sun
Upon his cheeks.

John told about his plans...
The hot-bed frames. Yes, glass—
He knew where he could find the glass he wanted.
Yes. New greenhouse, too.
And water pipes—another pump. Yes,
Second-hand—but still the pipes were good.
The well worked fine. It didn't cost too much.
He'd build a little office, too,
Right by the driveway, so the customers
Would not be trooping through his house.

He showed the pictures. "Here's my kid. He's only six;
Not big enough to be much help, not yet.
My wife— Well, this is her. She's strong.

She helps me out a lot. I tell you, Mr. Stephenson,
You come out there some time,
She'll bake you up some *kolaches*
Just like her Aunt Violka use to bake."

Their faces smiled from out the dime-store frame:
The woman, firm-fleshed, clean and hearty,
Pleasant as a heifer;
The kid: a jolly little calf;
And Novak never base as any bull,
Nor brutal like a bull,
But with a solid calm and grace—
The godliness of cream and fat and wheat,
And all that vegetation in his eyes.
Al swore that he smelled moss
And apple blossoms,
As the young man went away.

You don't mix moss and apple blossoms
When you fill out forms like that. You shouldn't.
Such husbandry becomes absurd to other men.

"What collateral insures this loan?"
The glassy glance of Mr. Prew,
Assailing every numeral and cipher that he saw . . .
And Steese came spying too.
They clucked. There'd been too many things like this;
They whispered, put their heads together;
And then so questioning, so pained and disapproving,
They came and challenged Stephenson.

"But what collateral secures this loan?
Four thousand dollars! Holy smoke, my man,
You can't do things like this!"

"Collateral?" repeated Al.
(Well, oats and apple blossoms:
Good enough for anyone—
The best assurance in the world.
He didn't say those words aloud;
He muttered them within his mind.)

"You've got two thousand
Backed up by the government,
Or do you think I misinterpreted

The GI Bill of Rights?
They guarantee one half
Of every loan like this."

"But at discretion of the lender," Prew declared,
With Steese beside him, watching sad and sly.
"Good grief, my man,
I don't know what the Board will say
If you keep on like this!
Two thousand— Half the loan is unsecured—
Let's see what Latham has to say.
Why didn't you demand
A mortgage on John Novak's place?"

Al frowned, he dug a paper out.
"Look here," he said. "To men like that
A mortgage is a handicap.
I think I know this guy. I know his kind.
He signed this. See? It's plain as dirt:
Agreement not to mortgage any property he owns
Until this loan is paid."

And Prew laughed bitterly,
And Steese essayed a little smile
Around his pearling lips.
"No, no," said Prew. "This paper— See, my friend,
This paper can't secure the loan: two thousand dollars.
Now just suppose this fellow Novak died,
Suppose he got in trouble with some other creditors,
Suppose they swooped down with attachments,
      judgments,
Just suppose they got there first.
Why, if they grab his property—
We haven't got a mortgage. We haven't got a thing!"

"I told him," Al said angrily,
"I'd not demand a mortgage.
This loan's already made,
So far as I'm concerned."
The metal clanged within his tone. He said,
"Am I the manager of small loans in this bank,
Or am I not?"
                  Steese fluttered off in fright.
But Prew still stared; his eyes were bright and bitter
As they peered beneath their thickened lids.

"I don't know what the Board will say.
But, when I had your job, I used discretion.
In matters of this kind, I talked to someone else."

The cold embattled glance
That spoke in sharper words than those;
The somber censure in their tone;
The little words a-flit from desk to desk;
The grapevine, girl to girl;
The whisper, under proper click of keys
Or petty sound of levers pulling down;
The smirk and gossip:
                    "Helen, did you hear
What Prew was telling Steese?
Look out . . . he's watching . . . Mr. Stephenson
Is mad. Oh, boy! I'd hate to have old Prew
Just even *look* at me like that!
If looks could kill—
Did you hear what he said?"

And so Al stood again before the desk of L.D.M.
And Milton sent his secretary out
And had her close the door.
He tapped his fingers on the blotter pad.
"Now, Alton, I am sorry
That I have to speak to you like this again.
I must request that you consult with Prew
On all transactions such as this."

He pressed a button. "I am telling Prew
That I'll approve the loan this time—
This Novak thing you made last Monday—
But in the future—"

Prew came in, and Latham found
An errand at that time to bring him close.
And Milton pressed another buzzer.
Steese appeared.
"Now, all of you—" said Milton.
He smiled his rigid smile.
"Please listen. This is childish.
We can't have disharmony, misunderstandings. . . .
I want it understood that Mr. Stephenson
Has full discretion in the matter of small loans—
Two thousand— Nothing more than that—

That he will answer only to the Board—
That he will not receive authority
In any case concerning larger sums, unless
With the complete approval of another ranking officer."
He said some more. He spoke his wretched platitude
Of Putting Shoulders to the Wheel.

"And, Alton—" when the rest were gone,
And Stephenson still stood indignant there,
"The GI Bill of Rights does not empower
Any officer of any bank
To grant a pension or distribute free
Largesse to every man requesting it."

"Two thousand bucks," said Al. His lips were dry.
He touched them with his tongue.
"Now, here's a man, a worker; honest; property;
Ambition; family. A solid citizen. You'd call him
Back-bone of a nation— Things like that.
He goes out, fights. He gets some stripes.
He gets a bullet in his hip;
They ladle out a chunk of bone;
He's through, he's safe, a solid risk,
If such a thing there is!
And all I get is criticism
For propping up ambition of a man like that."

This was an evil moment in the life
Of L. D. Milton. He'd have to face the Board
And tell them Prew was right,
And he, the president, was wrong!
We need someone with youth.
You've seen the world; the war
Has broadened you.... It's you, not Steese....
He snapped at Stephenson,
"I'm sorry, Alton, but I can't embrace
Your attitude. You seem to think, per se,
That any man who's served in combat in this war
Is better than a man who hasn't!
Entitled to a richer benefit and—"

Al Stephenson stared hard at Milton.
"Yes, I do," he said. "That's what I think."

"Indeed. Well, in the future, please
Secure our loans," said Milton, just as mad as Al,

And suddenly unwilling to prolong
An interview like this,
And feeling Al impertinent,
And liking it no way.
"Secure our loans," he said again.

xli

FROM day to day, from time to time
Went Derry, Fred,
Ex 1st lieutenant, ex the 3-0-5th,
Ex ardent, jaunty, dangerous—
And now condemned to dismal servitude
In serving only self,
Or hunting seemly masters he might serve.

The first was war work . . .
Led him up to the machine
And showed him how the levers worked
And where the switches were.
He bought himself blue denim, wore a cap.
He felt cut off and amputated from existence—
Never part of this steel-stamped community
Where earnest Negro women did their jobs
Far better than Fred Derry might do his.

He worked two days.
The second night, two men were waiting
When he came out through the gate.
"Here, Bud. We want to talk to you."
They talked to him, they told him what.
"The hell with that," said Fred.
"It's open shop. I got it straight on Tuesday:
Open shop. You'll never get
That forty bucks from me."
He walked away, he heard the muttered talk
Behind him. He was scared.
He heard the men's feet coming fast.
And then a prowl-car, green and white,
A little Ford with officers, came round the corner.
Both men turned calm; he saw them strolling leisurely.

They went into a corner grill:
The Men Behind the Men
Behind the Men Behind the Gun.

The next day Gus, the foreman,
Met Fred in the washroom—followed him.
"Say, guy," Gus said. "I like you.
I don't want to see you have no trouble, see.
I know they call it open shop. You better pay
That forty bucks. Don't ask me why, or how I know.
It doesn't matter. You can make it up
On overtime; you work next week on overtime;
You make it up, the forty bucks."

"Thanks, Gus," said Derry.
"But I guess that's all I want to hear.
So long." He hung his denim clothes
Abandoned in his locker; got his money;
He became an Absentee.

White-collar job? Ah, here it was:
A man was getting out a magazine,
He called it *Western Wings*—an aviation journal.
He talked with Derry. Well, he'd try him . . .
People with experience . . . hard to get.
And three more days, this time,
Fred Derry messed with photographs
And yards and yards of proof . . .
The hot close office—
New name lettered on the door—
And one old lady, lame,
To answer telephone.

"*Western Wings*," said Fred.
"That sounds like fiction—
Like a wood-pulp magazine.
I thought about it, Mr. Heath:
Why don't you change the title?
Call it *Age of Wings*, or some such name—?"

"You think too much," said Mr. Heath.
"When I want such suggestions, I'll inform you.
And another thing: I've got some sinus trouble;
I'm allergic. I can't stand tobacco smoke.
You'll have to give up smoking
While you're on this job."

"Ten-hut, All Personnel!" said Derry.
"I know one much better:
Why don't I give up the job?"

xlii

Accountant? No, I can't account for anything.
An aeronautical designer ... what design
Might they desire? Combat box? Or echelon? ...
An artist, all around, air-brush and lettering.
State salary, experience ... what's a bushelman?
A buffer, buyer, butcher, bookkeeper or boy:
One time I was a boy, a boy was I
Before I got my old Observer's wings—
Now I must be a chauffeur-handyman
Or cabinet-maker, carpenter or cook;
Because I'm not a dentist, doorman, draftsman, engineer,
Exterminator, fireman, or feeder—job—patch-up—,
Make ready ... not a floorman, foreman, fitter, furrier.
I'm neither hotel manager nor operator of an IBM.
What is an IBM? And does it have some toggle-knobs?
And do I have to use the double grip?

So why not be a jeweler, a kitchen help, a lacquer man,
Or operate a lathe, a laundry, lithographing shop?
Could I pretend to be a locksmith?
(Love has laughed at me.)
A lobby clerk? Or run a linotype?
Or merely be a Man?
Man, handy, must have car, intelligent;
A Man with truck; Man 45 to 50; Man to learn
The woolen business. Opportunity!
Man to deliver laundry ...
Does his grandma do the wash?
And does he draw it on a wagon through the street?
Who are these nymphomaniacs who scream,
"A Man, a Man! My kingdom for a Man!"

Therefore I'll be a packer-shipper, shipper-wrapper,
Wrapper-packer— Name your own.
Go name your own, go roll your own,
Go roll your leg.

Roll your leg over,
Oh, roll your leg over,
Roll your leg over the Man in the Moon!
I wish all the Wacs were wittle white wabbits
And I could go out and teach them bad habits—

Remembered melody makes sad
An echo through confusion in my mind.
A drink, a babe; the bobby pins upon the sheet—
They put their imprint in my flesh.
And where's that extra hundred bucks from Uncle?
Here it is.
            I'll tear the envelope,
And cash the check, and pay my hotel bill,
And buy the bottle, buy the sickly gifts.
I'll go to see Hortense and see my dad.
I'll take the salted peanuts, take the gin,
And leave them there, and take no thing away—
Not even wish to ever come again.

With six Q.D.M.'s
And a lot of good luck
They'll reach the Limey shore—

Lie flat and read—
And read detective tales, and shun
The many other books I know that I should know. . . .
Move to the floor when Homer comes,
And let him have the bed, and let him mumble, snore—
I'll lie upon the dirty floor, and hear the hot wind blow,
And let the curtain move against the gritty screen.
The wind tells bitter stories—
Hot and rusty roofs it tasted on the way.
And Homer, bathed in sweat . . . torpedoes in his dream.
The tough tin fish are hunting him again.

Another Homer? Long ago in school—
The bust with wide blind eyes and marble hair,
And less than half remembered, Homer's Odyssey:
The grim report, the correspondent's tale,
With words come back to haunt me in the heat:
"But all the other ships went down together there."

October afternoon, and two hurt Fortresses come home.
The people swear; they stand and search the sky;

Red-red the flares are shot.
The 17's are landing. Smoke
Seems drifting from their fins
Like vapor trails they left when far aloft.

"Those bastards sure were on the ball today,"
Says Homer, blind reporter, harness in his hand.
"The flak was like a feather bed.
I never saw so many 1-0-9's
With these white eyes; I never saw
So many fighters; never saw so many ships go down.
Yeh. We got back—we two—
But all the other ships went down together there."

xliii

HE MADE the rounds; he stood in line;
He filled out forms.
He brought his papers all along,
He sat before four different desks
And told his tale.
He answered questions.
He was getting sick and tired of this stuff.
The Veterans' Administration; the U. S.
Employment Service. . . . People talked to him.
His name was typed in files
And strung in ink on neat-ruled cards.
He went with chip on shoulder, bitter, terse,
But never once across those desks
Did he meet surliness or boredom fit to match his own.

He saw them all in memory when lying on his bed:
The chubby face, the jingly-laughing man
Who'd lost his leg beside the Marne
Just twenty-seven years before;
The kindly senatorial face;
The weary martyr, yellow-bald, who carried all the woes
Of every client on his shoulders,
In his heart, and did the best he could for them.

Their very patience sickened Fred:
The white humility of nuns

Who tended sobbing children
In an orphanage of war.

But still they could not set him right,
Because the crookedness was not outside alone
But in his spirit too.

"Let's see what Uncle has to say . . .
Now in this paragraph here—Number Seven—
In this pamphlet . . .
Now, here. If you want psychiatric help—
But just the same, if I were you,
I'd never bother with that stuff.
Now, here— Let's see what's in the file.
Assistant in a pet shop . . .
Here's one. You think that you
Would like to learn embalming?"

They offered Fred their cigarettes.
One noon he went with two of them to lunch.
They talked about the war.
And one had flown in Jennies years before,
And he knew Spaatz when Spaatz was just a major;
Things like that. And he knew Arnold, too.
Not Benedict, but Hap!

They told their stories, talked of families.
One fellow lived two streets away from Derry's dad,
But still they couldn't set him right.
They said, "It's tough . . .
Say, why not go to college?"
"With a bunch of kids?" asked Derry.
"Sorry, but I'm not a college boy.
I'm not the type.
I finished school the time I finished
Combat Preparation. No,
I guess I'll never make the team;
I'm not the frat-boy type."
They tried. . . .
        They couldn't steer him right.

From time to time, from place to place
Fred Derry walked. He stood in other lines.
And no one barked—nobody yapped at him,
Or called him misfit, malcontent

Or freak. (He knew that he was all of these,
And flogged himself
With limber whip of realization.)
He felt that he was hardening inside,
Was growing grimmer, week by week.
... No place in Boone
Or in the whole wide warm soft world
Of civilized affairs—
No shield on which to hang his D.F.C.
He saw a sign in front of every door
In big black letters:
"Bombardiers Need Not Apply."

And thinking things like that,
And feeling always lashes of the little whip
He wielded at his flesh—
A tight-mouthed *penitente*—
So he stood by night in bars,
And swallowed drinks.
He cared for liquor less and less.
He'd found it good to drink in war
To make forgetfulness.
He didn't find it quite so good to drink at Home;
He couldn't find the happy opiate.

Fred sent his nickels through the slot;
Once more he toyed with pin-balls at the Daniel Boone,
And thus he got the note. A waiter
Brought it up, on half a menu torn.
"A lady in the dining room—
She said to give you this."
He read the lines of square-cut script,
The tracks of her, the racing scrawl
He'd never read before:
"I saw you in the lobby when we came.
How have you been? A man
Is being very nice to me.
I wish for you instead.
He's gone to hunt for cigarettes.
Oh here he comes Oh damn."
And signed P.S.

So what's P.S., and who's P.S.?
A postscript

To a letter never sent
By her or me?

He walked. He stood within the dining-room,
And he saw Peggy sitting with a Navy man—
From submarines, this time.
                                        She shone
More beautiful, more charged with limpid life
Than all the courtesans of history . . .
More fruit within her bosom, sun in hair;
She was the mistress every mortal wants,
The mother who would comfort him,
The nurse who'd feed, the Sister
Who would talk to him of Light,
And make him feel a Peace and hear a Voice.

He went back to the lobby,
Sent his note to her:
"I'm lousy, thank you.
There's a moon upstairs.
I'll meet you by the elevator. Come whenever
You can make it."

He watched and worried. . . . Ten o'clock.
She came. They rode up to the roof,
Not saying much, but holding hands.
"Who's Submarines?" asked Fred.

"It's Marty Warren. I knew him in school.
And what a wolf is little Marty now!
My knee's worn out from being rubbed,
And I'm worn out
From sitting sideways in my chair—"

"Look here," said Fred.
"I'll take you home—"

"Oh, heavens, no! There'd be a scene,
And Marty's rather tight. No, no.
It's quite all right. It's bark—no bite.
Don't worry, dear."

They walked across the roof.
There used to be a garden on that roof,
There wasn't any more.

They stood beside the parapet,
And breathed the desert of their town,
And tried to sniff the countryside beyond,
And feel the moonlight beating down.

They grappled tight. Their mouths were one.
And all desire lived in Fred,
And all response was waiting in this girl.
He pushed her off.
"By God, I'm nuts." He tried to laugh.
"Believe me, this will never do."

"Oh, Fred . . . oh, darling . . .
Please—let's kiss like that
Just one more time."
They kissed. The one more time was long.

They broke apart again,
And both were close to tears.
"Oh, what's the matter?" cried the girl.
"You say it! Say it!
What's the thing that's wrong?
What's wrong with me? With you?
You haven't called.
I haven't seen you since that day—"
Her face, her voice were hurting her
And hurting him.

"It's really not so far," she said.
"About five miles. . . . We've got a sign;
The sign says *Cherry Hill*. I might put up another sign
All printed with my name!
I could tear up some paper—leave a trail—"
Her words were tart and sour as she spoke
With acrid laughter, telling him the way:
Out west on Grand . . . take Highway 17 . . .
The turn, the bridge beyond . . .
She printed sharp a road-map, pressed it on
The clear white paper of this night.
She made the map indelible
With tears she shouldn't shed.

Fred held her hand.
He looked: the moonlight on her hand,
Her birthstone flashing shrill. The ring

Seemed studded with the pure wild metal of this girl.
The moonlight on the little stone
Made sparks to sting his eyes.

He muttered, "Listen, hon.
You'd better keep a little dignity!
Play Hard-to-Get or—"

"No, I won't," she said.
"I won't play silly little tricks:
No artifice, no acting cute!
The world's not made that way today.
I'd only sicken both of us
In being too-too coy about a thing like this!"

He stood awhile and hunted up his words;
He tried to find an honesty to match her own.
In broken phrase, in whispered curse
He spoke the selfish, ingrown ailment
Which infected him.
                    "Oh, Christ!" he said.
"I came back ... everything was wrong.
Our poverty, our kind of coarseness got me down—
The dreariness, the ignorance.
I guess I'm dreary, yes, and ignorant.
But— That's the home I always had—
The sort of people that we were.
In England— Well, I lived a different kind of life:
The first time in my life that I—
That I could do the things
I'd always dreamed of doing.
They paid us pretty well.
We had big crap games at the Base.
I had a lot of dough.
I made some friends—some English people—
Went around with them in London:
The first time I amounted to a damn....
You don't know what I mean; you've always had
The things you wanted; all the clothes and stuff;
A decent house.
               Oh, hell, don't say it!
Sure. I know just what you want to say:
That lots of people never have a shilling—
Still they keep their souls alive.... O.K. for them.
But me—I came fresh out of that

And into this. My father and his second wife—
They make me feel all second-hand
Just being in the room with them!
It isn't only me. They feel the same—
The same as me— So they're uncomfortable with me,
And I'm uncomfortable with them!
That girl I married— Some day, maybe
I'll be rid of her. I gave her money,
Ordered her to get a lawyer, wash the whole thing up.
She may have started. I don't know. I haven't heard."

He turned away, he saw the pale green glow
Like radium around—
A marsh-light over wise and patient sky
With mean electric signs to ruin it.
And Peggy followed to the parapet. . . .
Fred Derry turned once more.

"It's all a mess, the way I tell it, Peg.
But I can't see where I'm to go, or how to live,
Or what to do. . . . I'm crazy for you.
I could love you half to death.
                              But here's the score:
I haven't got a job; was never trained to do a thing,
Except to twist those knobs.
I know a Norden bombsight, not much else.
And from the first day that I landed here,
There was the question: how much bombing
Would they want in Boone?
I went back to the drugstore, took that job.
I washed up. Then I tried some other things.
They didn't work. I'll go somewhere.
I can't ask you to go along.
I don't know where I'll go, or how I'll live,
Or what I'll eat, or if I'll eat.
I can't go to the war again;
Pacific stuff . . . the lousy medics . . .
Diagnosis that they made—
They say my reflexes aren't right,
That I could never be a bombardier again.
Hell's bells! Why, I could ride a 29
To any target anywhere
And put the bomb-load on a dime!
But no, no, no, I'm through, I'm Out!

It's all a fluke: they washed me out,
And here I am, and it's like this!"

He held and kissed her.
Peggy's face was wet.
                    "Just promise me,
Before you go— Sometime you'll see me?
If anything should happen; anything
To make you feel a little different—
Promise that you'll come?"

"Sure, sure," he muttered.
"Well, let's go downstairs—
And see if Submarines has made a dive."

Lieutenant Warren hadn't made a dive.
He waited by the crowded door,
He glared at Fred,
He took the girl away.

xliv

G OD shot His firecrackers in the sky,
    And cocked His celebrating cannon at the clouds;
    He tore the clouds in two.
The rain of angry old July came out
And walked, and washed Boone City's streets.
There was no bunting on the buildings any more,
But if there'd been, the bunting would have run.
And women hurried, ducking heads against the storm,
To lower flags and furl them, take them in;
And lazy men on porches moved their chairs
To keep from getting wet.
They let the canvas curtains down.

And programs on the radios
Talked dryly on, despite the summer storm,
Invoking echo of a fife and drum,
And Yankee Doodle ditties ... quoted Jefferson,
They aped at Patrick Henry's lines;
Ticonderoga boomed again in tired parable

With great Jehovah's name.
                    And fathers said,
"When I was just your age we had those big ones:
Yellow Kids. We had the Thunderbolts—
We had those red Salutes six inches long—
You should have seen the Ladyfingers that we had!"
The noise of past America ...
To never boom again,
No more than guns that shot the buffalo.

Young Homer Wermels sickened on his porch,
The awning soggy overhead,
The chairs turned up with seats against the wall.
He drank his coke, he swallowed aspirin,
He went inside. The house was quiet.
Radio squawked on in low and stuttered tones,
Neglected, burning up the juice
For two slow hours. Father, mother, sister gone
To movies; Aunt Sade gone away
To intellectual pursuit with spinster friends;
So Homer lived alone on Independence Day.
The thunder grumbled, sky was gray,
The trees were tossing wet.

At four p.m. he walked the porch again,
And in that moment saw a stir—
The movement of some shining hair.
He saw a young girl's figure
On the porch next door.
The shades were part-way down. ...
He limped, he went,
He hadn't gone for two whole weeks,
But now he went; he knew that he was sober;
He could go.

Perhaps he wouldn't say the bitter words again;
Perhaps the satans of his soul would not provoke
A nastiness to plop from off his tongue
Like toads and adders of the fairy tale.

He went—he wanted her
Not as a husband, lover—
All unprepared for that, because
The twisting of his body had disturbed
Maturity within his mind.

But wanting her for comfort, company,
For schoolboy squeak, for moron joke,
For necking in the night, for fudge,
And little games, and notes they'd write;
And later, in a dream, for more important things—
But wanting her to be his guide and marvel now.
He limped upon a lonely planet, limped alone.
He wanted Wilma Jacobson much more
Than any other peace and promise he might name.

The wind blew wet his tufted hair,
The thunder thickened in the clouds—
Contrived a brilliance in the sky—
Exploded ash-cans in the depths of sky.

This was a day of hallowed record:
Lives and fortunes, sacred honor pledged
By nervy youngsters long ago
Who dreaded dark the weeks that lay ahead,
And never knew they made a legend of themselves....
The radicals, the roughs, the rebel hearts
Condemned to pious servitude as proper saints,
Dressed up in lacy cuffs on calendars,
Confused with Jesus, called Conservatives!

This was the day for venerating Valley Forge,
And Paul Revere, and Boston tea, and tricorn hat—
For leaving bloody tracks in long-imagined snow,
For ringing fervent bell in Philadelphia,
For dying on the deck of John Paul Jones,
And snipping stars with Betsy Ross's shears—

The rainy day when Homer Wermels went
To Jacobsons' front porch.
                          Wet day;
Warm day; July; there was no snow
For him to leave his bloody footprints in.

He climbed the steps, he knocked his feet around,
He opened up the screen and gazed at her.
She smiled. He thought she started,
Seeing him. He saw her put a book away;
She slid it underneath a pillow on the swing,
And there were other books around.

"Hello," said Homer.
                    "Well!" she said.
He said, "It's quite a rain and—"
"Yes. My folks are gone—
They went to Cousin Ole's. Gee,
I hope that they're not getting wet!"

God shot His Roman candles
Up among the clouds. The rain came harder.

"What you reading?" Homer said.

"Oh, nothing," and her face was pale.
"Oh, nothing, Homer!" and her voice went high and
    tight.
He moved a little closer, lurching; saw one book
Which lay upon the table top.
He saw the title, read the words:
A Study of Spasticity.

"You reading—?"
And the mucilage was on his chin.
He took his right wrist, wiped the wet away—
"You reading stuff like this?"

"No, no!" she cried. "I wasn't, Homer. Honest!
That's just a book I had— It's just—"

In sultriness he shambled
Up to her. She drew away.
He wouldn't touch her—no, not he!
He didn't want to slap her face,
Or anything like that,
Although she shrank in fear
As if she thought he might.
He burrowed underneath the cushion,
Tore that other book away—
The one she'd hid:
The Brain from Ape to Man.

"You reading books," he said, "like this?
You reading books like this?
This thing; ataxia . . .
So you think, maybe—?"
And he sucked his breath

As if he sucked a distillation
Of a lethal gas instead.

"The Brain
From Ape to Man!
So what? You think I'm kind of like an ape—
A monkey, huh? The hell with you.
I hope you're having lots of fun!
Oh, sure. Keep on, and read some books like this.
Spasticity— It must be fun for you.
Keep on. Amuse yourself!
Buh-buh." He slapped his loose
And shaking fingers at his lip,
And made the legendary sound
Of idiot in obscene tale.

She didn't say a single word.
She couldn't say a single word.
She'd only lived for eighteen years:
Those years had never taught her what to say
At such a time as this.
She put her head down on the seat.
It wasn't pleasant when she cried.
She didn't sob politely, but she bawled.
And when he kept on—jeering, long insulted,
Hating her—she raised a white face, streaming tears.
She shrieked, "Oh, go away!
My God! Why don't you go away?"

He went away. He tottered off next door.
He swore. The toads and adders issued forth
In every word he spat.
He got his raincoat, yammered on the phone
And tried to call a taxicab.
No taxicab.
                    He reeled away
Along the street, forgot his raincoat after all.
And up in heaven, where the powdered Washingtons
And Jeffersons and John Paul Joneses all were gone,
The rockets of the Lord still made
Their thunder sound.

xlv

"HIT ME," said Derry, "light."
 The card flicked out.
 He put his finger on it,
Waited a split second, praying hard.
He had a jack and four-spot in the hole.
He turned the corner of the card.
"A six," he thought at first,
Because he saw it upside down. It wasn't.
It was nine;
And nine and fourteen came to twenty-three.
"Busted," he said in his flat voice.
The dealer took the two blue chips away.

Fred Derry measured close his little stack:
Ten-dollar chips. He had four left.
I'll try them all at once.
No. . . . Wait—try two—
I'll have another chance.
And then he felt a funny hunch;
He saw that blackjack coming fast,
And eagerly he slid the four chips out.
He waited. People on his right were taking cards,
And one went Down for Double.
Derry watched. The fellow won both hands.
Some people had the luck—
The kind of luck he didn't own tonight.

They called it Harry's Smoke House:
Cigarettes were sold in front—
Cigars and drinks. If you were known,
A buzzer thrilled within the door. . . .
This wasn't waving bank-notes with a laugh
Before you faced Infinity,
And saying, Yes, you'd drink that rum-and-coke
As soon as you had lost the wad you owned.
This was a business—weary little round
Of prying small amounts from meager men.

And so Fred shoved it all across the board;
The fresh cards flew.

Fred Derry read his cards:
A ten—a two.
"Hit me," he said.
The queen came out
And slapped him. Thus
The chips were gone.

Fred stood bereft, and watched.
He heard the mutter; heard the wise-cracks made . . .
The big man who was winning, at the end:
"Some days you can't lay up a cent!
Some days you can't lay up—"
He said that, every time he won,
And he had three rich stacks in front of him.

No succulence in all this wealthy world
Was ever made for Fred to taste.
He'd had his luck the year before,
And still another year before.
He was alive. He'd traveled back to Boone,
And traveled back to what?

To what? To Midway Drugs;
And all the nickels that were earned
By other hands for other men;
Translated, on and up the scale,
And melted into dollar bills, and Tens and Fives.
This little increment they'd offered Fred
Each day at ten o'clock:
A canvas bag with printing on,
Stuffed tight with rolls of bills,
And copper, silver, nickel weight.
"You got a gun?" asked Mr. Bullard.
                                        "Yes."
He brought it from his father's house—
A .38. It wasn't much—
An old-style .38,
A nigger-gun, they called it:
Hammerless, short-barreled, mean,
But still wet-oiled,
And able still to kill a man as dead
As tommy-gun could kill him.

Strong-armed to guard
The crumpled, jingling food of this his firm,

He put the canvas sack inside another,
Marched into the Cornbelt Bank,
And stowed the stuff away.
The entries in the little book;
The checks, the paper slips . . .
He leaned beside the window, wishing often
That this loveliness belonged to him.
They'd give him back a hundred bright new bills,
A hundred more in paper rolls—
He'd take them to the Midway Drugs again,
And Mr. Luce would welcome them.

Each Saturday
Fred got his thirty-seven-fifty.

Now, here at Harry's, slot machines
Stood silent and unused along the wall.
Fred wandered over, dredged his pocket out;
He took two quarters, put them in.
He pulled the lever, saw the lemons
Whirl and stop; he saw the bells go by.
He wondered vaguely . . .
Yes, his rent was paid—
Except for laundry, phone calls—stuff like that.
He'd paid it up to Saturday,
And this was Wednesday night.
He could take twenty-seven dollars—
He could take all his worldly wealth—
And try to earn his losings back.
                              Oh, no,
It wouldn't work. He had to eat.

Fred went away. The water lay
In fresh black pools, with bloom of lights
That smiled upon the surface. There was still
The mutter of more storm to come,
More squibs to fizzle in the damp,
And pin-wheels of the Lord lit up
To honor Independence Day.
Fred went dull-wounded to his den,
He crossed the greasy lobby tiles,
He asked the night clerk for the key.

"Say, Mr. Derry. Here's a man—"
He pointed.

Now the man was getting up.
He wore a raincoat, had a wet hat
In his hand.
                    "Are you Fred Derry?"
                                        "Yes."
"I got a present for you here."
He put a paper in Fred's hand,
And went away.

"I'm sorry," whispered dry the clerk.
"I hope it ain't a judgment or a—"
Derry held the thing unfolded,
Saw the rows of type, and names
Inserted on the form.
                    He read.

All bright elation in the world
Began to shine around him.
This thing, this very simple thing,
This lovely thing... the processes of law...
"Oh, boy," he told the clerk,
"This isn't hard to take!
I'm getting a divorce. I mean, she is!"
He heard the words come banging out
And didn't try to stop them.
Still the old man stared.
"It says if I don't come to court
They'll hold me in default,
And give her the divorce.
Willco! I mean, will not!
I'll never go."

He crossed the lobby, liberated.
Air outside smelled thin as tonic, tasty as
A nutmeg crust. The ginger of his strong young years
Was on his tongue... he licked it, swallowed it with
     joy.

"Somehow I'm freer than I felt before;
I'm free for something, something great and good.
Oh, boy. I'll talk to Peggy.
God, I'm dizzy. I don't care.
Oh, God, it's barely after nine.
There's time. I'm going there."

With rubber underneath his feet,
With springs that sank and spread within his heels.
He moved...gigantic strides...
No more the doleful rat, no more the alley-Tom.
He was a buck. The antlers shivered on his head;
And lightning shivered in the sky.

Fred found a cab, and headed west.
The driver talked about the weather;
Derry didn't want to talk.
But still he grinned.
                              Oh, now that dawn
Had burst...some kind of dawn...
So what? He didn't have a job;
He'd get one somehow, toil inspired...
Nervous, crazy, grinning to himself,
And feeling thunder was applause
For this, his happy madness,
Thus he rode. He knew the way.
The map she'd made was in his heart.
So many things had held him back:
Fear, shame, uncertainty, suspicion—
And now in ecstasy he shook them off,
And told the driver where to go.

"Out west on Grand.
You cross the Elk Creek bridge—
At Highway 17 you swing to right."
"Oh, sure," the driver said.
"That's where you go to Highland."
"Yes, the road to Avalon.
You turn right once again,
Across the tracks beyond the river—
Up the hill—the first place on the left.
They've got a sign."

                              A swinging placard
Like the sign of any inn in Bedfordshire.
The driver stopped,
And water dripped from trees,
And still the lightning sped
In open wonder up above the western hills.
Two-twenty-five. Fred Derry paid.
He gave the driver thirty cents.
He wished that he could make it more.

The taxi turned and fled away.
Fred didn't know how he'd get home.
Perhaps (he smiled in his conceit)
Perhaps she'd drive him home.

His feet crushed sodden gravel of the drive,
And then he saw the cars:
Black, brown and gray and green—
The pleasant cars—coupés, sedans—
It might have been a country club.
They sat in phalanx all before the door,
They rested tires on the grass.
The house was gleaming, gay with lights;
Fred heard the Capehart playing—Artie Shaw—
He recognized the tune.
He stood, and felt his eagerness dissolving,
Draining out through fingertips.
He went on, slowly.

Clear, sweet the windows spread their glow,
And scent of summer everywhere. . . .
A light still shone upon the porch:
Perhaps more guests?
                                   Oh, wait—
Please, wait (he tried to tell himself),
It isn't her, it's just her folks.
They've got some friends. They've got—

MacDuff appeared,
All wet and rowdy in his fur.
He made a *woof*,
And Derry spoke the Scotty's name.
The dog came on, he wagged around
And shook his bell, and made some marks
On Derry's trouser-leg. The Scotty led the way—
A fat and gusty little guide,
Who took Fred to the side and let him see
A merriment he might not share.

No shades drawn down in windows of that house:
They did not hide their living from the owls and mice
Who sat as chaperons amid the shade.
O handkerchiefs with happy lace—
O little slipper toes—
O laugh that ran around the room!

Fred Derry stood, a tired tramp, a mendicant
Who held his hat, and asked the world to take
The pencils out, and put the pennies down.
He looked. The windows stood ajar, turned on their
    hinges.
All filled with life and glow, the room beyond:
The eager lamps, the flowers in their sheaves,
The girls who crossed their pretty legs
And pulled their dresses down.
The men with glasses in their hands,
And others, dancing in the hall beyond.
The uniforms, the rare civilian suits,
The wisp of red chiffon
That one girl dangled from her hand.
The hubbub and the talk.
Secure their youth, if not their lives—secure their pride,
And clear and proper-tuned their song.
Fred Derry saw and heard it all.

In loathing, he disturbed the scene—
In full repugnance visualized himself
Led in politely through the door,
And introduced to peerless company
He'd seen in *Town and Country, Spur,* and *Country
    Life*
When he put parasitic eyes, in other years,
Against the glossy pages of the magazines.
Ah, this was it, translated into terms of Boone:
Not rich as Newport; never smart
As fabled drawing-rooms he'd read about
In far resorts, in bigger towns—
Yet essence of a life he'd never dare to claim . . .
Not he, who'd hauled the washings on his cart,
And seen his grandma pour the bluing out,
And plant her board beneath the steaming suds
To launder linen for the families of these.

He saw the girl he'd come to see.
He heard the skip and patter of her feet,
The viol of her voice.
He saw her beauty . . . slightest V of shadow
Marking breasts he'd dreamt that he might kiss
In future joy.
           He couldn't kiss them now.

He didn't have the necessary cash.
He didn't have a sly ambition in his eye,
Or promise in his limbs,
Or strong assurance that a man should have
Before he might enchant a bride like this.

MacDuff still nuzzled by his trouser-leg.
Fred Derry turned.
He twisted up the collar of his coat,
He found the road. The lamps were gone behind,
The little dog was left behind.
Fred Derry strode in blackened wind—
In summer wind, all soaked with breath
Of rich and simple grains that made the land.
He walked a mile, his shoes were sodden;
Mud came through, a chilly paste.
He reached the pavement, turned the way he'd come.
There wasn't any taxicab to take him now.
He walked another mile. A truck slowed down;
Fred got a ride to 46th and Kiowa,
And waited at the corner till a bus came by.

He jolted, watched the weary riders of the bus.
He thought, "I wish those people out at Cherry Hill—
I wish they could have seen the folks
At Flight Lieutenant Grace's house:
That old fat butler with his silver hair,
Air Marshal Ackerson, and all the rest—
That little countess, and the girl who starred in shows,
And all the brass and all the rank. I wish
They could have seen us under tables
When the bombs came by!
By God. One time I lived, one time I lived!"

And so he tried to cry a plaint
Against the only girl he'd ever loved;
He couldn't make it stick.
Deep in a hidden chapel of himself,
He couldn't hate, he couldn't polish up his fangs
To bite in envy and in bitterness.
He only hated his infirmity,
Because he'd come so close to her
And, terrified, had run away.

He found the sour-smelling place
Where he might lay his spirit down, and body too.

Where he might wash himself within the stained old tub,
And wipe his shoes, and set them out to dry,
And see the ruin of the suit he'd worn.
He snapped the light, he flung the window up,
And heard new water rinsing rust
From off the iron ladder in the court.

So tense and nervous, that it seemed he'd never sleep—
With anger as a bile exploding in his brain,
And rising up each time he drifted off,
To stain and taint the gentler thoughts he'd have—

Fred slept. He found his refuge in a dream,
A danger that made life and death
Two years before, when all the air
Was rugged with dismay.
Once more he walked a cinder road
Beside revetments. Still again
He hurled the darts, he shook the snooker cue.
He rode his bicycle,
And passed beside the door of Squadron Operations.
Still again he got his canvas bag;
He tried the mask and made it fit,
And put his body into flying clothes;
He wore the Mae West once again,
And twisted hooks of harness on his thighs.
He swung up through the hatch; the hatch was closed.
They shook and ambled on perimeter,
And voices crackled on the inter-phone,
And once again he made his bomb run,
Saw the soapy clouds. . . .
And more than that: the mystery of vanishment
Had swallowed up too many people whom he loved.

xlvi

UP THERE on oxygen,
   Up above everywhere,
     Ten of you trained and projected for bombing,
Wrapped in your mission and in dural metal:
Eighth Air Force Bombers—the Heavy Command.

Secret the numbers of Wing and of Squadron:
Busy with guns.... Let us open the breeches
Of the big Fifties, the hardy machine guns—
Let us go back to the Gunnery School.

First Position Stoppage:
Failure to feed,
Failure to fire.
(Did you burn up, Bailey?)
Broken the striker,
Broken the firing-pin
Or broken the firing-pin extension,
Or broken the belt-holding pawl arm.

Faulty ammunition,
Faulty this or that;
A broken sear;
Something jimmed or broken:
The good clean steel
That never before had broken, and now broke
And let that single Messerschmitt come in.

No one at fault. Not you.
Not another one of the gunners,
Nobody back at the Base,
None of the ground crew.
No one who helped you vicarious—
No one who wished you victorious—
Nor the man nor the woman back in the States
Who constructed that piece for the gun.
(Did you burn, was it you,
The chute on fire?)

So this was the way: I shall tell how it happened,
As others hard-eyed of the Squadron observed.
Now wisely I tell you, young Bailey, I tell you
You could never observe, you were busy as hell!
Still flying behind in such perfect formation,
Not far from the wing-tips of others that flew—
The bombing run done, and the bomb-bay wide open,
The blockbusters puffing in patterns beneath—
Down into that mix-up, that mingled illusion
Where dozens of bursts had already appeared.

Then the swoop, and the fighter deflecting on in—
O swift like a fish, he is trout coming in,

Drawn taut by the line of his own tracer-bullets—
An ME 1-10, with his two engines mooing:
And so he got in, and he put all his Twenties,
He put his death into the B-17.

So you turned, lazy-daisy, all ten of you people,
The living and dead, with four engines asleep,
And one of them stringing its wet-wash of flame.
(Did you burn, and if not you,
Who was it that burned)?
Flame hanging across, torn behind you in laundry:
Slips of fire, skirts, scarfs and a kerchief of flame.
While everyone else went away, went away,
Still keeping invincible in their formation,
Conducting their war by immutable rule.
And you gentlemen turned, jumbled round,
The ball-turret transformed to mid-upper.
And endless you hung there
Before the B-17 started on down.

Did you burn, did you burn up, O Bailey the Kid?
One of you went with all haste to the ground.
Seven white parachutes, now morning-glories
(Lilies of France on the Fourth of July
Over Nantes, the poor city. O lilies of France,
O sorrowing prisoner, swallowing tears).
The chutes they were magic, and fair morning-glories.

But one was on fire: a little flame chewing,
Eating the glossiest silk of the chute.
Who was it had waited not near long enough?
Who let his hand tremble too eager and wild?
Who managed his handle too soon, so the cord
Tossed open the fabric to kiss the high fire?
Somebody's chute was a little red rose—
Somebody's chute and his life were a crumple,
Little black crumple, all the way down—
Twenty-two thousand feet deep into Nantes.
Six of you wistful and six of you sailing,
Sailing and swinging,
All the way down, four full miles to the ground.
Bailey. Who burned?

This is the way that I think of you always:
Cocky and walking untrammeled and quick.

This is the way I shall see you forever:
Tough face and monkey-mouth wrinkled and pert.
Leather arms swaying, you walk at the Base,
Dingy gold bars on the loops of your jacket;
Childish forever you swagger and sing.
Always your cot with its rumpled gray blanket,
Always your pin-ups with lingerie leer,
Always your silken-limbed blondes on the wall,
Always your tongue running loose, and some fellow
Hauling you off of the bed on your fanny,
All the way down to the floor with a bump.

All the way down
To that checkerboard Nantes!
(Tell me, O Bailey, who burned?)
All the way down to the barbed-wire fences—
You, who said, "*Heil!*" for a comical greeting—
Down to the *Achtung!* and *Blitzspiel* you gabbled.
Six of you drifting, three dead in the ship,
Or battered so badly they couldn't bail out,
And another, lone flower, a-burning.

Somewhere forever among the cloud strata,
Somewhere aloft of the patterns and railroads,
Off there we bomb, and go bombing persistent.
Off there, a Mystic, you look up and hear us—
Secret and shapeless, named Missing In Action....
Ask for the news, and I'll willingly tell you:
Driscoll has salted down twenty-two missions;
Webb has done his, he is through, he is Home—
Drawling tall Webb, with his souvenir pistol,
He is alive and is gone back to Texas.
Springstun's still with us, and Bower, and Greene,
Whisky and Whiskers are living with Greene,
Barking and wagging back under his bed;
He gives them food in an old peanut can.
Otis is with you, and with you is Scott,
With you in blankness, with you in your limbo.
Bailey—who burned?

So I will think, sitting silent in Briefing,
So I will wonder in looking at maps:
How did it happen, the thing that has happened?
Now I shall utter in whispers the Failures:
How did that Messerschmitt do it to you?

Second Position: the broken ejector . . .
Incorrect oil-buffer setting, or bolt-track
Burred and distorted to stop the smooth cartridge,
Or—Third Position—the burred cantileer. . . .
Still, he came up and he burst your hot engines,
All of his shells in the nose and the gas-tanks,
All of his death in your B-17.

Hitler was shouting, ten years were forgotten:
Chancellor new of the *Reichstag* and *Reich.*
You, in the limitless void of Kentucky,
Played with your bombs on the Fourth of July.
Hitler remote, just a name in the papers—
Papers you never would read at your age.
You were nine, you were ten,
And you liked to read funnies. . . .

Fourth of July: and you yell in Kentucky,
Shoot off your crackers and frighten the cats;
Wait for the rockets in dusk, and the candles,
Sparklers and flower-pots. Then you would sleep.
(I did not know you from Adam, Child Bailey,
Ten years ago.)
Then you would sleep with your yellow hair mussy—
Dream of the finger you fried with torpedoes—
Dream of the cap pistol popping so proudly,
And of the cherry bombs burst in a garden. . . .
Old Mrs. Allen . . . you frightened her cat
Ten years ago.
                    Go to sleep in the past,
Bailey the Kid, on the Fourth of July.
But where sleep you now with the imps in your spirit?
And who was it died in the B-17?
And who was it dented the deck with his nostrils,
When his parachute blossomed with flame over Nantes?
Over Nantes, over France on the Fourth of July,
Bailey . . . who burned?

xlvii

THIS nation used Fred Derry in the war,
   This nation found him powerful and wise
   In conduct of his portion of the war.
This nation gave him money, dressed him proud—
The rank, the choice display of ribbonwear.
This nation didn't use him well at Home
 (Or so at last Fred thought he'd come to see)
Nor found him worthy of a decent price.

And still Fred Derry knew his worth
(He was the best.
All of Fred Derry's past and future
Bound in Fred)
And he could cut the pattern he'd been taught,
And pin it fast upon the goods
That lay before him now: upon Boone City goods,
And take his sharpened shears
And cut the image of a war on Boone.

He'd make attack—
He'd do a private mission now—
The last he'd manage in this hateful town.
Alone, exalted, wholly dangerous,
All set at last to grimly grab
The luxury he felt he'd earned
And never had received since he came Home.
Alone and roaring with the punch of wind,
Absorbing strong the shock of altitude,
As on a single time when he rode tail . . .
All amputated from the rest
And not united now by any cord of inter-com,
And breathing oxygen in heavy whiffs . . .
Rare drug distilled with oxygen
And carried in a tank that others couldn't tap.
He swallowed it, he breathed it in.

Alone, alone and stepping off in space,
The way he'd done the one time he bailed out
And lay awhile in empty clouds
Before the chute suspended him,

He'd walk alone for good and all.
He couldn't have the life he sought,
He couldn't own the woman whom he wanted;
Oh, rather leave this life for good and all
And make a new one in the stratosphere!

It wasn't death.
He'd never contemplated self-abuse like that—
No more did he embrace the notion now.
He was too much alive,
Too able and too sharp;
He liked to eat too well
And make a love, and drink,
And catch the whir of living in his ears,
Its odor in his nose,
And let his eyes rove challenging.

It wasn't death,
Unless he had hard luck.

Then rising, dressing, opening the drawer,
And taking out the gun—the .38—
And touching whiskers on his chin,
And going in to shave. And getting out the bag,
And taking from among his ties and handkerchiefs
A cash-sack from the Cornbelt Bank
That he'd misplaced one day, and found again,
And never carried to the Midway Drugs.
He'd kept it—never knowing why.
But now he knew.
And if they wanted bombing here in Boone,
He'd give them all they wanted, on the nose.

And folding up his uniform and cap,
And putting on a khaki shirt and tie to match;
And conning, cannily and well,
Each pattern, icy-blooded, of the plot he made;
And taking notebook from a drawer,
And printing on its page in clear, bold capitals
(No matter if a fear had jellied both his lips
And made him dumb)—

"This is a stick-up. I'm not kidding, Mr. Dunn.
I know each move you have to make.
Don't make an extra move.
Count out ten thousand in small bills:

Fives, tens or twenties.
Put them in this sack.
Then wait five minutes
After you give me the sack.
Don't move for five more minutes.
Do your job. Don't leave the cage.
Don't touch that button. You are being watched.
My partner's watching you
For five more minutes."

He'd estimated Dunn.
Of all the tellers, Fred picked him.
One who was too nervous wouldn't do.
Nor would a man too dumb to catch the drift—
A man who'd think that this was just a joke.

The goof named Dunn should be the one:
Not nervous, but the kind that you could scare.
He'd do exactly what you wanted him to do
When you were holding death before his eyes.
Dunn had a wife and kid. He knew the ropes,
And how that cash was all insured;
Dunn wasn't anybody's hero.

...The crowd—the 5th Street crowd,
On this hot day that followed on a holiday—
A crowd to wrap around him like a cloak.
The alley to the Hotel Seneca,
Two short blocks down—
The little room behind the elevator shaft,
Where mops and brooms were kept,
And no one ever went, except the scrubbing folks at
     night—

Fred Derry was a weasel on the stairs.
He ran light-footed, never met a soul;
He left his suitcase with the brooms and mops.
He trod the alley trail he'd tread again;
He'd be civilian as long as he was thief—
And then revert to Air Force officer
When once his thievery was done,
For he could go away, away,
In uniform to give him anonymity—
Good green and pink disguise
For nightmare banditry...

So many other 1st lieutenants
Wandered up and down this weary land.

The sun came clean, the buildings didn't sway,
The people didn't move.
Fred thought that not a wheel of traffic turned....
Suspended, chilled, entranced, immovable,
Boone City's life stood silent, waiting him,
As up the alley, down the street he turned.

He saw the heavy clock above the entrance.
Doors stood open, wide.
The only life that lived for Fred
Was in the Cornbelt Bank;
And there the people whirled,
They seemed to waltz and glide
By dozens and by hordes.
A hot day after holiday:
With docile lines before each window—
Women, men, depositing and drawing out.
And so would Derry draw his money from the bank—
His printed, rich reward....
Engraved the visages of Lincoln, Jackson, Hamilton,
Engraved the little fronds,
And numbers stamped in green!

"Long, long ago," Fred Derry might have said,
"I put this wealth to wait me here.
I earned it bit by bit and day by day,
I earned it with my terror,
With my secret blood;
I earned it in my shift
In awful factory where death
Was manufactured by the ton,
Sold dear, delivered here and there—
I was my own deliveryman!
I put the wealth away—
My fingers cold inside their gloves—
They counted nickel, dime and dollar,
Profit, surplus, bonus, wage,
Deposited when war was my assembly line.
On days and nights I did my overtime!"

And slyly in his soul he smiled,
(But never wiggling his mouth)

To know how he had made a nest-egg for a rainy day,
And now he'd have that egg served up to him.
"Too bad," he thought, "you foolish folk of peace—
Too bad that you will never understand!
Too bad, perhaps, for you
That you have never died
Your busy little deaths the way I have.
Too bad for you: you raised me up so strong,
And taught me that I must survive,
And taught me worthiness
That none of you admits is worthy now."

O grille, O glass, O desk, O icy door,
O name-plate made of bronze—
Memorial not to the dead,
But to the walking dead.
O bars, O windows keeping robbers out—

"But they will never keep me out.
I walked in through the door.
I caught the grin the guard gave me.
He'll smile again when I go out;
He'll call me friend;
He'll never spot me for an enemy."

Fred saw the face of Stephenson;
Dark, sullen, grim and taut—
And Stephenson saw him, and bowed.
Fred Derry saw the sergeant trapped;
An evil customer was hounding him—
Enameled white, her thin and foolish face,
And all the diamonds on her wrinkled flesh displayed—
A nausea and hate for such as her
Was rising in Fred's throat.
Oh, Al was captured. Bars had hemmed him in,
The chain was on his leg, and stapled to that desk.
But he, Fred Derry, he'd be free and gone.

He stood in line . . . the cash-sack, notebook
In his hand—his left hand.
His right went deep, and jammed within his coat,
And grew around the metal of the gun.

Eleven people on ahead, and two behind him now.
He waited . . . line went fast, then stopped awhile,

And some, annoyed, went off to other lines.
Now there were six ahead.

"I briefed myself," he thought.
"So how's the weather? Good.
And how's the wind above the target?
Not so bad. . . .
No, no. I have no escort: 47's, Spits—
No 38's or 51's are saving me."

He saw the inside clock, with ornamented hands
That turned in solemn pace,
But never seemed to turn.
And he was Home. And coming Home to what?
And coming Home to this!
To gather up the life that he had saved,
And breathe upon it softly, walk away
And vanish in the days and nights to come.

"So what's the cue?
And where's the queue?
Ah, here it is; and I am part of it—
Queued-up as I have been so many times before—
Queued-up for mess, for bus rides, for PX,
For King's Cross trains, for papers, telephones,
For shots, for cherries in the street.
And I am regulated to the quick; I know
The queuing ways as well
As any shacked-up, HQ major buying meat
To take home to his babe from Selfridge's!"

And four between him and the window now:
Three men, one girl. . . . Fred lifted feet.
He put his feet ahead, he moved again.
He heard the chatter of the teller in his cage.
The dismal little voice; the *How are you?*
The talk of holiday, and how
The customer had spent it.
                              Three ahead.
And later, later there were only two.

And one ahead: one man.
Fred Derry held the cash-sack tight,
But now unscrewed his fingers from the cloth,
And from the binding of the notebook—

Saw the moisture there. So this was sweat?
He hadn't known that he was sweating . . .
Hadn't known . . . all concentration, chill intent.
The target was a window just beyond.
Come in at twenty-seven thousand.
How's the flak?
The teller saw him—nodded, smiled,
And kept on counting money for the other man.
The gun, the gun—
His pocket was as deep
And roomy as a flour sack.
Each finger weighed a thousand pounds,
And there was concrete hardening his jaws.
He wouldn't say a word—
Just shove the notebook in.

A screech went up—a piercing yell—
A cougar-cry among the cages.
Derry felt his fingers on the gun;
He thought he'd shot someone.
He turned; the woman screeched again;
And everyone had turned . . . the bobbing heads,
The staring eyes, the spectacles that gleamed
In shocked amazement. So the world had ended here,
Here in the Cornbelt Bank. At crack of doom
The beasts were loose, the seals were torn away,
And Revelation opened with its noise.

Men started up from desks, and women rose
With papers in their hands.
The guard was hurrying.
But Fred saw only Stephenson, who strode,
Who glared, whose face seemed black-and-blue.
It was as if he'd bared his teeth
While clutching on his gun—
The way Fred Derry'd felt his own lips drawn
And twisted, iron cast beneath his rubber mask
When jets, when 2-6-2's attacked.

Behind the bar, beside the desk of Stephenson,
The witch was holding her hysteria.
Her hands were shaking—
Glassy stones and glassy nails—
The light descried her there.
Her eyes were rolling in her head,

Her voice was shrilling, wire-thin:
"No one has ever talked to me like that
In all my life!"

Al Stephenson turned by the gate.
He shot his words across the desks between:
"It's high time that they did!"

He turned again; his eyes met Fred's;
And Stephenson advanced in rapid pace,
He seemed to come a mile before he jerked
Fred's arm, and drew him from the line.

"Come on, come on!" said Stephenson,
"I'm getting out of here."
Al swung, he leaned his weight.
"Come on," he said again, in lower voice
Beside Fred Derry's ear. "I'm sorry . . .
Let's get out of here. Let's go!
I left my hat—the hell with it.
I'm never coming back."

Fred Derry walked, impelled, and drawn away
As if a truck were taking him,
For Stephenson was half again as big as he.
The desks and windows reeled, the people leered
And gaped. The witch cried carnival behind.
The door was wide, and sun was on the world;
The street noise rang and whistled;
They were in the air.

xlviii

I BLEW my top," said Stephenson—
Not Stephenson the banker: Stephenson, GI.

"I'm tough. I'm Tarzan. . . . Hero! Boy, that's me.
I'm not afraid of anything. Can lick my weight
In wildcats. No, I'm not afraid
Of Mrs. Jenninger. I'm What-a-Man!
A poor old bag like that—a mangy hag—

But Stephenson the Fearless did his stuff!
He ought to get another Silver Star today."

The tap-room of the Black Hawk Club;
Ten-forty-five a.m., and no one else around.
The calm mulatto answered to the name of Nat;
He went behind the bar, and came with ice,
And bourbon—soda—
                    "Thanks.
Just leave the bottle, Nat."
He left the bottle, shuffled soft away;
And Stephenson was counting bubbles bitterly,
And Derry staring blank against the wall
Where Custer and his cavalry found faded death,
And yelling Sioux found faded victory,
And all achieved an alcoholic immortality.

"I'm sorry that I pulled you out of line.
But still, I had to talk— I saw you standing there
And wanted you to have a drink with me.
I'm sorry, Derry . . . just a little balmy.
Please excuse. And please to have
Another drink?"
                    The 7th Cavalry
Was fighting hard, but losing scalps
Before Fred Derry's foggy eyes.

"I'm sorry—taking up your time," said Al.
"I guess you've got a new job. Where?"

"I haven't got a job."

"But in the bank—? You had a cash-sack—?
What the hell," said Al, "forget it.
Just let me go on and on. You're not compelled
To listen; but I've got to talk.
Too bad," he said, "it had to be that woman.
Should have been a heavyweight—a male
With feathers on his chest—so I could brag.
Too bad!" he said, and took another drink,
And shook his head.
                    Poor Yellow Hair—
The Indians were ganging on him still.

"I blew my top," said Stephenson.
"Then I got up; I saw you standing in the line.

I'd seen you all the time and I kept thinking—
That first day, when we came here
From Welburn in the plane—
And that first night at Butch's when we talked—
You know the score. I had to talk to you—
A guy who knows the score—
If there had been a man from my platoon,
I would have talked to him.
I had to talk to you," said Sergeant Stephenson.

"Derry," said Stephenson. "My father—he was swell—
I guess he had me wrong.
I guess I've had myself all wrong since I came back.
I thought that I could take it;
Well, I couldn't. So it's happened now.
I'm out like—who is it, that you say
In Air Corps slang?"

"Like Flout," said Derry.
Still he had the gun;
It lay in hidden heaviness
Against the cushion next to him.
He didn't try to use it on the Indians.

"Look here," said Al, "when you came in the bank
Perhaps you noticed— Did you see that woman?
Mrs. Jenninger? You've heard of her—"
"The rich one?" Derry asked.
And Stephenson was nodding:
"Yes, she's rich; she's rotten rich;
You see her in the papers: always on committees,
Always reformation, councils, causes,
Always leagues for this-or-that.
Her husband—patent medicine.
Before he died he made the fortune—"

Al Stephenson spat out the tip of his cigar.
"I couldn't help it. Christ, I hate a scene.
I guess my father's turning over in his grave.
The hell with it; it can't be helped.

"She came to me, this Mrs. Jenninger;
She crapped around, she talked about her nephew:
Twenty-two—from engineers. He came back Monday.
So his aunt— They had a row.

I guess he hasn't any people other than his aunt.
The nephew married some young girl
Whom Auntie never liked.
She said she wouldn't give him any money—
Not one cent; that she'd attach
Some other funds he should have had.
Perhaps she could—it's problematical.

"Well, anyway, the kid from engineers—
He took a wife; the girl whom Auntie didn't like—
He married her on Tuesday at the City Hall.
He has a job; and they were planning for a home.
He told his aunt, 'O.K., you keep your dough.
Marcella has a little—I have some—
We'll borrow more, and buy the house we want.'

"I guess that's more or less the tale . . .
She came in—Mrs. Jenninger—
She told me that her nephew possibly would try
To use the GI Bill of Rights
And swing a loan to buy himself that house.
She said I mustn't grant the loan.
As Mrs. Jenninger, who felt she owned
At least two notches of the Cornbelt Bank,
She told me what to do, and what to say,
And how to spank her nephew on my knee!
I bit my tongue; I couldn't talk to her.
By God. It got me suddenly—the selfishness,
The hate, the bitterness, the triviality . . .
You know, beside the processes
Of life and death, they're pretty small.
And then she talked about that league they've got—
She's something: national vice-president,
Or national committeewoman—something—
'The Friends of Liberated Germany.'
Oh, certainly, she'd give her cash
To help the Krauts, but not the kid!
And all because his girl had slept with him
Before he went away, and Auntie didn't bless the bed.

"I can't recall exactly
What I said. But I let loose.
And when I talked to her,
It seemed I wasn't talking just to her,
But to the whole gang—everyone

Who doesn't know, who doesn't understand:
Old Prew, and Latham, Steese, and Mr. Milton too—
The people at the bank. 'They'll never mind,
They'll never mind!' Just like your song.
The people in the houses everywhere . . .
The people having things they couldn't have
If certain kids had not gone out
And had their balls shot off . . .
And owning this and owning that,
And hanging on to this and that . . .

"By God, I knew it suddenly:
That I would have to speak my mind,
And tell her off—and everybody else,
And tell them how we feel, and what we think,
And how we hit the beaches over there,
And how the Germans blew the roads away,
And how our engineers dug out the mines,
And lost their hands and feet and heads
To try to make a way for us to walk. . . .
The chlorinated water, and the itch,
And living like a dog, and dirtier
Than any dog; and having crabs and lice
Crawl round among your private parts;
And climbing, climbing in the rocks
Until you didn't know your name, or who
Your mother was. You didn't care.
And seeing kids with eyes that haunted you,
And hearing women cry, and smelling rotten men,
And having headache . . . little voices in your head,
In whispers.
                'Go to hell. I hate you—
Every bastard in the world who has it soft—
Who doesn't know what I have known!
I hate you all, because you aren't a part of this,
Because you'll never care about the ones who die.'

"You know the names; you had yours too;
And I know mine: there's Pascowitz, and Meade,
And Rosenberg, and Hancock—guys like that. . . .
Let's have another drink."

Fred Derry rose; he stood,
And Stephenson looked up with challenge, wondering.
And Derry whispered, "Thanks a lot

But I won't have another drink.
There's something else—I've got it in my pocket.
Here."
        He brought the notebook out.
"I stood in line, you dragged me loose
Before I reached the window...
Dragged me out, and here I am.
I didn't do it, but I would have done it.
Now I can't. I'll never try again.
I had myself all briefed, and I was ready."

"Christ sake, Derry,
What on earth—?"

"Right here," said Derry. "Here it is.
It's all in here—this notebook.
Does it look just like a cash deposit book?
Well, not exactly. Anyway, that's what it was.
That's what I mean: not cash deposit—cash withdrawal.
Here, you read it." Then he went away
And left the stick-up note
For Stephenson to read.

xlix

AND SO your brain has gone from man to ape,
        And like an ape you've huddled in your cage.
        You've drugged and fed yourself,
You've chewed the yellow fruit,
And swallowed down the nuts that people tossed
Because they found you singular—
Because they held compassion for your captive state,
And thought you most afflicted in your cage.
They chortled when you climbed upon the swing,
Or put the water bucket on your head!

And so, the mandrill pose,
The baboon crouch have tired you;
But you have been asleep,
And now awaken stiff within your den.

The den is Papa Pappas's café,
With all-night lights
To probe the murk of 2nd Street.
You wake and sigh. The morning sun comes in.
It tries to melt your arm, to soften
Every kink that prisons it.

You sit erect; your arm flies out
And spills the salt, the paper napkin, glass.
And Papa Pappas mutters by the coffee urn;
He sends young Bill . . . the greasy paws
Are kind as nurse's hands.
"It's nine o'clock. You want some coffee now?"
You shake your head. You try to say, "No coffee,"
Make a sound. And young Bill shrugs;
He moves the table things,
He makes them right again.
And Papa calls across the solemn heads
Of brakemen eating chili at the bar:
"Hey, kid, it's nine o'clock.
You better go. You got a home?
Your mamma, she will want you, kid.
You better go."

You rise and stagger, walk.
The stuff is dry upon the sweater front—
The stuff you spilled
From out your aching innards, hours gone.
You lurch against the grimy glass
And fumble for your change.
"How much?" you say. "How much I owe?"
"No, kid," says Papa Pappas. "You have pay.
Remember? You come in and eat at four o'clock,
When you get sick—?" He snaps his fingers.

Up above the pyramids of breakfast food:
The photograph . . . his other son
Who died in dust of Iwo months ago.
And Papa knows nobility you owned;
He's seen your ribbons, knows about the Oerlikon,
The JU 88's. He's fed you more than once,
And let you sleep against the table top;
He's wiped the vomit off your chin.
He says, "Goodbye, old kid. You come back soon."
He waves you on.

You walk your plank
Amid the noise of 2nd Street. You go
To finish up the march you've made,
To take a last long swing on your trapeze.

The brain, from ape to man,
And man to ape—
It hurts you worse than it might hurt
Orang-outang or chimpanzee.
It bubbles, stews and swells,
And forces you to prance a path
More staggered than you ever walked before.
A taxicab? No. No. Not 2nd Street—
No taxicabs at nine a.m.
The busses roar, the trucks are loud,
And blue exhaust comes out to smother you.
The sun is wicked. Where is Home?
And what is Home? And why should you go there?

You cock your head,
You leer and squint. . . . The sky?
No 88's. No friendly Cats patrolling in a song.
The deck is never docile underfoot,
The overhead is pushing tight,
The bulkheads sway,
And all the street is one long ladder.
You would climb it, holding rungs,
But rungs dissolve beneath your hands today.

Somehow you've climbed without a rung to squeeze;
You're on another deck;
You see the sign you've seen before—
The old marquee with broken bulbs—
The Hotel Seneca.
You have a friend. He has a bed.
You're feeling sick again,
And—like the victim in the song
That entertainers sang in hospital—
You're poisoned. *Mother, mother . . .*
Eels and eel broth. Poisoned . . .
Far above there is a bed,
And you would fain lie down, lie down, lie down.

You clutch and shrivel by the desk.
The old clerk talks:
"No, it ain't here—the key.

I haven't seen him going out.
I guess that Mr. Derry's still upstairs."
You stagger in, past sliding doors
(Yes, yes, a cage— Gorilla in a cage.
The awful, angry brain—
From ape to man)—
The colored fellow takes you up;
Old cables creak and bang.
The door slides open . . . stagger out,
And navigate the hall,
And reel against the door.
You've wandered here before—
And you would fain lie down, lie down.

The lock unturned . . . no key, no bolt
To bar you out. You go inside.
(The mighty, kindly friend you had—
He isn't here. You don't know where he's gone,
Nor do you care.)
You pitch across the bed.
The tide of many oceans carries you . . .

. . . Takes you so far, and brings you back.
The lighters touch upon the landing stage,
The bos'n whistles, winches hum,
The chains are rattling round.
And motors in the sky above
Begin their menace. *Battle Stations* blares,
The buzzer: *rark-rark-rark,*
And running feet go fast and far.
You hang behind your gun again;
You hold the grips; you sink your hands
Within the wadded pillows on the bed.

Fred Derry tries to talk to you.
"I was asleep," you say.
You watch him slyly. Maybe he
Has felt his brain revert?
Ah, maybe he has mandrill manners
Waiting in his hide?
Long, long remote, your voice is piteous,
But recognized, transmitted back to you
By both your burning ears:
                              "You got
A suitcase. Are you going off somewhere?"

He's nodding. Yes, he's going far.
And you will be bereft, and left within your cage,
Abandoned in the zoo. He's going far. He says he is.
Does he need money? Derry hasn't any job.
He doesn't get a hundred-fifty every month.
You bring your money out:
The crumpled, torn and tired bills.
You want to give him money. Why should you
Have all this dough, and he have none?
He laughs; he shakes his head and swears;
He shoves you back across the bed.

You watch. Your brain is simian and wild.
You think that you'll get up
And swing upon the chandelier,
Or peel bananas...make him laugh...
Or solemn in your toes you'll take
The peanut, if he'll only throw it.
Now he reaches in his pocket—
Peanuts?
          No, he has a black revolver.
Funny...Derry with a gun.
You feel that you must ask him—
Ask the calibre. And has he got a job?
Is he a guard somewhere, and bearing that revolver?
You'd ask, if you might make your jaws behave.
They won't behave. You never ask. You lie and look.

He says it's laundry that he wants. He meditates,
And jingles coins upon his palm.
He swears again. The laundry at the desk downstairs—
He never got it, he explains—
They won't deliver to the room—
He has to get the laundry—pay for it.
And all these things he tells to you—
The paltry information you will never heed.

He vanishes, and you are sick,
And you would fain lie down.

But half of you is lying on the bed,
And half is going for the gun,
So clear, intent, with confidence
You've never known, in all confusion of the months
Since last you bounced, alert and sound,
Upon a slushy sea.

And saying now,
> Farewell, farewell,
To Wilma, Mother and Aunt Sade,
To Father and Luella.
> Long farewell
To Mrs. Engle and the lemon pie,
To Butch and Mr. Barleycorn!
Farewell the prom to which you never went;
Farewell the cigarettes; farewell the rum-and-coke.

Now you shall taper off,
And kiss goodbye to each illusion you embraced:
The cowboy dream, the hot flanks heaving sweat;
The ski-flight that you never made;
The trip to Yellowstone you never took;
The nifty night-clubs where you never went;
The New York Yankees that you never saw!
Farewell to travel, and the dollars which you never
    earned—
The country club, where you were never lord—
The shiny car you coveted but never drove!

Now see the eyes, the silky hair
Of formless children, eggs within your flesh
You've never pumped to her you love,
And let them grow to babies in her bulk. . . .
The kiss you never drank, the sleep you never slept,
The elder wisdom that you never cried—
Farewell! And stand stock-still
 (If you can manage it)
And let yourself become eternal.
Turn yourself to stone,
And press the muzzle up against your head.

l

THE GATE went click and latch, the elevator sang.
Fred Derry walked the hall,
A package in his hands.

The elevator'd gone two floors below,
And he was only ten feet from his door
When sound exploded in the room.
That one report, so final,
Puffing short . . . the thick old walls to case it in.
An accident . . . while still his ears consumed
The echo of the gun.
"He's had an accident! He shot it off—"
Fred Derry swam through space,
Broke loose the brief impediment
Of yards and lengthy inches strewn between,
And doorknob wrenching all too slow,
And door that banged
Against a chair as he crashed in.

Fred Derry smelled the powder which had burned,
And saw the frizzled place on Homer Wermels' head,
Where black the flame had scorched his hair.
And he saw Homer writhing, twisting,
Managing once more to get the gun aloft
And stiffen well his frame this time,
No matter how his left arm tried to fly away.

Fred went across, he went around, he didn't know—
He tussled loose the gun
Before it might discharge again.
And Homer snorted, made his monkey cry,
And one big bubble blew from out his nose
And tears intensified with fury
Flew from out his eyes—
He slobbered, moaned; his breath was hot as hate,
As Derry flung him hard upon the bed.

He lifted once—
He raised well up, upon his hands,
Then buried face. . . . His shoulders shook.
The powder flash still seemed to smolder,

Fry within his hair.
>   Fred bent and looked.
The bullet hadn't even split the scalp.
Fred raised his eyes. No, not the ceiling—
There. The bathroom door:
A hole that penetrated . . .
Flattened, pitted deep within a broken tile,
Bedraggled core of lead,
The pellet stared.

Fred stood beside the open door,
The outside door;
He held his breath, he listened to the hall,
But all the life that stirred
Was stirring sad in Homer as he cried.
A door banged. Derry listened;
Footsteps on the floor above; the elevator bell.
No, no one came.
He closed the door and locked it,
Stood behind the curtain at the window,
Heard the voices of some truckmen floating up.
They'd heard the shot. They talked of it;
They didn't recognize the sound.
They went to banging garbage cans again.

In golden dryness, sun of late forenoon
Grilled down the shaft,
And pigeons walked among the cornice bricks above.
They would have cooed and mooed the same,
If Homer'd held his balance true
And put the stupid bullet in his brain.

Fred Derry wouldn't try to estimate
The nastiness that lived in Homer's heart,
And made him want to murder this thin bag of bones
That he'd been sentenced to adorn.
Fred turned him over, saw the tribulation
Tight and ugly in the yellow face.
"You crazy bastard," Derry said,
And trotted out a drink.
>   He got the liquor down.
The thin throat swallowed, swallowed . . .
(So Homer Wermels couldn't manage anything –
Not even move to make an end to things,
When all beginnings better never were begun)!

The little sailor slept at last.
Fred Derry shook his head, and walked a path
From bathroom door to dresser . . .
Stopped a while, and leaned his elbows . . .
Looked against the glass
And saw the snapshots curling there:
The faces of the 3-o-5th.
And some were ringed—
He'd put an inky ring around the ones
He'd seen exploded, frying, going down—
But some were live and breathing even now.
And some he'd loved, and some he'd never liked,
But all made mural chronicle
When framed by mirror depth like this.
The tiny silver wings
Shone brightly from the past—
The frozen smiles, the cigarettes in hand—
The doorways that they leaned against—
The London cabs that waited always, always
Just beyond, and never moved.
Fox, Aber, Andy Anderson, Barrall,
Brazeal and Truesdell, Leslie Stone,
Rog Rodgers, Spitznagel and Sparks,
And Price, McGeehee, F/O Bower . . .

Oh, Tommy Thompson from the photo lab—
And there were Maxwell, Beaugureau,
And Kostal just before he got a leaf—
MacDonald with his eagle . . . line of scar
On face, and color on his blouse;
And Murray with his hair cut close;
And Kuhl and Melvin—men of early '45,
Of modern day, flak-apron day,
Chin-turret day, the day of Dillon,
Brooks and Kleppenger—
When few the Forts fell down.

"And were you coned at Hanover?
And are you angel in the air above?
And did you finish up?
And are you teaching Bomb Approach?
And are you mortal, mortal as my mind?"

His suitcase still unpacked—
The uniform half in, half out—

The laundry he had brought when he came in
And tore the weapon out of Homer's claw—

So now he took his .38,
Swung out the cylinder, ejected shells.
The empty one—he played with awhile.
He thought of greater guns,
And how the bags of smoky brass would smell.
He hurled the bit of metal (devilish one time:
A morsel of a doom for him,
And terminating fragment for the boy who lay
Beneath attacking flies upon the bed)—
He threw the spiteful little thing away,
And heard it scamper on a roof.
And now he thought, if he could only cry—
If he had knees to hug and cry upon.

O soft, O warm and comforting,
A mother lap, a tender lap, a sweetheart place,
A cleanly cloth to spread his tears upon!

li

BUTCH ENGLE strode into the Seneca,
And leaned his elbows on the slab.
He wagged his head at peering Mr. Mertz,
And old Mertz bowed and giggled,
Shook Butch Engle's hand;
He'd known him in the long ago,
When he had worked at other jobs,
In days when Engle carried bottles
Underneath his coat. He had no bottles now.

Butch shook his short cigar and said,
"Is this the house phone? Say,
You got a guy—Fred Derry—living here?
Well, let me talk to him,"
And Mr. Mertz put in the plug,
And tapped the little switch.

Butch leaned, and chewed his wet cigar.
"Hi, Derry. This is Butch. Say, how you been?

Say, what's the matter,
Is my joint too good for you?
You haven't been around. What's that?"
He laughed. He said to Mertz,
"He says my place is not too good,
But too expensive. What a laugh—
I'm charging sixty cents for highballs;
At the Daniel Boone it's eighty-five."
He talked again to Derry:
"Say, you know that kid
Who lives across the street from me—
Yeh—Homer Wermels—paralyzed—
Well, I just wondered
If you'd seen him anywhere.
His folks are scared. He went away;
Went yesterday, and gone all night.
They asked me if I'd look around.
What's that?" He said a word,
He hung up, frowned, and left the desk.

Six floors above, Fred met him in the hall
And told the story. Both of them
Were looking at the door of Derry's room,
As if the room contained a maniac.
They kept their voices low.
"Thank God," said Butch, "that you got there in time.
But why the hell," he muttered angrily,
"Did you leave that revolver—loaded, too?
Well, never mind. I wish that we
Could talk to him, and kind of wise him up."

"I've tried. No one can talk to him."

"Yeh, somebody could talk," said Butch.
"I know just who: that girl next door—
That kid of Jacobson's. But, hell,
We couldn't take him home,
Not when he feels like this...."

The hall was silent for a time.
The elevator came and went.
The walls were old and yellow-stained.
The ugly lamp upon the wall
Made hissing sounds, as if the bulb would burst.
"How many times like this," thought Fred,

"Have people stood and reckoned, in some cheap hotel,
And added, multiplied, subtracted all they knew,
And ended up by crying in a woman's lap?"

He went downstairs and made his call.
When he came back he never was the same,
Because of hope affecting him.
"Go get the girl," he said to Butch,
"And I'll rack Homer up. I'll clean him off;
He's out of uniform, to say the least.
You come back, bring the girl . . .
We'll take our little Homer for a ride."

He routed Homer from the bed
And cut the tumult of his snore.
He dragged him to the bathroom,
Pulled his trousers off, and other clothes.
He shoved the boy beneath the shower . . .
"Shave with that electric razor," Derry said.
"I'll give you half a drink, if you are good.
Come on there, Sailor. Rev it up!"

"Quit pulling rank on me," snarled Homer.
But he shaved.

Fred Derry wiped the stain from Homer's pants;
He draped him in a sweater of his own.
He talked hardboiled; he used the words
That Homer understood. He made him comb his hair.
They had a drink; they stood in unreality.
"Oh. Stingy, huh?" said Homer. "How about
Another drink?"
                "No, stupid.
We are going for a ride, instead."

Butch Engle brought the girl
With staring, frightened gaze.
He must have told her what was what. . . .
She twisted pallid hands,
And never spoke a word.
And Homer only growled when once
They'd shoved him in the car.

And sitting close beside the boy,
Fred Derry lived again

His conversation on the phone.
He heard the girl. He fondled
Every phrase they'd said.

"I'm having troubles, Peggy."

"Yes. I know. Dad told me . . .
Why don't you come out and talk?"

He said, "It's Homer—
Homer Wermels—you remember him.
Well, he just tried to kill himself.
He didn't make it. Look—
We want to let him talk—
That girl of his—somewhere, somehow—
And I thought— If you didn't mind—
Out there, it's kind of peaceful—"

"Darling," said the girl,
"You bring them here at once.
Please bring them . . . no, there's no one else
But Dad and Mother. They can talk quite undisturbed.
I knew somehow I'd hear from you. You're coming too?
Oh, Fred. You're coming, aren't you—
Fred. You're coming too?"
                                        "Why, sure,"
He weakly said, "I'm coming too."

lii

A LL RIGHT, all right, he'd show them up. . . .
      He'd baffle them, he'd have the death,
      He'd have the end, no matter if they wanted him
To hold to life and have beginning.

For there were still the razor blades,
And still another gun somewhere,
And still the windows looming high,
And still a train to mutilate his corse . . .
Oh, still the noose, the iodine,
The things on bathroom closet shelves!

There were a million ways to go—
A million doorways opening on dark—
A million ways to show them all.
He'd show them, given any chance.

But sun lay holy on his hair
Where little powder burns were crisp
(Although Fred Derry'd cut them off,
And trimmed the hair a bit—
But still the burning showed).

Thick clouds piled up in cream—the thunderheads;
An oriole was yellow in an elm,
And off across a sweep of country to the west,
Young Homer Wermels now beheld
A haze, a verdant hymn of afternoon.
Wet, warm—rich beauty of the prairieland
Provoked a musing in his aching mind
In every moment that he fought to stifle it.

. . . He'd felt like that when looking at the sea,
And not another ship in sight . . .
An organ tune one time in church . . .
His first dim frightened dream of sex
(The angel who had slept with him
Before he was fourteen) . . .
The wonder of the hot red seeds, the shells
Which flashed from battle-wagons in the dark . . .
Those mysteries reflecting now
In complicated memory
Among his summer prairies and his sky,
And thunderheads of barbers' foam.

But yet he willed to turn his back on them,
To seek seclusion, find destructive silence
Punctuated by a single shot or cry.

His girl was with him—Wilma Jacobson.
She tried to smile;
She tried to talk about the oriole;
Tell Homer what a pretty lawn
The Stephensons had made . . .
And oak trees overhead,
And battered canvas chairs.
She talked about a swimming pool—
"Down there," she said, "below that tree.

Oh, Homer, that would be so wonderful—
A good place for a pool!"
He looked at her with cold and ancient face,
And nervously she bit her fingernail.

She brought the book at last from her white bag—
The messy female purse, with crumpled handkerchief,
And compact, gum, and smell of powder,
Broken cards she'd saved from weight machines
That gave her fortune—

"Homer," she said, "this little book—"
"What's that?" he sneered,
"The Brain From Ape to Man?"
"No, no!" she cried.
"That's by another man—named Tilney—
This one—Homer, this is different;
I can understand it better."
"Yeh," he sneered again,
"I bet that's quite a book!
Does it tell all about a guy like me?
A spastic-athetoid, a hemiplegiac?
Does it tell all about ataxia?
I bet you had a lot of fun
With all that stuff."

She held the book
Squeezed precious in her hands.
"About a man . . . he used to be like you.
He wrote this book himself—a man named Carlson.
And I've read Helen Keller, too. But Carlson knows
Just how it feels to be like you,
And worse. He crawled around;
He couldn't walk, and he was born that way.
That's how he got the title for his book,
He calls it 'Born That Way.' You see,
It's better, Homer, if it happens to you late:
You have a pattern formed. He says
You have to re-establish it—the pattern.
All the motions that you make,
You have to *will* them—think them out.
And you can do it, Homer.
Yes, you can."

"A guy like me—" he mouthed at her.

The tears were sticky on her cheeks,
Her voice went on and on,
And Homer tried to interrupt;
She wouldn't let him interrupt.
"It's *you*," she said again, again.
"It's *you*. You've got to do it all yourself.
But you can't fear. No, you can't be afraid.
He says it's just mistaken kindness—
Acting like your folks have acted,
Trying to ignore the way you do.
You've done it too.
Oh, Homer, yes, you have.
You can't ignore— And drinking, too," she said.
"It doesn't say you mustn't drink.
The doctor tells about it in this book.
Just temporarily," she said,
"The alcohol eliminates
Those funny motions that you make.
But you can't take it all the time.
It's habit-forming. If you drink too much,
You're only getting worse. . . .
And only slight assistance!" Wilma cried,
"It's only slight assistance that you need,
Just like—I put my hand on you,
Like this. Just slightly—help your arm
To do the thing you want to do.
But still you've got to do it by yourself—
You've got to focus, think it out,
And walk or move the way you wish
Because you wish to do it. . . .
Homer, please," she cried.
"I didn't read those books to sneer at you.
I wasn't laughing. If the people laugh,
Well, just ignore it. Most of them
Won't laugh. He says," she cried,
"The doctor in this book—he says a blind man—
We don't pity him because he's blind—
A beggar, blind— We only pity him
Because he has to beg!
You've got to make a pattern for yourself. . . .
I guess I'm not so very bright,
But I could help you, if you'd only let me help.
Oh, please. Oh, God. Please, Homer,
Let me try."

Her eagerness, her tears, her charity and soul—
She gave them all to him,
Not only with these words recited fast,
But with a cool sobriety
From out a reservoir that had no depth
Which man might measure...
Pool...the ice-blue water of her hardihood,
A strength of mountains, pine, and rocky shore.
For she was speaking now, not as a child to child,
But with a nursing passion in her heart.
In whitest purity she offered up her breast to him,
And let him drink his nourishment.

He put his shaking lips
Around the nipple of her life,
And deeply took the milk she gave.

She said they'd take a walk. They walked.
She held his arm, not heavily;
She made no crutch of self,
She didn't caution him, or say
The green slope was too steep to walk upon.
She held thin fingers underneath his elbow—
(Powerful as block-and-tackle, hoisting him)
The inert weight, the flabby spasm of his weakness
Steeled by steady pull.

And probably he walked no better than before,
Perhaps he drooled, perhaps his mouth
Was twisting still, and devils stabbed his heel;
But still he walked, he didn't feel their jab.

She talked to him. She said they'd play
Some Chinese checkers on her porch;
They'd play that very night, and if his arm
Flipped out to throw the marbles far,
She'd make him go around and pick them up—
She wouldn't baby him.
She wouldn't let him drink too much.
Oh, let me try to help you.
Homer, let me try.

He said, "I've got a headache."
"Well," she said, "you need an aspirin."
"No, hell," he told her. "Let's sit down—

Just let me lie...." The grass was damp
Beneath the fuzz that sun had dried;
They felt its dampness soaking into them.
But still they sat ... and Homer's head
In Wilma's lap. She told him, "Go to sleep."
He didn't sleep; he only viewed
Athletic panorama of the past,
When he had run and cycled, sung and strode ...
And one day he would soar and stride again?

And sitting suddenly bolt upright, Homer knew:
The bullet—yes. Fred Derry hadn't hauled
That gun away in time.

The cap was dented, powder burned;
The bullet found the pudding brain
And opened it, and ended it.
Some sickly creature there had died.
The monkey-man was now embalmed in secrecy,
In fearful morgue forever best forgot.
And Homer Wermels, by the grace of God,
Might live appropriate in laugh
And ardor, mirth and miracle.
Because, if apes still quivered in his arms,
His brain was free of them at last.

liii

THAT was the day John Novak drove sedate
Past maple, hawthorn tree.

He took the long continuation—
Black Hawk Boulevard—past elms—
And turned by big box elders: Highway 17.
He noticed grapevines growing on a fence.
He passed the Highland golf course—
Creeping bent and stolons—
Saw them growing well, though much neglected
    nowadays.
The bluegrass in a yard across the way
Was being cut. John Novak smelled

The winy juice chewed up by mower blades.
He passed the oaks in that thin string of woods
Beside the railroad tracks.
He looked. Burr oaks. He'd thought them white before.
Just showed how you could make mistakes
With greenery you'd seen for years.

That was the day John Novak thought of palms
And long lianas, flowers red as paint,
With thickened water dark in boles of stump,
And all the insects humming round,
And butterflies of vitriolic blue
That turned to silver when they found the sun.
He thought of palms; rejected them;
Supplied the barberry instead,
And all the bushes—currant, wild,
And all the low growth: blue beech, ironwood.
He saw them. Novak found them good to see.

And, thumping in his rusty truck
Atop the hill, he turned.
He narrowed eyes . . .
That broken limb above
Was rotting at the base;
The tree would need a surgery:
The wood chipped out,
And treated . . . filling set within,
The way a dentist fills a tooth.
John Novak rattled up a drive,
He passed a terrace;
People there. . . . He was embarrassed—
Should have phoned. But still— Well, this
Was kind of a surprise.

He'd wrapped his presents good and tight.
He'd dug them out with lots of dirt,
And baled them up in burlap cloth
And fetched them here. And if it rained again
Why, that would be a good thing too . . .
With plenty dirt around the roots.

He stopped his truck, climbed down; he stood.
He rubbed his hands against his hips.
He didn't know just what to say.
Should he go up and ring the bell?

Or ask someone?
                    Al Stephenson
Came walking on the lawn.

Al smiled. "Hello."
"Hello," John Novak said.
He handed over a cigar,
Fat, brown and wrapped in cellophane.
"I owe you this," he said.
"And I have brought you something else:
That stuff there on the truck."

"Say—what you got?" asked Al.
                    "Well. Lilacs.
Like you used to get. But these are different—
Kind of hybrid. Some my Poppa fooled with,
Clear up to the time he died.
White Persian on the parent stem—
But he made cuttings: took some purple—
Most of them were not so hot; and many died.
But he saved just a few. They're pretty good—
These six I brought. Six bushes—
Poppa fooled with them for years.
When they come out
You'll see that the coralla's white,
But got a kind of bluish tinge."

"Say, they sound wonderful to me," said Al.
"I hadn't thought of more just now ...
More lilacs. But if these are good,
How much would they—?"

John Novak made a cigarette.
"No, honest, Mr. Stephenson.
I didn't mean to sell you anything.
These things are just a gift from me to you—
Account of how you helped me with the loan.
I thought I'd like to bring you some
To sort of show my gratitude."
And both were grinning,
Both embarrassed.
"God," said Stephenson,
"That's swell!"

"Well, ordinarily
I wouldn't recommend that, in July,

We transplant stuff like this—
But I have done it several times.
I got a lot of earth inside those sacks.
I took up quite a spread with every bush—
And plenty deep. They'll do all right.
I thought that you would like to have them."

They took the truck across the yard,
They found a special place where these
Should grow forever. Then they dug.
They toiled together;
Moving, shifting, shovel, grunt.
John Novak had his spade and other tools,
And Stephenson brought more.
They dug, they put the bushes down,
They set them solid in the soil.

They cocked their heads and watched the sky,
And scented other rain this night.
They did their tricks of gardening,
And all the time the sun went low.

They talked of root and moisture,
Fertilizer, bug and spray....
"First thing," John said,
"I thought I'd stop in at the bank some day,
And give my thanks. I hope that you're not worried—
All that dough— I'll do all right.
My leg is better now.
Yes, I am having quite a summer—
Lots of trade. Did I tell you about my glads?
You ought to come and see—
I've got the best glads that you ever saw.
Now, take about three weeks from now
As soon as all my Lady Gays come out—"

"Of course I'll come," said Stephenson.
"You call me here; not at the bank;
I'll not be at the Cornbelt any more."

"You mean—" said Novak,
"You have quit your job?
You going to another bank?"

"Not any bank," said Al.

And Novak held his silence for a time.
He cleaned the clay from off his spade.
"So I suppose that you will take
Another job somewhere?"
"Well, I don't know just what," said Al.
"If anyone's got money," Novak said,
"I guess he'd think that it was nice
To rest a while, and not do anything.
I know I felt that way when I came back—
But, hell, I couldn't leave the stuff alone."

"This kind of stuff," said Stephenson,
"I guess that I could never leave alone."
And then a notion seemed to strike him
So importantly and quaintly, tenderly and sane,
So natural, so pleasing all in one ...
He stood and grinned; he looked at Novak.
Red was in his ears,
And underneath the skin of his dark face;
The grim hard face that wasn't grim,
When you looked at the whetted edges
Of his eyes.

"Look here," said Stephenson,
And all his words were tumbled on his tongue,
"Look here— I wonder if you ever thought—
I mean— Well, I don't know so much
About a nursery—
But still, you're thinking of expanding—
I could bring a little dough;
As much as you might need.
Would you consider me?
I mean—a partnership?"

John Novak stood in caution.
All his thoughts were slow and steady
As the swell of germination in the soil,
But just as certain to emerge
When he'd attended them.
"Well, I don't know.
I never thought about a partner—
Not since Poppa died.
It's funny. You, a banker—
And I don't know why—"

"I'll tell you,'" Al said,
"Some day. Not right now."
"O.K.," said Novak.
"Let us think about it.
Guess I'd have to talk
To my old lady.
So would you."
"Yes, sure we would," said Stephenson,
"To both of our old ladies!"
"Sarge," said Novak,
Holding out his hand,
"I'll tell you what:
Let's think about it.
Maybe in a day or so
You drive out, take a look,
And see the place?
Then we can talk."

Each shook the other's hand, and well,
And liked the crush of bone
And muscle, flesh and earth, and mold
And dew and moisture . . . living blood
Of soil exchanged between them, mingling when
Each shook the other's hand.
Al Stephenson stood looking at the lilac trees
Fresh planted there.
Rob Stephenson rode up, and dumped
His bicycle upon the grass;
He grinned with scarlet face.
He'd ridden cultivator since the dawn
In Carl Van Bussel's cornfield.
"Gee," cried Rob, "more lilacs, Dad?"
And calmly, soberly, John Novak
Climbed into his shabby car,
And closed the door,
And drove away to 52nd Street,
Past plum and cottonwood,
Past hackberry and willow tree—
(White willow in that first ravine—
Mostly white willow;
Only a few were red)
And past the ample breadth of oats
Now turned increasing yellow with July.

liv

"COME sit by me
And be my love," said Peggy Stephenson.
She lured him to the sofa. Derry went
Resentful, shy, but wanting to be near to her....
The battered wicker couch, with cushioning of blue;
The faded couch, serene on tile and hemmed by screen,
The summer wind to move beneath the awning shade;
The couch that bore a battle scar. (A gun emplacement:
Wicker hacked away by Rob when he was six,
To arm this Chinese junk, and sail with friends,
And sweep the Japs from off the yellow seas.)
The little stains of drinks spilled there;
Depressions in the cloth and padding underneath
Where bodies rested through the years ...
And love had silvered with delight
Upon that sofa when the moon approved.

"Come sit by me upon this couch," she said.
"Belong to me."

Fred looked at her with tired face....
"Take off your coat," she said. "It's hot."
He hung the brown coat on a chair, and sat by her.
"I want to talk to you," she said.
"I want to tell a story. No—
This isn't right. Don't look at me like that;
And don't you gaze so grandly at the distance! Here."
She drew him down, she put his face against herself,
Against her limbs, against the light loose black—
The dirndl skirt she wore.
"That's better," and she held him there.

"Look here," he said. "Don't be a fool!
I'd feel ashamed, if someone came...."

"But why?" she asked. "Why be ashamed?
And as for someone's coming, that's impossible.
Rob's working on a neighbor's farm,
And Homer—Wilma— Well, they're on the lawn.
MacDuff? MacDuff's a kitchen hound

With shortcake on his nose—
And Butch and Dad— Quite likely
Mother's pressed them into service by this time!
They've got their fingers red with juice—
The strawberries won't wait—
And I won't wait. I'm going to keep you here.
Do I feel nice?"
     Fred growled a word.
"Thank you. Do I smell good?"
      He growled again.
"I want to tell a story," Peggy said.
She told the story well.

That week another warrior ran
Upon Boone City grass once more—
A handsome male, with good Clark Gable face:
The lengthened ears, the brows, the strong brown eyes,
And tendons strung like wire on his bones.
His name was Duke. He'd loved a woman once,
He'd loved some children, and a man.
But all the age he spent with them was now confused,
Mixed up in disarray with orders, smells of other life,
With clack of guns and killer talk,
And all the process he'd been taught
Of doing well with his great shoulders and his teeth
(The fighting heart behind to drive them on).
They'd set him in a dragon shape,
And armed him with iniquity.

And then one day they shipped him back.
He felt his paws on quiet turf again;
With collie living close, and Newfoundland beyond,
And on the other side, a German shepherd of his kind.
The weeks went by. . . . They tried to teach him not
To tear the living flesh, to find the throat,
To bite the ankle, bring the runner down.
They tried to tell him that the world was not alive
With enemies to be subdued—that every human form
Before him did not walk in curse and danger.

Now the weeks were months.
Duke wagged his tail. His ears were up,
His eyes were willing . . . telegraph of his black nose
Put pleasant understanding in his brain,
"O.K.," they said. "He's ready for discharge."

The printed paper with his name set down;
The proud certificate to worship on a wall,
And indicate with laughter and with love.
O long, O long ... to fade within its frame
When he was gone, when Duke was old
And dead and gone!

They brought him back, so panting and so hot.
He jolted in his crate across Boone City pavement.
Thus he smelled his certain home-rich earth again—
The soil that he had dug in puppyhood.
The crate came down, the catch was lifted,
Door was bent. He heard a voice ...
They smothered him with squeals and rapture.
All the neighborhood came close to meet him.
Duke remembered now—remembered much—
Though puzzled still at finding all these folks.
He licked a hand. He saw a cat: his ears went up.
He ran around, his big nose leading on.
He wet the ground; his able legs
Tore grass and leaves to cover up.
He danced and galloped; did a trick
That he'd forgotten how to do,
When men made killer out of him.

That night he slept. He sank serene
With eyes squeezed shut, in his old place
Upon the parlor rug ... the people there ...
He lifted now and then from sleep.
His tail slammed on the floor.
He slept again.
                    A child
Bent over him to kiss goodnight.
He leaped to life with open jaws,
And slashed. The screams arose; the blood ran red;
The feet were running.
                    Dr. Cooper came.

They put Duke in the dark garage.
He drooped his tail, he moaned a little,
Sniffed round the box they placed for him
With old coats on its floor.
He lay in darkness, wolfish, pondering ...
Twice in the night a flashlight burned his face.
He stared; he saw the light; he wondered,

Wagged his tail, and lay alone in gloom once more.
Next morning he was taken far away—
Perhaps in time he'd learn,
Upon that farm they took him to—
Perhaps. Nobody knew.
He'd loved the child when she was younger still,
And softer, frailer . . . when her fingers hurt his hair
And twisted uncomplaining ears. He had endured,
Accepted all the torment that she gave,
And never cried, and never bit before.

But he had been away to war, and he was not the same.
He'd have to study sanity
In better fashion than the K-9 men could teach,
To qualify for comfort on that rug again.

"They told me at the Red Cross rooms . . .
The child's not badly hurt.
Too early yet to tell if she is scarred. . . . "

And Peggy played with Derry's hair and ears.
"How are you, Duke?" she asked.

"Bow-wow," said Derry dreamily.

"And will you bite?"
                                    "Bend down and see."
She put her face down. Derry didn't bite;
Their mouths grew warm together.

Like all the infant paupers of their kind
They lived deluded . . . cut out paper dolls.
They nibbled gingerbread from off the witches' eaves,
And ate a sugar of the window panes.

They played with poverty—
Imagined it to be a toy—though both were realists,
And born amid the terror of this time,
And nourished by depression, long confused
By politics . . . long suffering, observing how
The others of their complicated era found
Destruction in the flush of dawn.

They'd heard, in fact or echo, somber symphony
Of bomb-bursts in this century.

And yet, and yet
They had the bud of living in their teeth;
They squeezed and tasted—
Touched with pointed tongues,
And felt the nectar of their youth come out
In bee-stung tininess.
                    It tasted sweet.
They jested, jeered, they found the scheme
Of all economy and history in talk
About the cracker-box they'd use for table—
Soap-box that they'd use to build a chair.
They sought adventure (in a sober dress,
And running out to meet them fast).

"What if we had a kid?" Fred Derry mourned.
"Don't ask!" said Peggy, rolling up her eyes.
"Don't talk of that. We can't!
We simply can't—not for a hundred years."

And yet, and yet they knew
That if such climax came to them
Despite the sharp sophistication of their years—
Despite the drugstore—quite in spite
Of all the rules put down in secret books—
Despite each preparation yet devised
To turn a procreation into play—
If all astringent never slew the germ—

If new life met and touched,
And cells united, swelled and grew,
And lust became fecundity—
If this would happen, still they'd manage it,
As other generations managed their mistakes.
They'd see the sapling grow from empty soil,
And sit one time beneath its shade.

They cried with softness or with slang,
And juggled hope and high ambition in between.
Each threw, each caught, each threw and caught again,
And saw the emblem whirling back and forth,
The gilded club which they must spin and keep aloft;
The wand that neither must let fall.

She bullied him. She was the law,
As women always are the law in end.

She talked; she slapped him once;
She kissed him with a fever, ruffed his hair,
She stifled words of self-reproach that Derry wailed,
And stuffed them back into his throat.
She wise manipulated him, and sat aloof
Again, to let him worship her.

lv

BUTCH ENGLE licked the berry stain
From off his lips, and solemn held
The hand of Milly Stephenson.
"You sure can make a shortcake, babe," he said.

"Well, stay for dinner—have some more!
I'm certain that Al wants you to;
But he's still digging on the lawn."

Butch Engle shook his head.
                              "No, thanks.
I got to get to work down at my joint.
It's cocktail time."
                        He wanted very much
To speak the gratitude and pride he felt
In claiming women of this kind as friends.
"By God," he thought. "This Mrs. Stephenson:
She's got a chassis just as good
As Claudette Colbert! Yet she's kind of noble—
Like my mother, too. . . . They're pretty swell,
These Stephensons."
                        He said,
As gruff and menacing as he could manage:
"Take good care of all them kids."
                                    He drove away.

lvi

FRED DERRY, Peggy Stephenson,
They talked to Al and Milly, four alone;
They laughed with them.
(Oh, people laugh within a house where one has died;
And wander in the kitchen, pour a drink,
While in another room lies stiff the waxen form.)

They'd lived in desolation. They were born of it,
And tempered by a heat no other generation knew.

Fred Derry, twenty-one and killer of a hundred men—
And bound for school with books in strap—
Not with a bunch of kids, the way he'd said,
But with the tanker men, the Liberator crews,
The infantry, the Gyrenes coming home
And opening a tome that told
How they must ever think and act
Now they had emptied out their gaunt Garands
And only felt a kick and thud in memory.
He'd go, he'd try to learn a life—
He'd try to prune and mold himself
The way a million others might.

"Good grief," said Milly, whistling soft.
"Just fifty dollars every month? You'll starve to death."
"Great heavens, mother! No," cried Peggy Stephenson.
"Not fifty. It's seventy, if Fred has a dependent—"
"Seventy-five," her father said.
"The government pays everything for college:
All the books, tuition, stuff like that;
And you two live on carrots and on rice."

His daughter looked at him and smiled,
With her superior wisdom, better plan.
"I figured it," she said. "Oh, yes. Can do!
My clothes will last at least two years.
I have so many. Freddy's got
Two suits, and pants and sweaters....
Mrs. Rafferty, down at the Red Cross—well,
She's renting rooms. She lives across the street,

Right by the campus ... get her rear room with the
   porch
For only fifteen dollars, by the month,
If Fred took out the ashes, cut the lawn,
 And things like that. She told me all about it."

Derry closed his eyes and groaned.
"And going back to Midway Drugs
Until September ... look:
Suppose that Bullard doesn't want to take me back?"
"Oh, yes, he will," said Peggy Stephenson.
"He's glad to have you back.
I called him up, before you came today."

When she and Milly'd gone away,
Fred stared in stubbornness at Al.
"She's not quite wise," said Derry.
"Peggy doesn't know what gives—not yet."
"Well, hell," said Al. "She wants to try it."
"Look," said Fred. "That thing today, down at the
   bank—
I just can't understand— Why don't you throw me out?
A guy like me— The thing I tried to do,
The thing I would have done
Unless you'd pulled me out of line—"

Al lit a cigarette.
"I might have done the same myself.
Yes, you were lucky that I blew my top just then.
Perhaps we both are lucky ... you know how it went:
Some guys were lucky, just because
Their names weren't on the hand-grenade or shell—
Because the primer wasn't made-to-order, marked for
   them."

"I know," said Fred. "But sticking up a bank—"

"God damn it!" Al said sharply. "I don't want
To hear you mention that again.
Two pages on that notebook—well—
I tore them off
Before I left the Black Hawk Club.
I burned them in the ashtray;
Now they're gone—they're burned up, all forgotten.
Not a soul knows anything about them but we four.

Forget it, please."
                    "Roger," said Fred
Across their private inter-com.

They took Martinis to the world outside;
MacDuff munched five illicit crackers;
Peggy hunted Homer and his Wilma down.
She led them in, with Homer sulky still—
And frightened—crispness showing in his hair,
And Wilma watching him with nervous eyes.
"Just one Martini, Homer. *One*," she said.
Her voice was shrill.
Al brought some cokes for her and Rob.

They chatted, said their dull and simple things.
They talked of food, and Peggy planned
That she and Derry'd make the meal—
And then they'd drive the others home.
They had a little gas;
If they ran out of gas they'd have to walk!

(The fright and woefulness, the loathing of themselves,
The feel of never fitting in—
These elements no longer jailed them tight
But stood like guards along the terrace end.)
They watched the day across a dusky field;
They saw it vanish, swaddled by ascending clouds.
Last light made copper plating on a crown of elms,
And nighthawks hunted wild ahead of wind.
"Another storm," said Milly. "Thar is rain
In them-thar clouds."
                    "Rain,"
Said her husband, "makes the lilacs grow."

He frowned from out predicament.
He felt they were a lost battalion, huddled close—
The three who'd known destroying flame,
And still perceived its blisters on their hide—
The boy, the elder boy, the man
Who'd felt exploding flare of doom
That women only guessed; and yet
Imagined properly, as women may,
When spreading tannic dressing of their tears.

They looked, they saw an angry past
Commingled with the future in a storm.

Oh, they would feel the lightning part their hair,
And hear the thunder deafen them once more.
A war? Perhaps. Or maybe not. . . .

But savage too the weather of a peace—
When glare exposes class and race
With bludgeon lifted for a blow—
When staring flash reveals a blackened face
As monster to the babies in their beds,
And to the blacks reveals a monster pale.
When Star of David is a curse, a jeer,
A lodestone and a sacrament in one.
When grasping claw goes round a neck
And strangles song before the singer sings—
When jealousy is hail to sting your eyes,
And love is hurricane to blow the lilacs down.

In suit for fending flak, in helmet hard
They needed now to dress themselves—
To stand formation, fire bursts
To ready up their guns—
And keep the ditching packets close,
And treasure well the benzedrine.
A keen voice yelled, "Attention!" in the sky—
For, mounting out of prairie rim
And sunset glare,
The wild-west clouds were galloping again.

"WHEN YOU HAVE READ HIS BOOK YOU FEEL THAT YOU KNOW WHAT IT WAS LIKE TO SNEAK THROUGH THE FIELDS OF VIRGINIA, IN FOGGY MARCH NIGHTS, WITH EVERY SOUND AN ENEMY, WHEN LEE AND GRANT WERE MAKING HISTORY."
—LEWIS GANNETT

Arouse and Beware

A NOVEL OF ESCAPE DURING THE CIVIL WAR

MacKinlay Kantor

PULITZER PRIZE-WINNING AUTHOR OF *ANDERSONVILLE*

Published by SpeakingVolumes

Visit us at www.speakingvolumes.us

MacKINLAY KANTOR
PULITZER PRIZE-WINNING AUTHOR
OF *ANDERSONVILLE*

VALLEY
FORGE

VALLEY FORGE is grandly conceived, but the quality is
equal to the concept. The climate of the war, its taste and
smell and the harsh texture of its life, are evoked with
mystery. Neither souped-up nor toned-down under
fashionable pressures, this is an extraordinarily honest
and human book. I am greatly impressed.
—*MARY RENAULT*

Published by SpeakingVolumes

Visit us at <u>www.speakingvolumes.us</u>

Sign up for free and bargain books

Join the Speaking Volumes mailing list

Text

ILOVEBOOKS

to 22828 to get started.

Message and data rates may apply